T0301290

National Accounting and Capital

National Accounting and Capital

John M. Hartwick

Professor of Economics, Queen's University, Canada

Edward Elgar

Cheltenham, UK • Northampton, MA, USA

Published by
Edward Elgar Publishing Limited
Glensanda House
Montpellier Parade
Cheltenham
Glos GL50 1UA
UK

Edward Elgar Publishing, Inc.
136 West Street
Suite 202
Northampton
Massachusetts 01060
USA

A catalogue record for this book is available from the British Library

Library of Congress Cataloguing in Publication Data

Hartwick, John M.
        National accounting and capital/John M. Hartwick.
        1. National income—Accounting. 2. Capital. I. Title.
        HC79.I5H375 2000
        339.3'2—dc21   99–16006
                                                                    CIP

ISBN 1 84064 206 8

Printed and bound in Great Britain by Bookcraft (Bath) Ltd.

Contents

List of figures   vii
List of tables   ix
Acknowledgments   xi
Introduction   xiii

1   The national accounts and capital   1
2   Integrating financial-capital accounts of firms into
    the national accounts   17
3   Welfare considerations in national accounting   49
4   Exhaustible resources   83
5   Renewable resources   124
6   Green national accounting for an economy with a
    free access distortion   145
7   International trade   158
8   Labor, leisure and human capital   178
9   Technical change   186
10 Recapitulation and questions about implementation   204

Index   213

Figures

4.1	Optimal current extraction of oil deposits	85
6.1a	Isoquant map with satiation of input S	147
6.1b	Outputs with satiation of input S	147
6.2	The steady-state first-best solution (no satiation of S)	151
6.3	The steady-state free access solution (satiation of S)	152
6.4	Two equilibria in free access	154

Tables

1.1	National accounting matrix (stationary, one-commodity, two-factor economy)	4
1.2	National accounting matrix (two goods, semi-durable K-capital)	8
1.3	National accounting matrix (intermediate goods)	10
1.4	National accounting matrix (knowledge capital and K-capital)	12
2.1	A national accounting matrix	18
2.2	National accounting matrix (two goods with intermediate flows, two primary factors)	20
2.3	One-sector stationary economy with financial accounts	22
2.4	National accounting matrix (a pure lending institution)	24
2.5	National accounting matrix (real representation of bank services)	28
2.6	National accounting matrix (interest rate spreads and dollar stocks)	32
2.7	National accounting matrix (real representation of bank and equity services)	37
2.8	National accounting matrix (rate spreads as prices)	41
2.9	National accounting matrix (costly banking services)	44
3.1	National accounting matrix (an economy with only K-capital)	51
3.2	National accounting matrix (K-capital and knowledge capital)	63
3.3	National accounting matrix (K-capital and oil stock capital)	66
4.1	National accounting matrix (oil-exporting nation)	87
4.2	National accounting matrix (exhaustible resources)	93
4.3	National accounting matrix (oil and labor produce output)	95
4.4	National accounting matrix (oil used in goods production)	97
4.5	National accounting matrix (semi-durable exhaustible resources)	104
4.6	National accounting matrix (recycling durable extracted material)	107
4.7	National accounting matrix (durable goods extraction and recycling)	111
4.8	National accounting matrix (exploration and extraction activity)	114
5.1	National accounting matrix (harvesting timber for fuel)	129
5.2	National accounting matrix (harvest used in goods production)	131
5.3	National accounting matrix (harvesting contributes to a pollution stock)	136
5.4	National accounting matrix (stationary OLG (overlapping generations) model with land)	139

5.5	National accounting matrix (forest clearing for agriculture)	142
6.1	National accounting matrix (labor/leisure and harvesting)	150
6.2	National accounting matrix (free access)	153
7.1	National accounting matrix (consumer goods exported)	160
7.2	National accounting matrix (oil importation)	161
7.3	National accounting matrix (unbalanced commodity trade)	164
7.4	National accounting matrix (specialized oil exporter)	166
7.5	National accounting matrix (an oil-exporting nation)	168
7.6	National accounting matrix (Norwegian model)	173
8.1	National accounting matrix (knowledge embodied in labor)	181
8.2	National accounting matrix (endogenous population growth)	183
9.1	National accounting matrix (labor-augmenting, exogenous technical progress)	189
9.2	National accounting matrix (exogenous technical progress)	193
9.3	National accounting matrix (Romer, 1990)	198
9.4	National accounting matrix (high-tech intermediate goods)	201

Acknowledgments

My colleague, Dan Usher, has been a sounding board for most of my ideas over the years, including many here. He did not 'sign off' on this material and should not be blamed for my approach or particulars. Thanks to him. Dan combines great insight with bemused skepticism, and possesses a special gift for getting into the topic at hand and forcing an interlocutor to sort out his/her thoughts more clearly. We, the current members of Queen's economics department, hope he hangs out in the department for years to come, in spite of being formally cut loose with compulsory retirement. Another large debt I owe is to Geir Asheim, University of Oslo. His work on some of my papers inspired me to do new and productive things, but he also read a key section of this monograph, in typescript, and guided me away from a serious misunderstanding. He too should not be implicated in errors or opinions. I accumulated a core of notes for this monograph, in preparing some lectures for presentation at Hans Werner Sinn's Center for Economic Studies, University of Munich. My four-month stay there, January to April 1993, was most rewarding, in many dimensions. Thanks to Hans Werner and his colleagues for making my stay pleasant and productive. Ray Rees and family were kind enough to provide a home for me in Munich, a new and strange town.

While working on a project with Jeff Vincent at the Harvard Institute for International Development, I was introduced to Social Accounting Matrices or SAMs. My wife, Anya Hageman, a student of Erik Thorbecke at Cornell, provided me with some detail and I quickly decided that the SAM was the correct way to set out the ideas that I had been accumulating on valuation and national accounting, over the years. One cannot peddle an attractive-looking expression for net national product, given the discipline forced on one by the SAM form, without having it pass the fundamental test of value of output or product having to end up equal to the value of inputs. The SAM obliges one to get one's accounts right, in principle, as well as in practice. It does not do basic valuation, but it provides a check on valuation because the separate micro-components must end up being consistent at the aggregate level. It is an extension of the principle of double-entry book-keeping. Thanks then to Jeff Vincent and to my wife. Elaine Constant did most of the word-processing of this document in her usual careful, quick and cheerful way. Thanks to her. In fact Elaine typed at least three very different versions of this monograph, each involving extensive revisions. Thanks to the Edward Elgar company for taking this project on, on the basis of an inadequate early draft.

Introduction

In this volume, we incorporate capital, person-made and natural, into the national accounts in a consistent way. We preserve the linearized, dollar-valued current-value Hamiltonian as the net national product (NNP) and this allows us to observe economic depreciation terms in the NNP clearly. For natural capital these terms are generally disinvestments in the current stocks. The novelty of our approach lies in the simultaneous accounting for national product (NNP) and national income (NNI) at all stages. We do this with a national accounting matrix (NAM), a variant of Richard Stone's (1951, 1973) social accounting matrix (SAM). Incomes to factors are always in balance with values of outputs, including investment goods, positive and negative. NNI mops up anomalous income terms such as residuals accruing because of the absence of constant returns to scale in production. Somewhat novel anomalous terms here are capital gains or capital goods price changes emerging because the ratios of physical stocks of capital are generally changing over time, and residuals emerging because the natural growth function for renewable natural stocks typically exhibits non-constant returns to scale. It is the discipline of being forced at every stage to account for the current value of output and the corresponding value of inputs that then forces us to deal with apparent anomalous terms in the final accounts.

Chapter 2 deals with financial capital as in loans from banks to widget producers. There is a long-standing controversy of how to measure the activities of banks and other financial institutions. The easy way is to measure the value of their activity by the value of their inputs used but this is an obvious 'ad hocery'. An alternative is to turn to interest rate spreads such as that between the lending rate at a bank and its rate paid on the capital it lends out. These mark-ups should be representing the cost of producing services in some sense and we investigate this intuition in depth. There turns out to be a dual price system for financial services, implicit prices represented by unit production costs, and explicit prices represented by interest rate spreads. Households lend directly to widget firms via equity purchases and we investigate the rate spreads for this channel of lending as well. In other words, households are direct producers of financial services (ownership supervisory services) when they hold equities in widget firms or even banks. An old issue in valuing financial services in the national accounts is what fraction of such services is intermediate to the economy and what fraction is final, ending up as consumption by households. Clearly households have no interest in consuming financial services *per se* but they are interested in having a good financial system if only for facilitating check-writing. We make clear that financial services are completely intermediate to the economy and are specific about exactly where all the services get 'capitalized' in the prices of goods which do enter the final demand of households.

Somewhat less novel than the above contributions made in this volume is our consistent treatment of human capital, leisure and technical change including endogenous technical change, in our NAM framework. Leisure shows up in Chapter 6, which in fact is structured around an open access market failure, and technical change and human capital are focused on in Chapters 8 and 9. Chapter 3 links NNP to Hicksian or sustainable income and this is done with explicit constant consumption path analysis as well as the hypothetical constant consumption analysis set out in Weitzman (1976). The issue of translating from util valuation to dollar valuation is dealt with in detail.

A sustainable development path for an economy is touched on in many places in this monograph but is not singled out for special treatment. Chapter 3 deals with national accounting and welfare economics, and sustainability can be interpreted as a path deriving from a particular social welfare objective, namely a path along which consumption never declines. This path provides a benchmark, but it is one of many paths along which an economy can and may be moving. The logically complete treatment of natural resources in the national accounts is not really an issue in the economics of sustainability *per se*; rather sustainability is about getting depreciation terms right in the national accounts for natural resources that are involved in production and consumption in the economy. It is in Chapter 4, where the natural capital associated with non-renewable resources is taken up, that we lay out 'procedures' for dealing with natural capital, distinct from produced K-capital. We set out how to process the unavoidable capital gains terms which emerge and how to deal with the corresponding valuation of capital in net national income. Our 'procedures' work for knowledge capital, taken up in Chapter 8, as well as for renewable resource capital, taken up in Chapter 5. We observe that wage income disappears from the national accounts when labor services are represented as services from human capital, in Chapter 8. This results in dollar-valued NNP being interest on dollar-valued wealth. Hence NNP serves as a dollar measure of 'sustainable income' in the sense of Weitzman (1976). Although Chapter 6 is focused on accounts when a distortion exists in the economy, we make the case there for including leisure in the national accounts. In Chapter 7, we focus on international trade and apply our 'procedures' to the national accounts involved with our model economies. In Chapter 9, we focus on technical change and the national accounts for our model economies are taken up there.

Our procedures derive from a conceptual experiment involving 'capital goods dealers'. These hypothetical agents buy capital goods at the end of period $t - 1$, rent them out to users or producers over the duration of period t, and sell them at the end of period t. In having zero profits maintained on such a transaction, terms representing depreciation emerge. These terms value the change in the value of the capital goods themselves over the period. These are the terms we make use of in separating gross national product from net national product. They are Hicksian concepts because they represent sums that, if invested at the end of period t, would restore the value of the capital good to what it was at the end of period $t - 1$. And capital gains or asset price changes inhere in these terms, quite generally. And the interest foregone by the renting out of these capital goods is the term that values these stocks in net national income. This line of argument allows us to derive the traditional national accounts, as in Samuelson (1961, Table 1), as well as our national accounts extended to cover new types of capital. It becomes clear by the end of Chapter 5 that we are dealing with a unified approach to national accounting and capital. We can put a central aspect of this monograph differently. There is produced or K-capital, and national accounting practice has been developed around this concept of capital. But the view since about 1989 is that there are many other capital goods that should be 'processed' in the national accounts, and one has to extend current practice to deal with these other types of capital goods, for example. oil deposits, fish stocks, knowledge stocks and so on. We show how to extend current practice to deal with these other types of capital. Of course, our obligation is to show that our 'procedures' work to obtain the traditional accounts with their K-capital, and we do this in Chapter 1.

REFERENCES

Samuelson, P.A. (1961), 'The evaluation of "social income": capital formation and wealth', in F.A. Lutz and D.C. Hague (eds), *The Theory of Capital*, London: Macmillan, pp. 32–57.

Store, Richard (1951), 'Simple transactions models, information and computing', *Review of Economic Studies*, **19** (49), 67–84.

Stone, Richard (1973), 'A system of social matrices', *Review of Income and Wealth*, **19** (2), 143–66.

Weitzman, M.L. (1976), 'On the welfare significance of national product in a dynamic economy', *Quarterly Journal of Economics*, **90**, 156-62.

1. The national accounts and capital

1.1 INTRODUCTION

We approach national accounting here by setting out a simple abstract economy and its corresponding national accounts. We address the matter of accounting under non-constant returns to scale but our focus is on capital. In our first model there is infinitely durable capital, a constant labor force, no accumulation and no technical change. This seemingly dull economy has a fairly simple national accounts and provides a framework for emphasizing the role of constant returns to scale in production and input pricing in accord with the value of marginal product. It is also the ideal setting for introducing our national accounting matrix (NAM), a central apparatus for organizing our thoughts and analysis throughout this monograph. We discuss the presence of a government sector in such an economy.

We then consider an economy experiencing the production of new investment goods and the accumulation of person-made capital. We derive its national accounts via two principles or equilibrium conditions: goods producers have matched *current* costs of production to *current* revenues at the prevailing prices of inputs and outputs (zero current profit) and capital goods dealers have driven profits on the buying and selling of capital goods *between periods* to zero (zero profit intertemporal arbitrage) at prevailing prices. Implicit is our assumption that the prices prevailing are equilibrium prices in the sense that expectations of agents are met. These assumptions allow us to derive the traditional accounts (Samuelson, 1961, Table 1). An essential entry in these accounts is the *market rate of interest*; we defer an analysis of this item until Chapter 3.

A key property of the traditional accounts is the absence of capital gains or asset price changes and we observe this in Table 1.2. However, with more than one capital good, an economy typically exhibits changes in the ratios of the capital goods and changes in relative capital goods prices. These asset price changes are accounted for in the income side of the accounts. We introduce this topic here. Since green national accounting deals with stocks of natural capital, such asset price changes are a central part of the accounts analysis.

And we note five other accounting problems, as we label them, that emerge in this volume and in a sense represent departures from the traditional accounts. Two deal with special types of non-constant returns to scale. One is associated with imperfect competition, one with varying discount rates, and the last with exogenous technical change. These problems get a more detailed analysis later in this monograph.

1.2 ACCOUNTING IN A CLOSED, STEADY-STATE ECONOMY

This first economy has one commodity produced with constant amounts of labor and machine capital over the period. The output is consumed at the end of the period and the scenario repeats itself into the indefinite future. This is a stationary or steady-state situation. There is no investment and hence no accumulation of capital, and this immensely simplifies the analysis of valuing capital.

We abstract from the presence of other inputs into production, such as land (sites), and from the possible intermediateness of our goods. We take up intermediate goods in Chapter 2. We abstract from foreign trade, government and a monetary system (currency and banking). We abstract from the use of natural inputs such as oil flows, which are drawn from shrinking stocks, and/or timber flows which are drawn from renewable stocks. We abstract from pricing problems or imperfections associated with, say, externalities and/or imperfect competition. The question of what to leave out is somewhat arbitrary. In abstracting from x, one is implicitly saying it is of less importance than y, not abstracted from. History and tradition often dictate what constitutes the core model and what is to be abstracted from. For example, natural resources have been abstracted from in national accounting in part because national accounting was developed in nations which considered themselves to be 'industrial'. Labor and machine-capital services were considered to be the dominant inputs in production in 'industrial' countries. The impetus for moving to include natural resources in the national accounts has in large part arisen from the 'application' of national accounting to nations specialized in, say, oil exporting. In an oil-exporting nation, depletion effects and sustainability are central issues for the national accounts to deal with. We move on to these matters after we have set out our accounts for a simple, closed 'industrial' economy.

Each firm i has a constant returns to scale production function $f^i(k^i, n^i)$ which captures its technical-engineering 'constraints'. The production process involves transmuting the services of M-capital k^i and labor n^i into q^i amount of goods over the accounting period. Since all firms are assumed to be the same, we consider the aggregate 'input–output' relation

$$Q = F(K, L).$$

It is generally assumed that firms have some flexibility in their choice of 'techniques' or engineering specifications. Hence $F(\cdot)$ is assumed to exhibit substitutability among inputs. Different combinations of M-capital and labor can produce the same flow of Q. (If this substitutability assumption were not in effect, the production process would be as

$$Q = a^K Q + a^N Q$$

where a^K is a parameter defining the amount of services of M-capital required per unit of consumer goods produced. Such technical specifications are often referred to as 'fixed coefficient' or 'Leontief'.)

For our case with substitutability and constant returns to scale, we can express the relationship $Q = F(K, L)$ as

$$Q = K \frac{\partial F}{\partial K} + N \frac{\partial F}{\partial N}$$

where $\partial F/\partial K$ and $\partial F/\partial N$ are partial derivatives of the production function $F(\cdot)$. (The so-called 'Euler's Theorem' allows us to express our production relation as above.) We have in turn

$$pQ = K \frac{\partial F}{\partial K} p + N \frac{\partial F}{\partial N} p$$
$$= Krq + Nw$$

where p is the price (dollars per unit) of consumer goods and w ($= p \, (\partial F/\partial N)$) is the wage ($\$$ per unit of labor services). q is the price (capital value) of a unit of M-capital. It is the market price of *buying* a machine for use in production. rq is the rental price for renting the services of a unit of M-capital for a year, the accounting period. r here is the interest rate. q can be thought of as the cost of *replacing* a machine being used as distinct from the original outlay for the machine (its so-called 'book value'). q here has come to be referred to a 'Tobin's q'. In Chapter 3, we report on q in detail. There are many delicate issues in valuing capital goods because their value changes over time as they wear out in use and lose value because of obsolescence. We do not intend to dwell on these important issues at this time. Our formulation here is not intended to be novel or innovative. Innovations will be taken up later. The point to note here is that we have moved from a representation of goods production in physical flows terms to one in dollar value of flows terms. The national accounts 'function' in terms of dollar flows so that, roughly speaking, all magnitudes are comparable and can be summed to yield familiar aggregates.

The statements

$$w = p \, \frac{\partial F}{\partial N} \, , \, rq = p \, \frac{\partial F}{\partial K}$$

are so-called 'value of marginal product input pricing relations'. Under competitive conditions in input markets (many buyers, many sellers), inputs are said to be valued in use according to the value of their marginal products. This value in use, in equilibrium, becomes the same as the cost or payment in use. This approach to valuing (pricing) inputs is known as the marginal productivity theory of input pricing.

We can summarize what we have presented above in a national accounting matrix (NAM), a particular case of a social accounting matrix (SAM) developed by Richard Stone (1951, 1973) and others.[1] A NAM is an accounting framework for all accounting for flows in a general equilibrium system. Value sum in a specific row (receipts) must equal the value sum in the corresponding column (expenditures). This rule of construction of the table constitutes a disciplinary feedback mechanism which forces the models to have the value of primary inputs (value-added) in the economy in balance with the aggregate expenditures on final product. In a sense it makes double-entry book-keeping at the level of the nation internally consistent. The result emerging in the NAM in Table 1.1 is aggregate household expenditure, pQ equals aggregate household income, $wN + rqK$. Or the value of expenditure on final goods produced over the accounting period equals the value of incomes accruing to all primary inputs, ultimately owned by households. $wN + rqK$ is often referred to as total primary factor income or total value-added over the accounting period. Other terms relevant are gross national product on the expenditure

Table 1.1   *National accounting matrix (stationary, one-commodity, two-factor economy)*

Expenditures ↓ Receipts →	Consumer goods	Labor	M-capital	Households
Consumer goods				pX
Labor	wN			
M-capital	rqK			
Households		wN	rqK	

side and gross national income on the income side. One can also refer to the expenditure side as the value of final demand.

1.3 SCALE EFFECTS AND PROFIT

In the absence of constant returns to scale in the technology of production, the value of inputs does not equal the value of product under marginal cost pricing of inputs. For example, with decreasing returns to scale we have

$$pQ = \pi + wN + rqK,$$

where π denotes profit. Profit is essentially a residual income category here after inputs have been paid the values of their marginal products. This is a straightforward way to obtain a profit entry but fails to capture the intuitive notion of profit as a return to entrepreneurship or risk-taking. We observe below, when we introduce financial institutions, including equity holding in firms by households, that natural profit entries emerge. These 'profit' terms are capturing a return to shareholders for risk-taking. Nevertheless there remains the central problem of spreading revenues of firms back onto inputs when returns to scale in production are not constant.

A characterization of technology under non-constant returns is

$$Q = F(\lambda K, \lambda N)$$

$$= \lambda F(K, N)$$

for function $F(\cdot)$ homogeneous of degree λ. When λ equals unity, we have constant returns to scale. λ greater than (less than) unity is associated with increasing (decreasing) returns to scale. Under marginal cost pricing of inputs and $\lambda \neq 1$, we obtain

$$pQ = \pi + wN + rqK$$

with π positive (negative) under decreasing (increasing) returns to scale. The import of this is that marginal cost pricing of inputs ceases to yield 'product exhaustion' when the technology exhibits increasing returns to scale. We have then

Accounting Problem 1: Non-constant returns to scale in goods production complicates the linking of the value of product to the value of inputs.

One approach is to introduce a 'residual' productive input such as land which gets residual income after others have received the values of their marginal products (for example, Starrett, 1974). Another approach is to introduce mark-up pricing of outputs in order to have firms obtain sufficient revenues to cover off total input payments in accord with marginal cost pricing, as in Romer (1990), reported on in Chapter 8. There is, however, no standard procedure for dealing with this central issue. One usually falls back on the assumption of large quantities being produced and of those quantities being produced under constant returns to scale. Unless explicitly indicated, we too shall assume that constant returns to scale and marginal cost pricing are in effect.

1.4 A GOVERNMENT SECTOR

One can view the government as a large firm producing government services such as law and order, and national defense with inputs of M-capital and labor. One could envisage a production function underlying this production activity but we shall proceed in a somewhat *ad hoc* fashion and simply say that government uses the services of labor in N^G and M-capital in K^G and balances its budget by collecting the appropriate tax revenue T from households. Household expenditure gets a new entry, in T, corresponding to a new row, labelled 'government' in Table 1.1, and a new column, capturing government expenditure on inputs, gets added with entries wN^G and rqK^G. The assumption of budget balance has row sum T equal to column sum $wNG + rqK^G$.

Given the fixed endowments (K, N) for our economy, the effect of a new user of inputs, namely the government, is to 'crowd out' inputs available for use by the other (consumer goods) sector. National income will remain at $wN + rqK$. National expenditure will be $pX + T$, where X is reduced because government co-opted some of the inputs formerly used to produce X. When the government's current expenditure exceeds revenues, T, a borrowing activity must be added and this brings financial considerations into the flow accounts. (Certain intrinsic financial relations are introduced in Chapter 2, in order to incorporate commercial banking firms into the accounts.) We shall, however, for the most part, leave government out of the accounts from now on.

1.5 AN ECONOMY WITH K-CAPITAL BEING ACCUMULATED

A textbook characterization of an economy (Samuelson, 1961, Table 1) has current aggregate output Q produced under constant returns to scale with the services of K-capital, K, and labor services from N. That is, $Q = F(K, N)$. K-

capital decays at exogenous rate δ and consumption goods C and gross new capital I^G are jointly produced or share identical technologies. This latter assumption means that the market price for a unit of C and a unit of I^G must be the same. At any date t, we have

$$C + I^G = F(K, N)$$

and

$$C + I^G = KF_K + NF_N.$$

We treat N as constant. Let the price of C and I be unity, then F_N is referred to as the value of the marginal product of labor and gets equated to the market wage rate w under competitive conditions.

Net new capital is $I^N (= I^G - \delta K)$. An equilibrium condition for this economy is that 'competition' results in zero profits by goods producers. Hence a key accounting relation is

$$C + I^G = KF_K + NF_N.$$

Since K is durable, producers are said to rent the K over the production period and to pay rentals to capital goods owners. Workers own their 'human capital' and rent themselves and their human capital out for 'rentals', $NF_N (= wN)$, or wage payments.

A coherent way to close the accounts is to postulate the existence of a group of capital goods dealers (CGDs) who live by buying K capital at the end of period $t - 1$, renting it out to goods producers for period t, and selling the remaining capital at the end of period t. The CGDs must make zero profits in equilibrium by this arbitrage activity. (We refer to this condition as zero profit intertemporal arbitrage (ZPIA) activity.) That is

$$K_{t-1} = \frac{F_K(t)K_{t-1} + (1 - \delta)K_{t-1}}{1 + r_t}$$

or the purchase price of K_{t-1} at the end of period $t - 1$ equals discounted returns from the end of period t. r_t is the *market interest rate*. $F_K(t) K_{t-1}$ is rental income accruing at the end of period t. This ZPIA condition serves to *define* what r_t must be in order to preserve coherence in the accounts.[2] Hence

$$r_t = F_K(t) - \delta.$$

We gloss over time subscripts now and present the accounts for this classic economy in Table 1.2.

National accounting and capital

Table 1.2   National accounting matrix (two goods, semi-durable K-capital)

Expenditures ↓ Receipts →	Consumption goods and investment goods	Labor	K-capital	Households
Consumption goods and investment goods				C I^G
Labor	NF_N			
K-capital	KF_K			$-\delta K$
Households		NF_N	Kr	

Gross national product (GNP) is $C + I^G$ in the households column and net national product (NNP) is $C + I^G - \delta K$, the sum of entries in the households column. Given, by construction, the row sum equal to the column sum, we have net national income (NNI) as $NF_N + Kr$ in the households row. GNP differs from NNP by 'depreciation', $-\delta K$, of K-capital over the 'period' of production. If amount δK were taken from GNP and put into investment in K-capital, we could say that K-capital was being preserved intact. NNP would then constitute current product that *could* be consumed, while leaving K intact. This view of NNP, as potential consumption, makes NNP an instance of *Hicksian Income* (Hicks, 1939, Chapter 14) defined as a level of consumption that could be pursued, while maintaining capital intact.

To summarize: static zero profit conditions for 'goods' production and dynamic zero profit conditions for capital goods dealing yield our national accounts. The rules which we use repeatedly below in obtaining our accounts, product or expenditure on one side and income or value-added on the other are: (1) set out current revenue equal to current expenditure or inputs for 'goods' production (use value of marginal product pricing for inputs and pay attention to constant returns to scale or a lack thereof), (2) multiply each first-order condition including Euler equations or zero profit intertemporal arbitrage conditions by its real variable (for example, K_{t-1} for the K-capital condition) and insert these conditions into the national accounting matrix, and (3) make sure that the discount rates in the accounts are market interest rates, not social discount rates.

We need additional behavioral relations to determine how current aggregate output gets divided between consumption goods and investment goods, and how the market interest rate is linked to 'time preference'. We take these matters up below. The accounting associated with our economy was made easier by the assumptions of (a) constant returns to scale in goods production, (b) a single commodity produced (consumption and investment goods share the same technology), (c) competition in production and capital goods dealing, and (d) an exogenous rate of decay in K-capital.

1.6 INTERMEDIATE GOODS

Such goods play a large role in our subsequent analysis. We illustrate with the case of K-capital maintenance. Suppose our K-stock does not suffer 'decay' as in δK but instead gets oiled and polished each period at cost $g(K, N_1)$ in terms of goods produced. N_1 is labor in maintenance activity. Thus goods production becomes

$$C + I + g(K, N_1) = F(K, N - N_1).$$

K only accommodates so that I is both the net and gross increase in K. We assume that goods production takes place under constant returns to scale. Hence

$$C + I + g(K, N_1) = KF_K + (N - N_1)F_Z \tag{1.1}$$

where $Z = N - N_1$. And we assume that maintenance takes place under constant returns to scale. Hence

$$g(K, N_1) = Kg_K + N_1 g_{N_1}. \tag{1.2}$$

Goods producers and K-capital maintenance firms compete for labor. Hence

$$N_1 F_Z = -N_1 g_{N_1}. \tag{1.3}$$

The market return r_t resembles our previous case in that it is net of maintenance per unit:[3]

$$r_t = F_K(t) - g_K(t).$$

Hence

$$KF_K - Kg_K = Kr_t. \tag{1.4}$$

Equation (1.1) is our first row–column pair in our national accounting matrix in Table 1.3. Equation (1.3) gives us our third row–column pair in Table 1.3 and equation (1.4) gives us our second row–column pair.

Table 1.3   National accounting matrix (intermediate goods)

Expenditures ↓ Receipts →	'Goods' production	K-capital	Labor	Households
'Goods' production				$C + I + g(\cdot)$
K-capital	KF_K			$-Kg_K$
Labor	$(N - N_1)F_Z$			$-N_1 g_{N_1}$
Households		Kr_t	NF_Z	

When the entries in the households column are rationalized, we end up with

$$NNP = C + I$$

because $g(\cdot) = Kg_K + N_1 g_{N_1}$. Maintenance here is an intermediate activity, not appearing in net product. GNP is $C + I + g(\cdot)$. Hence maintenance activity washes out in the households column in the same way that depreciation δK washed out in the households column in Table 1.2. We shall observe that extraction costs for oil and/or harvesting costs for fishing or timbering operate in an accounting sense in the same way as our maintenance costs, here. A huge amount of economic activity is intermediate in precisely the sense that our maintenance activity was. Such activity uses up resources in the current period but contributes only indirectly to creating consumables, C. The whole transportation sector of an economy comes to mind. In Chapter 2, we focus on the banking or financial sector of an economy which is also intermediate to the economy. Consumers derive no direct utility or pleasure from banking activity but the financial sector facilitates the production of consumables for citizens.

A problem arises if $g(\cdot)$ above does not exhibit constant returns to scale. For example, $g(\cdot)$ might take the form of simply $g(N_1)$ with $g(\cdot)$ now concave in N_1. Then

$$g(N_1) - N_1 g_{N_1} > 0$$

and we would not get the washing out in the households column that we achieved. Then a surplus would get entered in national income, an obvious accounting awkwardness. We have then

Accounting Problem 2: Non-constant returns in intermediate goods production creates problems in linking the value of product to the value of inputs.

A related problem arises with renewable resources in the model. The renewability function is typically *concave* in the stock of the resource and this concavity shows up as a surplus income flow in national income. See Chapter 5. Let us refer to this as

Accounting Problem 3: Non-linearity in natural stock renewal functions leads to a surplus income flow in national income.

1.7 PRICE CHANGES OF CAPITAL GOODS

When an economy with multiple capital goods is not in balanced growth (balanced growth being a very unusual state), capital goods will be in changing proportions to one another and relative prices of such goods will be changing. These price changes cannot be netted out and must be accounted for in the accounts. We shall illustrate with a simple model involving K-capital and produced knowledge capital, A. The latter requires N_1 workers in

$$\dot{A} = aAN_1$$

where $\dot{A}$ is new knowledge capital and a is a positive parameter. K-capital is produced in the usual way, so that

$$C + \dot{K} = F[K, (N - N_1)A]$$

where N is the fixed labor endowment in the economy and $\dot{K}$ is newly produced K-capital. There is no shrinkage or wear and tear in K. C is aggregate consumption. Knowledge capital makes workers more productive. In this economy, there is a market interest rate r_t and

$$r_t = F_K(t).$$

The price of K-capital is wrapped up in r_t and the price of A-capital is m in relation to the price of K-capital. m will be moving over time because A and K

will, in general, be growing at different rates. This change in the price of A-capital can be expressed as

$$(r - r^A)m$$

where r^A is an own-rate of interest on A-capital. Such rates are discussed in Chapter 3. The ZPIA condition on A-capital is

$$A(N - N_1)F_Z + \dot{A}m = mAr^A.$$

where $Z = A(N - N_1)$. Since own-rate r^A is not observable in the marketplace, one rewrites this as

$$A(N - N_1)F_Z + \dot{A}m = (r^A - r)mA + rmA.$$

This forms the third row–column pair in our national accounting matrix in Table 1.4. Entry $(r^A - r)mA$ is expressing the relative decline in the price of A compared with the price of K. It can be written as $-\dot{A}m$. This will be observable in the market place.

$\dot{A}m$ in the households column is the economic depreciation (here appreciation) in the A-stock. The households column is net national product. The households row is net national income and includes the A-capital current price change. We have then

Table 1.4   *National accounting matrix (knowledge capital and K-capital)*

Expenditures ↓ Receipts →	'Goods' production	K-capital	A-capital	Households
'Goods' production				$C + \dot{K}$
K-capital	KF_K			
A-capital	$A(N - N_1)F_Z$			$\dot{A}m$
Households		rK	$(r - \dot{m}/m)mA$	

Accounting Problem 4: Multiple capital goods involve relative capital goods price changes which are generally entries in national income.

This model with knowledge capital being accumulated is reported on in somewhat more detail in Chapter 9. We repeat: the asset price entries are not present when the proportions of capital goods are unchanging or as in balanced growth. There is a long-standing rule in national accounting: no price changes in NNP. We have been discussing changes in the values of capital goods not flow goods and we are sticking to keeping such price changes in the income side of the accounts. A case can be made for inserting such changes in the product side of the accounts but we do not pursue this line of thinking at this point. Above we added knowledge capital A to a model with K-capital. One view of green national accounting is that it involves adding stocks of natural capital to models with K-capital. And our Chapters 4, 5, and 6 do that directly. Much attention is focused on natural capital in Chapter 7, 'International trade', as well. Chapters 8 and 9 deal with a capital stock associated with technical change. And in Chapter 9, we deal with two vintages of one type of capital. Hence, from one perspective, this is a study of models with multiple capital goods and thus, capital goods price changes is a central part of the analysis.

1.8   EXOGENOUS TECHNICAL CHANGE

Accounting both literally and figuratively for technical change has been a central activity for economists since the industrial revolution starting in, say, 1775. Much of prosperity derives from improved techniques and more productive capital goods and workers. Here we touch on exogenous technical change since it raises its own peculiar accounting problem. We draw on our model from the chapter on technical change. Goods production occurs in

$$C + \dot{K} = F(K, N, s)$$

where s simply grows under its own steam. s resembles a capital good getting larger and larger, with no resource using investment. Under constant returns to scale, we have

$$F(\cdot) = KF_K + NF_N + sF_s.$$

Dealing with s as a capital good is dealt with in Chapter 9. It has its own price F_s and its own interest rate r_t^s. See the preliminaries to Table 9.2. What the households row of Table 9.2 indicates is that there is an income entry for income ascribable to the stock, s, under marginal cost pricing. NNP there is $C + \dot{K}$ and national income (total value-added) is $NF_N + Kr_t + \mu s r_t^s / \lambda$ where μ / λ

is the price of a unit of stock *s*. Hence, though income should be flowing to owners of *s*, there are no owners to collect the income. Hence the income gets smeared somehow over the other inputs showing up as high wages or returns to *K*-capital. But these 'high' returns distort investment and labor allocation from their first-best values. Thus an economy with exogenous technical change has the value of product and the value of incomes distorted because extra income is being smeared over the owned inputs. We refer to this as

Accounting Problem 5: Exogenous technical change leads to a de-linking of the value of product and the value of inputs.

Such de-linking is much like that associated with non-constant returns to scale and the measurement person often has no way of distinguishing which cause is leading to a de-linking of the value of product and of inputs under value-of-marginal-product input pricing. We report on this in more detail in Chapter 9.

1.9   IMPERFECT COMPETITION AND VARYING DISCOUNT RATES

To round out our introduction to accounting problems, we note that in Chapters 6 and 9 we take up cases of departures from a first-best economy. Recall the simple case of price departing from marginal cost under monopoly. Such departures imply surplus income as monopoly profit or income not tied to a competitively priced input. In Chapter 6, we deal with so-called free access problems and underpricing of, say, fish stocks. In Chapter 9, we take up Romer's (1990) growth model with its distinctive elements of monopolistic competition. We have then

Accounting Problem 6: Departures from a first-best or the perfectly competitive paradigm lead to input price distortions and 'surpluses' in national income.

Finally we note that the assumption of a constant social discount rate makes doing accounting easier. In Chapters 3 and 4, we report on cases of non-constant discount rates. We have then:

Accounting Problem 7: Departure from constancy of the social discount rate creates problems in defining the market interest rates.

1.10 FINANCING A FIRM AND RULING OUT ARBITRAGE PROFITS

Treating current revenue of a firm as equal to current costs of production is a convenient approximation. We shall make use of this notion of equilibrium in much of the remainder of this monograph. In a sense it is an accounting rule of thumb that has become entrenched by long-standing practice. A superior approach has current revenue for the firm equal to current costs plus change in debt. A steady-state version of this has

$$pq^i = wN^i + r^L L^i + (r + \gamma^i)E^i - r^D D^i$$

where pq^i is current revenue, wN^i is current labor costs, $r^L L^i$ is current costs of loans to the firm, $(r + \gamma^i)E^i$ is current costs of equity, E^i, to the firm and $r^D D^i$ is current 'revenue' from bank deposits owned by the firm. γ^i is the risk premium and r^L, r^D and r are the loan rate, deposit rate and certain rate of the economy. This is the basic flow balance for a firm in a steady state. The corresponding asset balance or capital 'constraint' for the firm is

$$E^i + L^i = qK^i + D^i$$

or liabilities, measured in dollars, equal assets. If one multiplies this by r and subtracts from the one above, one obtains the alternative flow balance relation for the firm

$$pq^i = wN^i + rqK^i + (r^L - r)L^i + (r - r^D)D^i + \gamma^i E^i.$$

Here $(r^L - r)L^i$ and $(r - r^D)D^i$ are representations of the value-added in banks, generically defined, involved in providing lending services and deposit services to the firm. $\gamma^i E^i$ is a cost to households of providing equity to the firm. We link these banking entries to the accounts of banking firms in the next chapter. This financial approach to national accounting represents a substantial departure from current practice.

1.11 CONCLUDING REMARKS

Two tasks were taken up in this chapter. We introduced our national accounting matrix (NAM) and related various versions to somewhat different economies. The NAM yields a straightforward representation of net national expenditure or product in the households column and of aggregate value-added or net national income in the households row. Second, we obtained precise representations of net investment, economic depreciation of capital, and value-added from capital by incorporating the standard zero profit intertemporal arbitrage (ZPIA) condition into the national accounts. We derived the traditional accounts (Table 1.2) for the classic textbook economy with homogeneous person-made capital. And we noted the place of government in our national accounting framework.

A classic result we observed in our derivations of accounts for our different economies was the absence of pure capital gains terms in NNP or in the terms for economic depreciation in NNP. Asset price changes do appear on the income side of the accounts, in general. We introduced seven problems associated with national accounting in complicated problems. If one departs from our basic dynamic model associated with Table 1.2, one runs into at least one of these seven problems. Three deal with non-constant returns to scale. One involves the departure from perfect competition or a first-best. One is associated with multiple capital goods and another is related to non-constant discount rates. The last relates to exogenous technical change. In a sense textbook or generic economic problems or complications lead to certain generic problems for accounting.

NOTES

1. Defourny and Thorbecke (1984) is an accessible introduction. Our NAM is a special case designed to focus on net national product (households column in Table 1.1) and net national income (households row in Table 1.1). In Table 1.2, we incorporate the zero profit intertemporal arbitrage condition into our NAM. This is a central innovation. Eurostat (1996) makes considerable use of social accounting matrices in their reporting of recommended national accounting practices.
2. One usually thinks of r_t as reflecting 'time preference', and we shall pursue that idea later.
3. This condition and the previous one in (1.3) are first-order or equilibrium conditions in planning or 'market replication' problems.

REFERENCES

Defourny, J. and E. Thorbecke (1984), 'Structural path analysis and multiplier decomposition within a social accounting matrix framework', *Economic Journal*, **94**, March, 111–36.

Eurostat (1996), *European System of Accounts, ESA 1995*, Luxembourg: Office for Official Publications of the European Communities.

Hicks, John R. (1939), *Value and Capital*, Oxford: Clarendon Press.

Romer, Paul (1990), 'Endogenous technical change', *Journal of Political Economy*, **98**, 71–102.

Samuelson, P.A. (1961), 'The evaluation of "social income": capital formation and wealth', in F.A. Lutz and D.C. Hague (eds), *The Theory of Capital*, London: Macmillan.

Starrett, David (1974), 'Principles of optimal location in a large homogeneous area', *Journal of Economic Theory*, **4**, December, 418–48.

2. Integrating financial-capital accounts of firms into the national accounts

2.1 INTRODUCTION

In this chapter we introduce banks, broadly conceived, into a simple one-commodity economy. Banks provide deposit services (check-writing services) for households and firms and lending services for firms. Associated with these services, produced with labor and K-capital, are dollar stocks, deposits and loan capital. These last three have interest rate spreads or mark-ups as prices. We set out a dual accounting and valuation system for economies with banks. There is the real system with banking services produced with labor and K-capital and the financial system with banking activities represented by dollar stocks and interest rate spreads as prices.

Firms, including banks, have two sets of accounts, flow or zero current profit relations, and capital accounts. The integration of these accounts leads to our valuation in terms of dollar stocks and interest rate spreads. The bottom line is that there are natural proxies for the direct value of labor and K-capital in banking services. 'Imputation' is straightforward. Equity financing of firms by households is a substitute for bank financing and we treat this financial activity in a fashion parallel to that of banking activity.

A central accounting issue associated with financial activity is: how much is purely intermediate and how much should be represented in NNP? We deal with this issue in complete detail.[1] In our view all of the activity is intermediate in an economic sense but some activity ends up in NNP and this is viewed as transactions activity related to the acquisition of final goods by households. In the broader sense, then, this transactions activity should be viewed as a cost to the households of acquiring the final goods. Hence all banking activity is intermediate. We take a few pages to set out the generic accounts for an economy, starting with intermediate goods.

Another form of financial activity is asset-trading, which one associates with the process of asset price formation. Roughly speaking, trading occurs as long as asset prices are away from equilibrium values. We explore this idea and close with a dynamic model, incorporating simple formulations of transactions activity and intermediation activity, this latter being resource-using activity involved in getting savings allocated to (invested in) good projects.

2.2   A STEADY-STATE ONE-COMMODITY ECONOMY

Recall from Chapter 1 that a steady-state economy, involving constant returns to scale in production $F(K, N)$ and perfect competition has its accounts as in Table 2.1. Under value-of-marginal-product input pricing, the wage is pF_N ($= w$) and the rental rate on K-capital is pF_K ($= rq$). The value of product, pX, equals the value of inputs, wN plus rqK. Inputs N and K remain unchanging over time.

In the national accounting matrix (NAM) in Table 2.1, the widget firm row sum is the value of output and the column sum is the value of inputs. Labor's column sum is dollars expended in the economy on labor and the row sum is dollars received by labor in the economy over the accounting period. Similarly for machine capital. The households column sum is net national product or the value of final product, final in the sense of ending up in households, not firms, and the households row sum is primary factor income or value-added or net national income. The row sum for labor (machine capital) is the aggregate demand for labor (machine capital) services. The column sum is the aggregate value of labor (machine capital) service supply.

Table 2.1   A national accounting matrix

Expenditures ↓ Receipts →	Widget firms	Labor	Machine capital	Households
Widget firms				pX
Labor	wN			
Machine capital	rqK			
Households		wN	rqK	

2.3   INTERMEDIATE GOODS

It is important to distinguish intermediate from final goods in order to avoid double counting. Traditional intermediate goods received a careful formalization in Leontief's input–output system. Financial services are a conceptually distinct class of intermediate goods and are treated below.

We have two produced goods

$$X^1 = F^1 (x^{11}, x^{21}, N^1, K^1)$$

$$X^2 = F^2 (x^{12}, x^{22}, N^2, K^2)$$

with constant returns to scale production functions $F^1(\cdot)$ and $F^2(\cdot)$, respectively. x^{ij} is the current flow of good i used in producing good j. Good i uses some of itself as intermediate input, x^{ii}. N^i and K^i correspond to flows of services of primary inputs into the production of good i. X^i is the flow of final product i over the accounting period.

Euler's Theorem allows us to write

$$X^i = x^{1i} \frac{\partial F^i}{\partial x^{1i}} + x^{2i} \frac{\partial F^i}{\partial x^{2i}} + N^i \frac{\partial F^i}{\partial N^i} + K^i \frac{\partial F^i}{\partial K^i} \ (i = 1, 2).$$

We can then write values

$$p^i X^i = x^{1i} p^i \frac{\partial F^i}{\partial x^{1i}} + x^{2i} p^i \frac{\partial F^i}{\partial x^{2i}} + N^i p^i \frac{\partial F^i}{\partial N^i} + K^i p^i \frac{\partial F^i}{\partial K^i}$$

$$= a^{1i} X^i p^1 + a^{2i} X^i p^2 + N^i w + K^i rq \ (i = 1, 2).$$

under the pricing of inputs in accord with the value of their marginal products.
In this step, we make use of the fact that

$$p_2 = p_1 \frac{\partial F^1}{\partial x^{21}}, \ p_1 = p_2 \frac{\partial F^2}{\partial x^{12}}, \text{ and } \frac{\partial F^i}{\partial x^{ii}} = a^{ii}.$$

Note that X^i measures gross flow of commodity i over the accounting period. By definition net flow is

$$C^i = X^i - a^{i1} X^1 - a^{i2} X^2 \ (i = 1, 2).$$

Also

$$p^i = a^{1i} p^i + a^{2i} p^2 + wN^i/X^i + rqK^i/X^i \ (i = 1, 2),$$

or the price of a unit of i fully embodies the cost of intermediate as well as primary inputs. (This same 'embodiment' shows up below, where the price of widgets embodies (intermediate) banking services.)

Table 2.2 *National accounting matrix (two goods with intermediate flows, two primary factors)*

	Expenditure ↓ Receipts →	Sector 1 firms	Sector 2 firms	Intermediate Sector 1 firms	Intermediate Sector 2 firms	Labor	Machine capital	Households
	Sector 1 firms			$p^1a^{11}X^1$	$p^1a^{12}X^2$			p^1X^1
	Sector 2 firms			$p^2a^{21}X^1$	$p^2a^{22}X^2$			p^2C^2
Intermediate	Sector 1 firms	$p^1a^{11}X^1$	$p^1a^{12}X^2$					
Intermediate	Sector 2 firms	$p^2a^{21}X^1$	$p^2a^{22}X^2$					
	Labor	wN^1	wN^2					
	Capital	rqK^1	rqK^2					
	Households					wN	rqK	

Endowments of flows of primary input services K and N must equal 'demands' over the accounting period. That is,

$$N = N^1 + N^2$$

$$K = K^1 + K^2$$

These lead to balance relations, values in equal values set in the NAM in Table 2.2 (labor (machine capital) column equals labor (machine capital) row). The household row entries contain values of primary factors supplied over the accounting period.

Recall that a row sum, measuring flows in dollars over the accounting period must equal the corresponding column sum. The bottom line, so to speak, is the household column sum (measuring national *product*) equals the household row sum (measuring national income or the sum of the value of primary inputs (value-added) used over the accounting period). Recall that there is no production of new capital goods in our model here. We are in a steady state, living off flows from durable K and labor services year after year.

Intermediate goods flows are in the middle section of Table 2.2. The costs of these inputs are embodied in the revenues received by firms in the final goods market but these inputs are intermediate in the sense that their presence is not recorded in the value of primary inputs used in production (the household row sum).

2.4   THE INTEGRATION OF THE FINANCIAL ACCOUNTS OF FIRMS AND HOUSEHOLDS

We return to our single-commodity widget economy. There is no saving or investment and no wearing out of machine capital. The economy is in a steady (stationary) state with no population growth or technical change. Recall Table 2.1. We now have firms owned by households, with equity capital or finance. The firm pays dividends $E(r + \gamma)$ on equity E where r is the certain rate (government bond rate) in the economy and γ is a mark-up demanded by equity holders as compensation for providing oversight activity to the firm.[2] We abstract from modelling stochasticity and investor uncertainty explicitly. We have then

$$\hat{E} = qK \qquad (2.1)$$

and

$$pX = wN + (r + \gamma)E. \qquad (2.2)$$

as the flow account of the firm. $\hat{E}$ is dollars of financial capital and E is a real flow of services provided by shareholders to firms. For the moment we link these two as $\hat{E} = E$. More detail follows below. We can retrieve the familiar flow account for the firm by multiplying (2.1) by r and inserting rE in (2.2) to obtain

$$pX = wN + rqK + \gamma E. \qquad (2.3)$$

The novel component of the right-hand side of (2.3) is risk flow, of γE dollars. Firms must achieve sufficient revenues to pay for the one-period rental of labor and capital plus compensation to shareholders for oversight services.

Our introduction of the financial accounts of firms, leads to a new NAM in Table 2.3 with a new purely intermediate flow, which we label financial capital, here for widget firms. The household column sum is national product for the period and the row sum is national income or aggregate value-added. Compensation for risk bearing, γE, is part of national income and ends up in the accounts for households. Although 'financial capital' in Table 2.3 is purely intermediate, it does not correspond to flows which remain in the upper left-hand corner of the table, as would traditional intermediate goods flows. 'Financial capital' corresponds to a new set of flows. The merit of this new approach is that it puts the accounts of firms and households on a more reasonable accounting footing. Households own the firms with an explicit tether, so to speak. And we end up with a new type of income accruing to households, namely compensation, γE, for 'supervising' the firms.

Table 2.3   One-sector stationary economy with financial accounts

Expenditures ↓ Receipts →	Widget firms	Financial capital	Labor	Machine capital	Households
Widget firms					pX
Financial capital	$r\hat{E}$				
Labor	wN				
Machine capital		rqK			
Households	γE		wN	rqK	

2.5   A LENDING INSTITUTION

Households now hold equities in a new group of competitive firms, which lend to widget producers. All widget firms are then debt financed, rather than equity financed as in the previous section. The lending institutions (LIs) have loan managers who place and monitor loans, and they collect interest payments.[3] The LIs' flow accounts are

$$r^L L - wN^L - (r + \gamma)E = 0 \qquad (2.4)$$

and

$$E = qK^L + L \qquad (2.5)$$

represents the financial capital constraint of the LI. L are loans in dollars and r^L is the loan rate. γ is the risk premium demanded of shareholders and E is equity in the bank. All loans are equity financed. There is an implicit production function relating inputs N^L and K^L, and E to output L, lending services associated with loan capital $\hat{L}$, placed with widget firms. We set $L = \hat{L}$ and $E = \hat{E}$ for the moment.

If we multiply (2.5) by r and substitute in (2.4), we get

$$(r^L - r)L = wN^L + rqK^L + \gamma E. \qquad (2.6)$$

The right-hand side is value-added in the lending sector and $(r^L - r)L$ is the value of output. $(r^L - r) \times \$1$ is the net price of a loan.

Widget producers are financed by the LI so that

$$\hat{L} = qK^W \qquad (2.7)$$

where K^W is machine capital in widget production. Flow accounts are

$$pX = wN^W + r^L L. \qquad (2.8)$$

Total labor services N, available equal total demanded in equilibrium, namely $N^W + N^L$. Similarly $K = K^W + K^L$. Multiply (2.7) by r and substitute in (2.6). Then substitute in (2.8) for $r^L L$ from (2.6). We obtain

$$pX = wN^W + wN^L + rqK^L + rqK^W + \gamma E. \qquad (2.9)$$

The cost of lending is fully 'capitalized' in the price charged by widget producers. Or lending is a purely intermediate activity in this economy. (Loan

Table 2.4 National accounting matrix (a pure lending institution)

Expenditures ↓ Receipts →	Widget firms	LIs	Financial capital — Widget	Financial capital — LI	Labor	Machine capital	Households
Widget firms							pX
LIs	$r^L L$						
Financial capital — Widget		$r\hat{E}$		$r\hat{L}$			
Financial capital — LI							
Labor	wN^W	wN^L					
Machine capital			rqK^W	rqK^L			
Households		γE			wN	rqK	

agents are intermediaries between savers and borrowers.) Lending here is direct resource-using whereas in the previous section, the savers (households) did their own 'loan' placing when they purchased equities. Nevertheless, lending in each case ends up fully 'capitalized' in the prices of output charged by borrowers. Recall that widget producers were the only agents 'demanding' finance in this economy.

We insert these accounts into a NAM in Table 2.4, where we have NNP in the households column sum, namely pX, and NNI in the households row sum, namely $wN + rqK + \gamma E$. The activities of the lending institutions are purely intermediate, except for the risk-cost of operating the LIs. This is standard in national accounting. The activities of financial institutions are resource-using but end up, from a valuation perspective, 'capitalized' in the prices of products of *firms* served. In this case loans are made to widget-producing firms and are turned over regularly into the indefinite future.

The other function which our generic banks perform is check-processing or the providing of services associated with cash held as deposits. Firms and households do check-cashing in their regular transacting activity. Thus our generic banks below do these two activities: loan-placing and monitoring, and deposit-taking and check-processing. We proceed now to explicitly link the real sides or representations of firms, banks and households to their financial representations. We have glossed over such detail to this point. For simplicity, we leave equity out in our first analysis. Equity is added later in a separate extension.

2.6   THE REAL (NON-FINANCIAL) FLOW REPRESENTATION OF THE ECONOMY

We assume constant returns to scale throughout the analysis. This simplifies valuation greatly and is regrettably at odds with what many observers argue for commercial banks.

Widget Firms

The zero profit condition is

$$p = a_{K,x}rq + a_{N,x}w + a_{D,x}p^D + a_{L,x}p^L, \tag{2.10}$$

where p is the price of a widget, rq is the rental price of a unit of K-capital, where r is the rate of interest and q is the price of unit of K-capital,[4] w is the wage rate, p^D is the price of a unit of deposit services, the latter provided by commercial banks, and p^L is the price of a unit of lending services, also provided by commercial banks. We conceive of deposit services as check-processing.[5] The firm pays its suppliers with checks drawn on its accounts at a commercial bank. The bank provides personnel and computers to process the checks and the cost of such inputs shows up in the price of deposit services. In fact price will equal the cost of inputs in our competitive, constant returns to scale framework. A lending service will take the form of monitoring of the borrower, a widget firm, by the commercial bank. We assume that we are in a stationary environment so that there is no expansion in K-capital and no new loans are being placed by the banks. Existing loans were let against earlier investment in K-capital by the widget firm. We treat the K-capital as perfectly durable. Check-writing will be linked to a stock of deposits held in the bank by the widget firm below when we take up the capital accounts of widget firms and commercial banks. Similarly, lending services will be linked to a stock of loan capital in the widget firm below. And households are assumed to consume real check-writing services.

The $a'_{i,j}$s are input coefficients, each a function of current input prices. Hence $a_{K,x}$ is the input of K-capital per unit of widgets X produced. And $a_{N,x}$, $a_{D,x}$ and $a_{L,x}$ are inputs of labor services, deposit services and lending services per unit of X produced. Hence

$$a_{K,x}X = K^x, \; a_{N,x}X = N^x, \; a_{D,x}X = D^x \text{ and } a_{L,x}X = L^x$$

where K^x, N^x, D^x and L^x are current use flows of K-capital, labor services deposit services, and lending services by the widget firms in the production of level X of widgets. A period in our stationary world is the time it takes to produce a batch of widgets. Households live on this commodity. It is our all-purpose, composite, produced final good.

Commercial Banks

The zero profit condition here is

$$p^L b_{L,Q} + p^D b_{D,Q} = w a_{N,Q} + rq a_{K,Q,} \tag{2.11}$$

where the $a'_{i,j}$s are input coefficients and the $b'_{k,m}$s are output coefficients, each a function of p^L, p^D, w and rental rq. We have in turn

$$Q b_{L,Q} = L, \; Q b_{D,Q} = D, \; Q a_{N,Q} = N^b \text{ and } Q a_{K,Q} = K^b,$$

where Q is an activity level for commercial banks, and L and D are flows of lending services and deposit services from the banks and N^b and K^b are labor and K-capital services currently used in the production of deposit and lending services. These outputs are measured in physical flows as in y checks processed per unit time for deposit services and z units of monitoring services done by banks with regard to their loans outstanding to the widget firms. We assume that the households have not borrowed from the banks.

Commodity Balance

There is a fixed endowment K and N of K-capital and labor services in the economy. Hence

$$K^b + K^x = K \qquad (2.12)$$

and

$$N^b + N^x = N. \qquad (2.13)$$

Also, the total output of lending services from the banks is consumed by the widget firms. Households consume some deposit services. They write checks when they acquire the final output, namely the widgets. Hence

$$D^x + D^h = D, \qquad (2.14)$$

where D^x is the supply of deposit services to widget firms.[6] Demand for deposit services by households is simply

$$D^x = \alpha X \qquad (2.15)$$

where α is a positive constant. The volume of checks processed in acquiring X is proportional to the physical amount of X acquired. This is a simple (simplistic) theory of transactions services. One might think of the analogy with transportation costs, as in resources used in transporting volume y of widgets from place A to place B is proportional to volume y.

Households

These entities supply the labor, own the K-capital and consume the widgets at the end of the production period. Hence

$$pX + p^D D^h = wN + rqK. \qquad (2.16)$$

The right-hand side is the value of all primary inputs in the economy and the left-hand side is the value of net product in the economy. Hence banking services are largely absent from net product. They are largely intermediate and are in a sense 'capitalized' in the price of widgets. That is, the price of a

Table 2.5 *National accounting matrix (real representation of bank services)*

Expenditures ↓ Receipts →	Widget production	Bank production (deposit and loan services)	K-capital	Labor	Households
Widget production					pX
Deposit services	$p^D a_{D,X} X$	$-p^D b_{D,Q} Q$			$p^D D^h$
Loan services	$p^L a_{L,X} X$	$-p^L b_{L,Q} Q$			
K-capital	$rq a_{K,X} X$	$rq a_{K,Q} Q$			
Labor	$w a_{N,X} X$	$w a_{N,Q} Q$			
Households			rqK	wN	

widget includes the cost of banking services required f28or the production of that widget. Since $p^D D^h$ are in fact the banking services needed by households to acquire the widgets, one can argue that the value of these services should be considered a part of the price of a widget 'at the home' of the consumer. There is a sense then that all banking services are purely intermediate in the final aggregate accounts for our economy. This an observation of long standing and was emphasized in Hartwick (1997).

Summary

Equilibrium emerges in a system that functions as if pX were being maximized, subject to

$$a_{K,x}X + a_{K,b}Q = K,$$

$$a_{N,x}X + a_{N,b}Q = N,$$

$$a_{L,x}X - b_{L,b}Q = 0,$$

$$a_{D,x}X - b_{D,Q}Q + D^h = 0,$$

$$aX - D^h = 0,$$

where of course the $a'_{i,j}$s and $b'_{k,m}$s are endogenously determined as functions of the equilibrium prices. See Table 2.5 for a national accounting matrix representation of this system.

We turn to representing this equilibrium with financial valuation for deposit and lending services. This is somewhat more complicated and more interesting than simply representing p^D and p^L with appropriate interest rate spreads.

2.7   FINANCIAL VALUATION

We take up the flow and capital accounts of widget firms and then commercial banks. The integration of the two sets of accounts for each type of firm yields the financial valuations of deposit and lending services. Interest rate spreads appear as prices in this valuation system. We are obtaining perfect proxy measures of the value of certain services of commercial banks. (The same approach works for the services associated with equity holding and we pursue this later.)

Widget Firms

The *flow accounts* of the widget firms are

$$pX = r^L \hat{L} - r^D \hat{D}^x + wN^x, \tag{2.17}$$

where r^L and r^D are the lending and deposit rate, respectively, and $\hat{L}$ and D^x are loans to and deposits of widget firms, respectively. These latter are stocks of dollars. The *capital accounts* of these firms are

$$\hat{L} = qK^x + \hat{D}^x. \tag{2.18}$$

If (2.18) is multiplied by r and inserted in (2.17) we obtain the revised flow accounts (RFA) in

$$pX = (r^L - r)\hat{L} + (r - r^D)\hat{D}^x + wN^x + rqK^x. \tag{2.19}$$

It is apparent in light of our real representation of these flow accounts above that

$$(r^L - r)\hat{L} + (r - r^D)\hat{D}^x = p^L L + p^D D^x. \tag{2.20}$$

Hence we have an insight into how financial valuation coincides with real valuation and the roles played by interest rate spreads and by financial stocks. But this is preliminary. More on these fundamental links below.

Commercial Banks

The flow accounts for the commercial banks are

$$r^L \hat{L} = r^D \hat{D} + wN^b \tag{2.21}$$

and the capital accounts[7] are

$$\hat{D} = qK^b + \hat{L}. \tag{2.22}$$

$\hat{D}$ is a dollar stock comprising deposit stocks owned by households and widget firms. That is, $\hat{D} = \hat{D}^h + \hat{D}^x$. When (2.22) is multiplied by r and inserted in (2.21), we obtain the RFA in

$$(r^L - r)\hat{L} + (r - r^D)\hat{D} = wN^b + rqK^b. \tag{2.23}$$

When (2.23) is considered in light of the real accounts for commercial banks above, we have

$$(r^L - r)\hat{L} + (r - r^D)\hat{D} = P^L L + p^D D. \qquad (2.24)$$

or financial valuation, $(r^L - r)\hat{L} + (r - r^D)\hat{D}$, is a perfect proxy for real valuation of deposit and lending services of commercial banks. We can be more precise if we combine the accounts of commercial banks in (2.23) with those of widget firms in (2.19).

Combined Accounts

The combining of the financial flow accounts of commercial banks and widget firms yields

$$pX + (r - r^D)\hat{D}^h = wN + rqK, \qquad (2.25)$$

which is the budget relation of households. The right-hand side is aggregate income and the left-hand side is the value of the consumption bundle. See Table 2.6 for a national accounting matrix representation of this economy.

When (2.25) is compared with its counterpart in the real accounts, we obtain

$$(r - r^D)\hat{D}^h = p^D D^h \qquad (2.26)$$

which represents the precise proxy relationship between financial valuation and real valuation of deposit services consumed by households. Note that $(r - r^D)$ is acting as a price of a unit of stock, $\hat{D}^h$. Note also that price p^D cannot be identified with price $(r - r^D)$ because each price is associated with a different quantity. $\hat{D}^h$ is a stock of dollars and $p^D D^h$ is the dollar value of the flow of deposit services being received by the household. Hence $(r - r^D)$ is the appropriate interest rate for translating the flow value into the stock value. That is, $\hat{D}^h = p^D D^h/(r - r^D)$. This is not a coincidence. The stock of deposits $\hat{D}^h$ is needed for the flow of services $p^D D^h$ to be realized, though the stock $\hat{D}^h$ is not an input in the conventional sense for 'producing' deposit services.

It follows that stock $\hat{D}^x$ is needed in order to obtain the services, $p^D D^x$ and hence

$$\hat{D}^x = p^D D^x/(r - r^D)$$

and stock $\hat{L}$ is needed in order to make service flow $p^L L$ happen. Hence

$$\hat{L} = p^L L/(r^L - r).$$

Table 2.6 *National accounting matrix (interest rate spreads and dollar stocks)*

Expenditures ↓ / Receipts →	Widget production	Bank production (deposit and loan services)	K-capital	Labor	Households
Widget production					pX
Deposit services	$(r-r^D)\hat{D}^X$	$-(r-r^D)\hat{D}$			$(r-r^D)\hat{D}^h$
Loan services	$(r^L-r)\hat{L}^X$	$-(r^L-r)\hat{L}$			
K-capital	$rqa_{K,X}X$	$rqa_{K,Q}Q$			
Labor	$wa_{N,X}X$	$wa_{N,Q}Q$			
Households			rqK	wN	

We are obviously observing here 'financial valuations' being perfect proxies for real valuation of banking services. But there is something more fundamental occurring here. The dollar stocks are produced at no cost in our formulation and thus are not scarce in the sense of services produced with primary inputs in, say, fixed supply. Thus the stocks are needed in order to complete the use of banking services but they do not show up as part of the production process of banking services. *They constitute part of a dual representation of the value of banking services.* We know that financial stocks are needed in order for banking services to be used but such stocks do not constitute inputs into the process of producing banking services, in large part because these financial stocks are costless to produce at the level of the economy.

If we *assume* a value for $\hat{D}^h$, then from (2.28) below we obtain a value for q, and given rq already solved for, we obtain a value for r, and from our equations immediately above, values for $\hat{D}^x$, L, r^L and r^D. Hence, given a solution to the real problem with, say, $p = 1$, and a value for stock $\hat{D}^h$, we can solve for q, r, $\hat{D}^x$, $\hat{L}$, r^L and r^D. Specifying a value for $\hat{D}^h$ is like choosing a stock of money for the economy. Given this stock of money, the values of the other stocks and interest rates must be solved, to be compatible with the solution for the real, as distinct from the financial, specification of the economy.

We can infer that

$$\frac{a_{D,x} p^D}{a_{L,x} p^L} = \frac{(r - r^D)\,\hat{D}^x}{(r^L - r)\hat{L}} \, . \tag{2.27}$$

The left-hand side is invariant to the choice of numeraire for the real solution. However the ratios $(r - r^D)/(r^L - r)$ and $\hat{D}^x/L$ *will change*, given $\hat{D}^h$ constant, with the choice of numeraire for the real problem. Given the numeraire fixed for the real problem, a change in the selected value for $\hat{D}^h$ implies a different value for r. Interest rates depend on both the choice of numeraire on the real side and on the choice of a value for $\hat{D}^h$ on the financial side. The central conclusion is that the value of the right-hand ratio in (2.27) is invariant to the choice of the numeraire for the real problem and to the choice of a value for $\hat{D}^h$.

2.8 HOUSEHOLD TRANSACTIONS BALANCES AND THE VALUE OF *K*-CAPITAL

From our capital constraints on commercial banks and widget firms, we obtain

$$\hat{D}^h = qK. \tag{2.28}$$

This indicates that household deposits are acting as loans to the commercial banks and ultimately, these balances represent claims on the K-capital in the economy. It is as if $\hat{D}^h$ were household savings and the savings end up as claims on the K-capital in existence. Of central importance is that (2.28) allows us to define capital goods price q. This is a basic link between the financial representation of the economy and the real representation. Since rq is solved in the real system as the rental on K-capital, we are able to extract the value of r for our economy and thus of r^D and r^L. We have a complete solution of the system given K, N, $\hat{D}^h$ and the production functions and parameter α in the demand by households for deposit services.

The exact nature of payments is relevant for the issue of the size of transactions balances, kept on deposit in commercial banks. It is reasonable to view the deposit accounts of households as getting filled up by payments of widget firms over the period in which widgets are being produced. Hence at the opening of a period, the deposit accounts of widget firms are full with approximately pX dollars. Near the end of the period, the deposit accounts of households are about full with these same pX dollars and households purchase the X widgets for pX dollars and fill up the deposit accounts of widget firms, for a new period of production. Hence, we assume that $\hat{D}^h$ is, say, $pX/2$ dollars as an average over the period of production. And similarly for $\hat{D}^x$. Then p could be set at unity and $\hat{D}^h$ would equal $X/2$. Then q and the interest rates would be defined. $\hat{L}$ would be treated as constant over time and the value of the firms would vary over the period as q varied in synchrony with variation in $\hat{D}^h$ and $\hat{D}^x$ over the period of production. It is clearly tricky to integrate the periodicity of payments of the period of production of widgets and we have simply sketched an approach. The relation in (2.28) remains fundamental, in any case. Transactions balances of households represent loans to the banks and end up as the claim on the K-capital in the economy. Hence $\hat{D}^h$ acts as both transactions balances of households and as savings of these same households.

2.9   BALANCED GROWTH

Given constant returns to scale, if K, N and $\hat{D}^h$ move at the same rate, the quantity proportions and price proportions, including interest rate spreads, will remain unchanged. There is an obvious sense in which growth in money, namely in $\hat{D}^h$, must move in synchrony with growth K and N for a balanced growth solution to obtain. We could endogenize the growth rate by postulating the maximization of $\int_0^\infty U[X(t)]e^{-\rho t}dt$ with $U(X) \equiv X^{1-\sigma}/(1-\sigma)$, $\sigma > 0$. Then $-\dot{U}x/Ux = \sigma \dot{X}/X$ and the growth rate $\dot{X}/X$ gets defined in $\sigma \dot{X}/X + \rho = r$.

2.10 EQUITY IN THE ECONOMY

On the real side of the economy, we treat the services of equity holders as arm's-length management inputs into the production activity. Owners of equity are owners of the firms in question and they exercise some arm's-length supervisory role over the activities of the firms. We shall use the term E^x for the equity services provided to the widget firms by the households who own equity in the widget firms.

Widget Firms

The real flow accounts get expanded to

$$p = rqa_{K,x} + wa_{N,x} + p^D a_{D,x} + p^L a_{L,x} + p^{Ex} a_{E,x}, \qquad (2.29)$$

where $a_{E,x}$ is now equity holder management input per unit of X produced and p^{Ex} is the relevant input price. Both of these terms are endogenously solved for, given the production function and perfect competition.

It follows then that

$$a_{K,x} X = K^h, \ a_{N,x} X = N^h, \ a_{D,x} X = D^h, \ a_{L,x} X = L, \ a_{E,x} X = E^h. \qquad (2.30)$$

Commercial Banks

The zero profit condition is now

$$p^L b_{L,Q} + p^D b_{D,Q} = wa_{N,Q} + rqa_{K,Q} + p^E a_{E,Q} \qquad (2.31)$$

where $a_{E,Q}$ is equity (management services from households) per unit of banking activity. We have now

$$Qb_{L,Q} = L, \ Qb_{D,Q} = D, \ Qa_{N,Q} = N^b, \ Qa_{K,Q} = K^b, \ Qa_{E,Q} = E^b. \qquad (2.32)$$

Commodity Balance

Inputs used by commercial banks and widget producers satisfy

$$K^b + K^x = K$$
$$N^b + N^x = N$$

where K and N are given. E^b and E^x resemble flows of skilled labor. We could have these flows come from endowment N or we could create a new endowment. We shall do the latter. Hence

$$E^b + E^x = E.$$

We also have demand for deposit services by households in

$$D^h = \alpha X$$

with α a positive constant. Then

$$D^x + D^h = D$$

where D are deposit services produced by commercial banks.

Households

Since households own the K-capital and supply the N and E, we have

$$pX + p^D D^h = wN + rqK + p^E E. \tag{2.33}$$

Again we note that most of the cost of banking services are embodied in the price p of widgets. Hence banking services are largely intermediate in the final accounts. $p^D D^h$ are the deposit services consumed by households in acquiring final goods, X.

The above equilibrium can be viewed as the outcome of pX being maximized, subject to

$$a_{K,x} X + a_{K,b} Q = K$$
$$a_{N,x} X + a_{N,b} Q = N$$
$$a_{E,x} X + a_{E,b} Q = E$$
$$a_{L,x} X - b_{L,b} Q = 0$$
$$a_{D,x} X - b_{D,b} Q + d^h = 0$$
$$\alpha X - D^h = 0$$

where, in fact, the $a_{i,j}$s and $b_{i,j}$s are endogenously determined. See Table 2.7 for a national accounting matrix representation of these relations.

Table 2.7 *National accounting matrix (real representation of bank and equity services)*

Expenditures ↓ Receipts →	Widget production	Bank production (deposit and loan services)	K-capital	Labor	Equity services	Households
Widget production						pX
Deposit services	$p^D a_{D,X} X$	$-p^D b_{D,Q} Q$				$p^D D^h$
Loan services	$p^L a_{L,X} X$	$-p^L b_{L,Q} Q$				
K-capital	$rq a_{K,X} X$	$rq a_{K,Q} Q$				
Labor	$w a_{N,X} X$	$w a_{N,Q} Q$				
Equity services	$p^E a_{E,X} X$	$p^E a_{E,Q} Q$				
Households			rqK	wN	$p^E E$	

2.11 FINANCIAL VALUATION WITH EQUITY

A principal result here is that 'interest rate' spreads appear as prices on dollar stocks of equity capital and the values of these stocks 'weighted by' prices are perfect proxies for the real management services provided to firms by households. Hence 'interest rate' spreads 'price' equity capital and the values here proxy for service flows (management services) provided by households.

Widget Firms

The flow accounts are

$$pX = r^L \hat{L} - r^D \hat{D}^x + r^E \hat{E}^x + wN^x \qquad (2.34)$$

where r^E is a rate paid on equity capital by firms. It will be the certain rate r plus a so-called 'risk premium'. $\hat{E}^x$ is a stock of dollars invested by households in widget firms.

The capital accounts of widget firms are now

$$\hat{E}^x + \hat{L} = qK^x + \hat{D}^x. \qquad (2.35)$$

If we multiply (2.35) by r and substitute in (2.34), we obtain

$$pX = (r^L - r)\hat{L} + (r - r^D)\hat{D}^x + (r^E - r)\hat{E}^x + wN^x + rqK^x. \qquad (2.36)$$

If we compare (2.36) with the zero profit condition above (2.29) and (2.30) for widget firms, we obtain

$$(r^L - r)\hat{L} + (r - r^D)\hat{D}^x + (r^E - r)\hat{E}^x = p^L L + p^D D^x + p^E E^x. \qquad (2.37)$$

Commercial Banks

The flow accounts are

$$r^L \hat{L} = r^D \hat{D} + r^E \hat{E}^b + wN^b \qquad (2.38)$$

where $\hat{E}^b$ is the stock of financial capital invested in commercial banks by households. The capital accounts for commercial banks are

$$\hat{E}^b + \hat{D} = qK^b + \hat{L}. \qquad (2.39)$$

When (2.39) is multiplied by r and inserted in (2.38), we obtain the revised flow accounts for commercial banks.

$$(r^L - r)\hat{L} + (r - r^D)\,\hat{D} = wN^b + rqK^b + (r^E - r)\hat{E}^b. \tag{2.40}$$

Households

Combining (2.40) and (2.36) yields

$$pX + (r - r^D)\,\hat{D}^h = wN + rqK + p^E E \tag{2.41}$$

which is another statement of household expenditure equal to household income. When (2.41) is compared with the corresponding budget constraint in (2.33) for the 'real economy', one obtains

$$(r - r^D)\,\hat{D}^h = p^D D^h \tag{2.42}$$

the key expression for dual valuation of financial services. Dollar stock $\hat{D}^h$ must equal $p^D D^h/(r - r^D)$, as in capital value equals the discounted value of flows associated with the stock. This stock valuation condition holds for other financial services. Hence

$$\hat{D}^x = p^D D^x/(r - r^D) \tag{2.43}$$

$$\hat{L} = p^L L/(r^L - r) \tag{2.44}$$

$$\hat{E}^x = p^E E^x/(r^E - r) \tag{2.45}$$

and

$$\hat{E}^b = p^E E^b/(r^E - r). \tag{2.46}$$

The new 'savings relation' derives from the capital constraints of commercial banks and widget firms, namely

$$\hat{E} + \hat{D}^h = qK. \tag{2.47}$$

Hence if $\hat{E}$ $(= \hat{E}^b + \hat{E}^x)$ and $\hat{D}^h$ are specified, q can be solved for. This implies a value for r.

We are able to solve for $\hat{D}_h$, $\hat{E}^b$, $\hat{E}^x$, q, r, r^D, $\hat{D}^x$, $\hat{L}$, r^L and r^E once dollar wealth $\hat{W}$ is specified in

$$\hat{W} = \hat{E} + \hat{D}^h,$$ (2.48)

and equal returns are specified in

$$r^L - r = r^E - r.$$ (2.49)

Clearly, the 'restriction' in (2.48) is analogous to our fixing of $\hat{D}^h$ in the model with no equity. Hence the addition of equity capital obliges us to add a new condition in (2.49), namely the net return to a dollar of equity capital must equal the net return to a dollar of loan capital. This means that a dollar of equity capital in the activity of households monitoring their borrowers (of equity capital), earns the same return of a dollar of lending capital in the activity of banks monitoring their borrowers (of loan capital). In terms of dollar capital, the costs of monitoring via the equity channel and the bank-loan channel are equal. A dollar lent, from households as equity capital or from commercial banks as direct investment, requires the same 'mark-up' to cover monitoring costs.[8]

Interest rate determination works the same way here as for the model without equity. Dollar wealth $\hat{W}$ is fixed and this determines q. Given q, r follows from the real model, since rq was solved for. Then, with (2.49), one can solve for $\hat{D}^h$, r^D, $\hat{D}^x$, $\hat{L}$, r^L, $\hat{E}^b$, $\hat{E}^x$ and r^E. Hence the determination of r depends on (a) the choice of numeraire for the real model and (b) the level of $\hat{W}$ selected in the financial model. Equation (2.49) plus the flow and capital restrictions on widget firms and commercial banks in the financial model immediately above allow us to obtain r^L, r^D and r^E. See Table 2.8 for a national accounting matrix representation of the equilibrium relations defining our economy.

In a narrow sense, the introduction of equity is associated with a new form of finance and a new channel of monitoring of the activity of commercial banks and of widget firms. There is a new real input in specialized labor, E and a new price of K-capital in $\hat{E} + \hat{D}^h = qK$. From a broader perspective, there is a quite different form of governance of firms. Households become explicit monitors of the activities of commercial banks and of widget firms.

The same two alternative approaches to normalizing prices make sense in this model, with equity. On the real side, set p is pX at unity. Then select $\hat{W}$ so that $r^D = 0$. Alternatively, since widget firms must write checks worth pX over the period of production, we set $\hat{D}^x = X/2$, this latter being the average size of deposits of widget firms over a period. This restriction on $\hat{D}^x$ is sufficient to allow us to specify $\hat{W}$. Uniqueness is an open question.

Table 2.8 *National accounting matrix (rate spreads as prices)*

Expenditures ↓ / Receipts →	Widget production	Bank production (deposit and loan services)	K-capital	Labor	Equity services	Households
Widget production						pX
Deposit services	$(r-r^D)\hat{D}^X$	$-(r-r^D)\hat{D}$				$(r-r^D)\hat{D}^h$
Loan services	$(r^L-r)\hat{L}^X$	$-(r^L-r)\hat{L}$				
K-capital	$rqa_{K,X}X$	$rqa_{K,Q}Q$				
Labor	$wa_{N,X}X$	$wa_{N,Q}Q$				
Equity services	$(r^E-r)\hat{E}^X$	$(r^E-r)\hat{E}^b$				
Households			rqK	wN	$(r^E-r)\hat{E}$	

2.12 HETEROGENEOUS AGENTS AND STOCHASTICITY

If checks written and checks deposited per day in a particular commercial bank were not in balance, there would be a need for borrowing or lending by the bank from or to another commercial bank.[9] This opens a role for a central bank, an institution that provides 'liquidity' to the commercial banking sector. A central bank would make use of labor, K-capital, and the monitoring input in its activities and an equilibrium would emerge in a new model, an extension of that above. Interest rate determination would be different in such a model. The central bank's 'liquidity' would be linked in some way to our crucial $\hat{D}^h$ level. This latter stock, $\hat{D}^h$, was characterizing 'liquidity' in, say, $\hat{D}^h/pX$.

The other large omission in our model is public debt and 'government' bonds held by commercial banks. And our model was explicitly stationary. In a world of positive household savings, there would be new equity to allocate to widget firms and to commercial banks.[10] Household wealth would be changing as would the levels of financial stocks and interest rates. In balanced growth, labor, N, equity-holder input, E, K-capital, K, and dollar wealth, $\hat{W}$ will be growing at the same rate. Prices will remain unchanging and output X will grow at the same rate as the inputs.

2.13 COSTLY BANKING SERVICES IN A DYNAMIC MODEL

We have considered three sorts of costs, usually linked to banking activity, broadly conceived. There are loan placing costs, loan monitoring costs, and costs of deposit servicing. These three costs have simple representations in a dynamic framework. γ can be a rate associated with check-writing or deposit-servicing or transacting, broadly defined. Then $(1 - \gamma)F(K,N)$ is current product left after transacting costs are netted out. Given a level of K-capital, αK can be conceived of as monitoring costs associated with loans placed. And $\beta\dot{K}$ can be considered a cost of placing new loans in productive projects. Current product left for consumption is

$$C = (1 - \gamma)F(K, N) - \alpha K - (1 + \beta)\dot{K}.$$

This implies an equation of motion:

$$\dot{K} = \Gamma F(K, N) - \Lambda K - \Omega C \tag{2.50}$$

where $\Gamma = (1 - \gamma)/(1 + \beta)$, $\Lambda = \alpha/(1 + \beta)$ and $\Omega = 1/(1 + \beta)$. The market acts to maximise $\int_0^\infty U[C(t)]e^{-pt}dt$ subject to (2.50) and $K(0) = K_0$. $U(\cdot)$ is our concave utility function with $U(0) = 0$ and $U_C(0) = \infty$ and ρ is the constant discount rate. The current-value Hamiltonian is

$$H = U(C) + \lambda[\Gamma F(K,N) - \Lambda K - \Omega C]$$

and the necessary conditions are

$$\frac{\partial H}{\partial C} = 0, \text{ or } U_C = \lambda \Omega \tag{2.51}$$

$$-\frac{\partial H}{\partial K} = \dot{\lambda} - \rho\lambda, \text{ or } -\lambda\Gamma F_K + \lambda\Lambda = \dot{\lambda} - \rho\lambda$$

or

$$r_t = \Gamma F_K - \Lambda$$

or

$$Kr_t/\Gamma = KF_K - K\Lambda/\Gamma, \tag{2.52}$$

where $r_t = \rho - \dot{\lambda}/\lambda$. Equation (2.52) forms the second row–column pair in Table 2.9, our national accounting matrix. Constant returns to scale in $F(\cdot)$ allows us to express the first row–column pair the way we do in Table 2.9.

The households column is

$$NNP = C + \dot{K}/\Omega$$

and the households row becomes

$$NNI = r_t K/\Omega + NF_N\Gamma/\Omega.$$

The complication here arises because of the distinct prices of consumer goods and investment goods. In simpler models, these two entries have the same price, but here costly loan-placing leads to separate prices for a unit of the consumer good and the investment good. Compare this NNP with that in the basic model associated with Table 1.2.

Roughly speaking, annual dollar transactions in asset trade, multiplied by 0.25 percent, constitute aggregate revenue to the suppliers of transactions services.[11] The volume of transactions represents a roll-over of existing wealth, possibly more than once over the accounting period, plus the placing of gross savings in assets, plus the cashing in of assets to gain income for consumption. Roughly speaking, total annual private sector transactions, divided by

Table 2.9 *National accounting matrix (costly banking services)*

Expenditures ↓ Receipts →	'Goods' production	K-capital	Labor	Households
'Goods' production				$C/(1-\gamma) + K\alpha/(1-\gamma) + \dot{K}/\Gamma$
K-capital	KF_K			$-K\alpha/(1-\gamma)$
Labor	NF_N			
Households		Kr_t/Γ	NF_N	

private wealth, equals the velocity of turnover of wealth. However, the meaningful measure of asset transactions costs is our 0.25 percent multiplied by annual trading volume. This should equal the wages of workers and the value of real capital rentals for machines, buildings and land in the financial sector of the economy. Of importance is that most of these costs should be 'capitalized' in the price of capital goods.

From an accounting perspective, one would like to say that x percent of the market value of firm j is 'consumed' each year by asset-trading costs. This measure implies the idea that resources are consumed to keep asset prices in line with fundamental values. (One has the rough analogy of a consumer searching for the best price and quality for his/her desired purchase. Resources are consumed in the linking of preferences to actual purchases.) It seems obvious that different assets will register more resources consumed by the process of keeping prices in line with fundamental value. Roughly speaking, some firms have more uncertain anticipated profits. This suggests, among other things, that 'market volatility', defined on some aggregate of assets traded, may be obscuring the mechanics of 'instability'. Speculative bubbles in aggregates may be driven by volatility in certain predictable constituents of the aggregates.

In recent years in the United States, the average equity has turned over every 500 days, well down from the seven years in 1960. These current rates are similar to those in other OECD countries (Organization for Economic Cooperation and Development, 1996, p. 155). The US turnover rate on equities (about 365/500) multiplied by the transactions charge (about 0.0025) implies that, on an annual basis, less than a fifth of a percent of asset price is represented by turnover or arbitrage costs. This seems a small price to pay for market thickness.

The issuing of new debt and equity by firms raises problems for measurement. Both the numerator and denominator of our measure of intermediation costs are raised. The timing of the new issues will have some impact on the value of our indicator. A naive view would have net savings flowing into new issues of debt and equity and the flows would move once in the year. Then τ would measure the fraction of savings 'consumed' in the placement of savings in new investment prospects. The reason that this is naive is that a once-over placement of savings over the accounting period is implausible. The savings is part of wealth and wealth gets turned over in arbitrage activity. New wealth gets an initial complete turnover and then becomes part of total wealth, a fraction of which becomes 'churned' in arbitrage activity. The initial complete turnover of new wealth (savings) imparts a bias toward more average turnover in arbitrage activity than would be exhibited by 'old' wealth. The turnover τ (brokerage rate) appears to be under the control of brokers and may not reflect true resource costs. But this is an open question. Ultimate turnover costs are represented by the capital and labor in the financial sector of the economy not engaged in transactions activity (check-clearing, loosely speaking).

2.14 MARKET INFRASTRUCTURE

Our view of 'the banking system', that system which allocates savings to investment projects, and which provides check-writing services to firms and households, is that it is a piece of market infrastructure. The banking system provides essential services to keep the market system functioning, but does not provide services that end up in final demand. The transportation system is analogous. It is not the travelling that yields utility, in general; it is the getting there. In both cases the costs of providing the service end up mostly in the prices which we pay for goods we consume as final demand. The wholesale and retail system can be viewed as a generalized transportation system and it too is a major part of the market infrastructure. The other major element of this infrastructure is the security system comprising police, the courts, judges, lawyers, penitentiaries and so on. The costs of operating this system show up in our own tax bills plus those of the firms we buy goods from and hence in the prices of goods in our final demands. One can think of this security system as being largely passive and its presence as sufficing to keep people moderately honest. The analogy with 'self-censorship' is appropriate. The threat of censorship keeps 'producers' from producing material that could get censored. It is the presence of the security system that keeps people from being egregiously dishonest in their 'market' activity.

Again we emphasize that much of seemingly final product, goods comprising 'market infrastructure', only appears in consumers' final goods as price 'mark-ups', not really as final goods consumed. Banking activity, the transportation system, the wholesale and retail sector, and the security system are means to getting final goods into our baskets. They are not part of final demand. And, of course, they are produced with capital and labor and are thus not primary inputs either. They form a special class of intermediate goods, goods with a system-wide dimension. Of interest is that 'the security system' is paid for largely by tax levies and fees, transportation and retail and wholesale services are paid for by the purchasers of final goods, and banking services are likewise paid for by the purchasers of final goods, but somewhat more indirectly.

2.15 CONCLUDING REMARKS

We started this chapter with the seemingly innocent innovation of combining the wealth or capital accounts of firms with the familiar zero current profit (real) constraints. This led to shareholder supervision terms showing up in national income or value-added. We pursued the idea that equity capital has its counterpart in services of shareholders being provided to firms and loan capital has its counterpart in lending services provided by banks and capital services provided to the borrower. Deposits or deposit capital has its counterpart in deposit services provided by banks and deposit services (check-writing services) provided to firms and households. Real accounts were linked to financial representations via zero profit relations and capital accounts for banks, firms and households. Interest rate spreads were identified with explicit prices on the dollar capital associated with loans, deposits and equity.

We discussed arbitrage activity as resource-using, asset price formation and set out an explicit dynamic model with transactions costs, loan-monitoring costs and loan-placing costs.

NOTES

1. See US Department of Commerce (1954), Ruggles and Ruggles (1956), Fixler and Zieschang (1991) and Inter-Secretariat (1993).
2. This is a different notion than the premium existing because owners are being compensated for incurring variability in dividends.
3. A lending institution can be viewed here as being in the business of rolling over a firm's debt (bank loans) each period. This is a component of intermediation activity. The other component of intermediation activity is the placing of the savings of households in *new* investment prospects. In practice it would be impossible to trace a dollar of current savings into the financing of debt roll-over or of new investments. One perspective on debt and equity roll-over is provided by Tobin (1998, p. 155). 'In 1993, for example, non-financial corporations raised about $370 gross from security issues but only $75 billion net'. Arbitrage activity which is resource-using can be viewed as a species of intermediation activity. We take this up toward the end of this chapter.
4. Until further notice rental rq should be thought of as a unit, say, R. Later we shall be able to solve for r and q separately.
5. Chia and Whalley (1999) present a formal model with transactions costs or 'intermediation services' in an empirical analysis of taxation.
6. We assume that banks consume or use no deposit services themselves. This avoids clutter and is clearly unrealistic.
7. This 'constraint' is usually presented in a double-entry table of Assets and Liabilities. See, for example, Kashyap and Stein (1994, pp. 236–8), Dewatripont and Tirole (1994, Chapter 7) or Tobin (1998, Chapter 7).
8. When explicit risk-bearing is considered, one can imagine that a bank can diversify better and would have on average a lower mark-up $r^L - r$ compared with the $r^E - r$ for households. Households can delegate their monitoring to a mutual fund manager by holding equities indirectly as in holding units of a mutual fund.

9. We have, of course, abstracted from reserves held by a commercial bank, reserves used for servicing the withdrawal activity of depositors.
10. This activity, placing savings in new equities, should consume primary factors. Allocating new savings is a different activity from monitoring the location of past savings.
11. Berkowitz et al. (1988, p. 103) estimate the costs of trading at about 0.24 percent of the value of the trade. This mostly comprises commission, but includes a small 'market impact cost' component. This measure is calculated without reference to bid–ask spreads. Stoll (1989) estimates about 0.57 of the bid–ask spread is input-using costs and about 0.43 is 'adverse information costs'.

REFERENCES

Berkowitz, Stephen A., Dennis E. Logue and Eugene A. Noser (1988), 'The total cost of transactions on the NYSE', *Journal of Finance*, **43** (1), March, 97–112.

Chia, N.-C. and John Whalley (1999), 'The tax treatment of financial intermediation', *Journal of Money, Credit and Banking*, (forthcoming).

Dewatripont, M. and Jean Tirole (1994), *The Prudential Regulation of Banks*, Cambridge, MA: MIT Press.

Fixler, Dennis and Kimberly D. Zieschang (1991), 'Measuring the nominal value of financial services in the national income accounts', *Economic Inquiry*, **29**, January, 53–68.

Hartwick, J.M. (1997), 'On imputing for financial services in the national accounts', *Economics Letters*, **56**, 63–70.

Inter-Secretariat Working Group on National Accounts (1993), 'System of National Accounts 1993', Eurostat–IMF–OECD–UN–World Bank, New York.

Kashyap, A.K. and J.C. Stein (1994), 'Monetary policy and bank lending', in N.G. Mankiw (ed.), *Monetary Policy*, Chicago: University of Chicago Press, 221–56.

Organization for Economic Cooperation and Development (OECD) (1996), *OECD Economic Surveys 1995–96 United States*, Paris: OECD.

Ruggles, R. and N.D. Ruggles (1956), *National Income Accounts and Income Analysis*, 2nd edn, New York: McGraw-Hill.

Stoll, H.R. (1989), 'Inferring the components of the bid–ask spread: theory and empirical tests', *Journal of Finance*, **44** (1), March, 115–34.

Stone, Richard (1951), 'Simple transactions models, informations and computing', *Review of Economic Studies*, **19** (49), 67–84.

Stone, Richard (1973), 'A system of social matrices', *Review of Income and Wealth*, **19** (2), 143–66.

Tobin, James (with Stephen S. Golub) (1998), *Money, Credit and Capital*, New York: McGraw-Hill.

United States Department of Commerce, Office of Business Economics (1954), *National Income*, 1954 edn: A Supplement to the Survey of Current Business, Washington, DC: US Government Printing Office.

3. Welfare considerations in national accounting

3.1 INTRODUCTION

What does GNP measure? What does NNP measure? What would we like them to measure? These questions have received serious scrutiny over recent decades, particularly in the 1930s in the United Kingdom and in the 1940s and 1950s in the United States.[1] A resolution of sorts was achieved by Hicks in Chapter 14 in his *Value and Capital* (1939). Hicks argued that 'income' should measure that level of potential consumption that could be sustained over a long period of time. Sustaining consumption meant preserving the capacity to produce intact and his notion of income is often linked to the phrase, 'maintaining capital intact'. If then one has 'maintained capital intact' and one consumes the remainder of the current product, and the intact capital is capable of yielding a new dose of consumption, at the same level as before, again while capital is maintained intact, one is on a sustainable consumption path and the level of consumption attainable is called 'Hicksian income'. At the level of the nation, NNP has the attributes of Hicksian income. That is, NNP should be a sustainable level of potential consumption. These thoughts have guided thinkers on national accounting and architects of the national accounts. And this is our perspective in this chapter. However, there is some distance between the ideas and the practice. Measurement problems abound and we address many of them in this chapter.

For example, when does one know that 'capital' has been 'maintained intact'? Current product used for capital maintenance is, of course, current consumption foregone. Hence investment must be measured in units of consumption goods. How is foregoing current timber harvesting related to foregoing current 'goods' consumption? Many issues turn on what is meant by 'the interest rate'. How is this related to 'the discount rate'? Different capital goods turn out to have own interest rates and thus in a multiple capital good world one has to relate one interest rate to another. These matters are reported on in this chapter. One might say that this chapter is about 'constant consumption programs' and interest rates. Related to the multiple interest rate problem are changes in relative prices of different types of capital as relative quantities of different capital goods change. The price ratio changes show up as capital gains associated with stocks and we report on these entries in the income side of the national accounts.

The basic unit in welfare economics should be the individual. Social welfare must deal with summing the welfare of different individuals and tracking relative welfares over time. We have nothing to say about this fundamental issue. We work at the aggregate level, *ab initio*, and thus leave the large question of aggregation over individuals unaddressed. This sounds like a cop-out but there is a long tradition of proceeding in this way. Our agenda is not sufficiently comprehensive to include all topics. Ultimately, the national accounts should communicate how well a nation is doing, over time and over space. We shed some light on this large question.

In Appendix 3A1, we take up economies with constant consumption paths, economies in a sustainable mode. In Appendix 3A2, we consider economies with stochastic discount rates and in Appendix 3A3 we report on the Chichilnisky–Heal critique of constant discount rates. In this chapter, we shall leave renewable natural resources aside. Much of our attention is focused on a traditional economy, one using machine capital and labor to produce a final product, which can be used as either a consumption good or an investment good. We take up oil use near the end of the chapter when two capital goods are considered. Natural resources are central in Appendix 3A3 as well, and are focused on in Chapters 4 and 5.

3.2   THE MARKET RATE, r_t, WITH ONLY K-CAPITAL

We shall take the next pages to restate the planning problem, with produced K-capital the only type of capital, and then consider market realization of the planning problem. Market realization or decentralization involves single agents, households and firms, optimizing in isolation and the 'sum' of the actions of all agents yields the market solution for the model. Somewhat tricky is the distinction between the market rate of interest and the social rate of discount. We pay attention to this. Once we have considered the planning solution and its market or decentralized counterpart, we turn to the question of how the national accounts measure or reflect 'sustainable income'. The issue here is, in what sense is NNP a measure of 'sustainable income'? For simple cases, our answer is that NNP measures 'sustainable income' well. We then take up a complicated case with a non-constant discount rate.

We formulate the planning problem as

$$\text{maximise} \int_0^\infty NU(C)e^{-\rho t}dt \tag{3.1}$$

subject to

$$\dot{K} = F(K, N) - C - \delta K \qquad (3.2)$$

$$K(0) = K_0, \ N \text{ constant}.$$

We are distinguishing N distinct households in this formulation. Each household is weighted equally in the planning problem. We assume that discount rate ρ and decay rate δ are constant. $F(\cdot)$ exhibits constant returns to scale. The current-value Hamiltonian is

$$H = NU(C) + \lambda(t)[F(K, N) - NC - \delta K] \qquad (3.3)$$

and the necessary conditions are

$$\frac{\partial H}{\partial C} = 0 \Rightarrow U_C = \lambda \qquad (3.4)$$

$$-\frac{\partial H}{\partial K} = \dot{\lambda} - \rho\lambda \Rightarrow \rho - \frac{\dot{\lambda}}{\lambda} = F_K - \delta \qquad (3.5)$$

and

$$\lim_{t \to \infty} \lambda(t)K(t)e^{-\rho t} = 0. \qquad (3.6)$$

Now $\rho - \dot{U}_C/U_C$ is the market rate as distinct from the social rate of discount. We label $\rho - \dot{U}_C/U_C$ as r_t. The first row–column pair in Table 3.1 corresponds to $F(\cdot) = KF_K + NF_N$ which implies that the value of inputs in production equal the value of product. The second row–column pair is essentially equation (3.5), multiplied by K.

Table 3.1   *National accounting matrix (an economy with only K-capital)*

Expenditures ↓ Receipts →	'Goods' production	K-capital	Labour	Households
'Goods' production				$NC + \dot{K} + \delta K$
K-capital	KF_K			$-\delta K$
Labor	NF_N			
Households		$r_t K$	NF_N	

The households column is NNP ($=NC + \dot{K}$) and the households row is NNI or valued-added ($= r_t K + NF_N$), the sum of wage income and K-capital interest flow. Note also that the households column is

$$NC + \dot{K}\lambda(t)/U_C(t) \tag{3.7}$$

which is H/U_C with CU_C substituted for $U(C)$. Hence NNP is the linearized, dollar-valued current-value Hamiltonian.[2]

3.3 DECENTRALIZED ECONOMY

Each household has wealth or dollar-valued assets $a(t)$, derived from borrowing and net savings. Current income derives from labor offered (one unit per household) and rentals from K-capital owned. Hence

$$\dot{a}(t) = w(t) + a(t)r_t - C(t) + \dot{b}(t)$$

where $w(t)$ is wage income, $b(t)$ is current borrowing, and $a(t) = k(t) + b(t)$. $k(t)$ is ownership of K-capital. Since there will, in fact, be no borrowing in the optimal solution, we shall ignore $b(t)$ and $\dot{b}(t)$. Hence a household maximizes

$$\int_0^\infty U[C(t)] \exp(-\rho t)dt \tag{3.8}$$

subject to

$$\dot{k} = w + kr_t - \delta k - C(t) \tag{3.9}$$

and

$$k(0) = k_0.$$

This problem has a present-value Hamiltonian

$$H^P = U(C) \exp(-\rho t) + \mu(t)[w(t) + k(t)r_t - \delta k(t) - C(t)]. \tag{3.10}$$

The necessary conditions are

$$\frac{\partial HP}{\partial C} = 0 \text{ or } \exp(-\rho t)U_C = \mu \tag{3.11}$$

$$-\frac{\partial HP}{\partial k} = \dot{\mu} \text{ or} - r_t + \delta = \dot{\mu}/\mu \tag{3.12}$$

$$\lim_{t\to\infty} a(t) \exp\left[-\int_0^t r(z)dz\right] \geq 0. \tag{3.13}$$

This last condition (no-Ponzi-game condition) rules out debt accumulation at a rate exceeding r_t in the limit. Differentiating (3.11) yields

$$\frac{\dot{\mu}}{\mu} = \frac{\dot{U}_C}{U_C} - \rho. \tag{3.14}$$

Hence, with (3.12), we retrieve the basic result

$$\rho - \frac{\dot{U}_C}{U_C} = rt - \delta. \tag{3.15}$$

This portrays households as acquirers of k. It is better to view them as savers and to imagine intermediaries who take the savings and allocate it to firms producing new k goods. These k goods are in turn rented, by arbitrageurs, to producers of consumption goods as well as to producers of new k goods. The intermediaries are obscured in this aggregated presentation. Goods producers in this view do not invest in new plant and equipment. They simply rent the K available at a rental rate which leaves them in a zero profit position.

Households and firms treat r_t and w_t as observable and immune to manipulation. Moreover they correctly observe the future paths of these prices and operate with perfect foresight. When the market solution and the planning solution are the same, agents' foresight is confirmed as time passes or their expectations are rational.

3.4 NNP AND SUSTAINABLE INCOME

We know from dynamic programming that

$$NU(C) + \lambda(t)\dot{K}(t) = \rho V(t) \tag{3.16}$$

where $\rho V(t) = \int_t^\infty NU[C^*(z)]e^{-\rho(z-t)}dz$ for $C^*(z)$ being the optimal value. Hence (4.1) is telling us that the current-value Hamiltonian is interest on wealth, where $V(t)$ is a measure of wealth and ρ is acting as an interest rate. Hence one could say that the left-hand side of (3.16) is a sustainable income flow.

Wealth is not reduced if the left-hand side were consumed. The left-hand side of (3.16) can be written as

$$NS(t) + NC(t)U_C(t) + \lambda(t)\dot{K}(t) \tag{3.17}$$

where $S(t)$ is consumer surplus for a household. Dividing by $U_C(t)$ yields

$$NS(t)/U_C(t) + NC(t) + \dot{K}(t) = \rho V(t)/U_C(t). \tag{3.18}$$

Now $S(t)$ is consumer surplus *per household* and should thus be a small number. The remainder on the left-hand side of (4.18) is our NNP, in dollars (the linearized, dollar-valued current-value Hamiltonian). Recall the households column in Table 3.1. Hence treating $S(t)$ as zero, allows us to infer that our NNP is measuring sustainable income. Since we expect $S(t)$ to be small in any case, we are certainly justified in inferring that our NNP in Table 3.1 is a good approximation to sustainable income.[3]

Supposing each surplus is zero, when we divide by U_C, we really end up with NNP as $F(K, N) - \delta K$. This is weighted by one dollar, the numeraire. This certainly implies sustainable income because it is reproducible period after period. Worn-out K is replaced so that productive K remains constant and N is constant. Hence output is constant over time or NNP is then 'sustainable income' or a potential maximum consumption level that could be achieved, indefinitely.

The simplicity of this 'result' is partly a consequence of U_C equalling λ. The import of this is that the current sacrifice of a unit of consumption, at util cost U_C, is matched by extra K so that extra output $F_K - \delta$ is produced into the indefinite future, period after period. This extra output is valued as a present value at

$$\int_t^\infty e^{-\rho(z-t)} U_C(z)[F_K(z) - \delta]dz$$

which defines $\lambda(t)$, which equals $U_C(t)$. Consumption sacrifice today, at the margin, yields discounted future output of exactly the same value as $U_C(t)$. This reflects the fact that consumption goods and investment (new capital) goods are produced with the same technology.

For example, $U_C[C(t)]$ does not equal $\lambda(t)$ when consumers have a rate of time preference that depends on the utility of current consumption. The maximand is

$$\int_0^\infty NU[C(t)] \exp\{-\int_0^t \rho U[C(z)]dz\}dt.$$

See Uzawa (1968) and the exposition in Blanchard and Fischer (1989, pp. 72–5). Dividing by U_C for this model yields a linearized current-value Hamiltonian

$$C(t) + \frac{\lambda(t)}{U_C(t)} \dot{K}(t)$$

Away from the steady state, this value will be changing over time, in part, because the price ratio, $\lambda(t)/U_C(t)$, will be changing. Hence the simple notion of sustainable income, which we observed above, does not obtain. Note however, that the national accounts for this economy, with its complicated discount rate, will be the same as those in Table 3.1. Thus though the accounts are the same, the interpretation of NNP as sustainable income is somewhat different.

3.5   WEALTH AS CUMULATIVE PAST INVESTMENT

Another concept of wealth is, roughly speaking, cumulative past investment. Above we worked with wealth as discounted future 'earnings'. We indicate here that these two concepts are 'opposite sides of the same coin' along the optimal path. Since

$$V(t) = \int_t^\infty U[C(v)]e^{-\rho(v-t)}dv$$

for $C(v)$s on the optimal path, we have, from differentiation,

$$\dot{V}(t) = \rho V(t) - U[C(t)].$$

From dynamic programming, we have

$$\rho V(t) = U[C(t)] + \dot{K}(t)U_C[C(t)].$$

Hence, combining these terms yields

$$\dot{V}(t) = \dot{K}(t)U_C[C(t)]$$

or 'new wealth' at t is the value of current net investment. We can integrate this expression to obtain

$$V(t) = \int_0^t \dot{K}(v)U_C[C(v)]dv + \text{constant}.$$

This current wealth is the value of cumulative past investment (Hartwick, 1994). This concept of wealth can be used above to obtain 'interest on wealth' relations.

3.6 CHANGES IN NNP

NNP or sustainable income only becomes meaningful in comparisons with
another NNP or sustainable income. What can we say about changes in NNP
and changes in the corresponding sustainable income? Do they move in synchrony? Consider then the simple sustainable income on the left and the
corresponding utility-based current-value Hamiltonian on the right.

$$\rho \int_0^\infty U[C^*(t)]e^{-\rho t}dt = U[C^*(0)] + I^*(0)U_C C^*(0). \tag{3.19}$$

We consider changes, to a first order in (3.19) induced by a change in endowments or by a small change in technology. We then have

$$\rho \int_0^\infty U[C^*(t) + \delta C^*(t)]e^{-\rho t}dt \cong [\delta C^*(0) + \delta I^*(0)]U_C(0)$$

$$+ I^*(0)\delta C^*(0)U_{CC}[C^*(0)]. \tag{3.20}$$

Now the term $[SC^*(0) + SI^*(0)]$ in (3.20) is the change in NNP and the term
on the left is the change in sustainable income. We divide by $U_C(0)$ to get
things in dollar units and we end up with

$$\frac{\rho}{U_C(0)}\int_0^\infty U[C^*(t) + \delta C^*(t)]e^{-\rho t}dt \cong \Delta NNP(0) + (r_t - \rho)I^*(0) \tag{3.21}$$

where

$$-\frac{U_{CC}[C^*(0)]}{U_C[C^*(0)]}\frac{dC^*(0)}{dt} = r_t - \rho$$

and $\Delta NNP(0) = [\delta C^*(0) + \delta I^*(0)]$. In balanced growth $U_{CC}(t) = 0$ and $r_t = \rho$.
Hence in balanced growth, a change in NNP is exactly matched by a change
in sustainable income. Away from balanced growth, we have a precise value
for the wedge between change in NNP and change in sustainable income,
namely $(r_t - \rho)I^*(0)$, which is negative in general. Hence *change* in sustainable income is in general overestimated by the current change in NNP. In
contrast, *current NNP* underestimates sustainable income because it fails to
incorporate the consumer surplus term.

Weitzman (1999a), following Sefton and Weale (1996), exploits the fact
that utility as a measure of welfare is an ordinal scaling with two free parameters to be specified. For a money metricization approach, he selects a and b
such that $V(C) = aU(C) + b$ or $V_C[C(0)] = 1$ and $V[C(0)] = C(0)$. Utility is

measured in dollars in the base year and thus in an intertemporal investigation of changes in NNP and changes in sustainable income, he obtains

$$\frac{\rho}{U_C[C^*(0)]} \int_0^\infty U[C^*(t) + \delta C^*(t)]e^{-\rho t}dt \cong \delta C^*(0) + \delta I^*(0) - S[C(1)]$$

where $S[C(1)]$ is consumer surplus in the economy at the second date, date 1. Consumer surplus at date 0 has been 'defined away'. Such a normalization is particularly compelling because the current-value Hamiltonian has a quasi-linear form and an argument can be made that income effects wash out in the intertemporal optimization actions of a representative agent. This argument has been developed in Weitzman (1999b) in order to make cross-country comparisons of change in sustainable income and change in NNP. For the case of economy 1 selected as the baseline economy, one gets

$$\frac{\rho}{\lambda^1} \left\{ \int_0^\infty U[C^{\cdot 2}(t)]e^{-\rho t} - \int_0^\infty U[C^{\cdot 1}(t)]e^{-\rho t}dt \right\} = \theta Y^2 - Y^1 + \int_{\theta p^2}^{p^1} D^1(P).dp.$$

The left-hand side is a difference in sustainable incomes and the right-hand side is a difference in NNPs plus a consumer surplus term. θ measures the ratio of expenditure on a benchmark basket of consumption goods

$$\theta(C) = \frac{E^{\cdot 1}(C)}{E^{\cdot 2}(C)}.$$

3.7   A DOLLAR-VALUED NNP PATH

To translate a util-valued optimal program into its corresponding dollar-valued NNP counterpart, Sefton and Weale (1996) introduced the base-period normalization, we made use of above. That is, $V_C[C^*(0)] = 1$ and $V[C^*(0)] = C^*(0)$. They then asked what discount rate could equate the value of the original program with its corresponding dollar-valued NNP program, at time 0. They introduced $\alpha(\tau) \equiv \exp[-\int_0^\tau r(z)dz]$ where $r(z)$ is the own rate of return on transformed consumption at time z. Then

$$V_C[C^*(\tau)]\alpha(\tau) = U_C[C^*(\tau)]e^{-\rho(\tau-0)}$$

at each τ. Then the maximization of

$$\int_0^\infty V[C^*(\tau)]\alpha(\tau)d\tau,$$

subject to the original constraints, yields the same $C^*(\tau)$ path. Obviously the $r(z)$s are carrying the burden of making the original and transformed problems (the $U(\cdot)$ and $V(\cdot)$ problems) yield the same $[C(t)]$ path. One has then

$$\int_0^\infty V[C^*(\tau)]\alpha(\tau)d\tau = \int_0^\infty [C^*(0) + \dot{K}^*(0)]e^{(\tau-0)\bar{r}}d\tau$$

for

$$\bar{\tau} = \frac{\int_0^\infty r(\tau)V[C^*(\tau)]\alpha(t)d\tau}{\int_0^\infty V[C^*(\tau)]\alpha(t)d\tau}$$

$C^*(0) + \dot{K}^*(0)$ is the stationary equivalent in dollars of the original problem, normalized at time 0. $\bar{r}$ is an average rate. One inference here is that this approach reveals the subtlety of asking that dollar-valued NNP represent the original problem.

3.8   SUSTAINABLE INCOME FOR NON-AUTONOMOUS CASES[4]

The above argument that NNP is interest on wealth needs amending when time dependence enters in ways different from that associated with the constant discount rate. Suppose there was an exogenously shifting parameter representing exogenous, labor-augmenting technical change. Then our current-value Hamiltonian would be

$$H = NU(C) + \lambda(t)\{F[K, NA(t)] - C - K\}.$$

For such a formulation, the dynamic programming expression is (Aronsson, et al., 1997, Proposition 4.1)

$$H = \rho V(t) - \int_t^\infty \lambda(z)F_z(z)N\dot{A}(z)e^{-\rho(z-t)}dz$$

for $Z = NA$. If H is measuring an NNP and $\dot{A}(z)$ is positive, we have the result that NNP plus an adjustment term is interest on wealth. Hence in such cases NNP is a poor estimate of sustainable income. The adjustment term breaks the simple link between NNP(t) and $V(t)$.

   This remains true when the discount rate is endogenous.

3.9 VARYING DISCOUNT RATES

Certain fairly general variations in the discount rate can be incorporated into the above analyses of the current-value Hamiltonian as measuring sustainable income. Kemp and Long's (1998) approach is quite general. They, following Uzawa (1968) and Epstein (1987), define the discount factor β, in

$$\frac{\dot{\beta}}{\beta} - \delta[C(t), K(t)].$$

This means that the discount rate is endogenous, depending on the current state, $K(t)$, a vector of capital stocks, and $C(t)$, possibly a vector of current consumption levels. (One can consider $C(t)$ and $K(t)$ as scalars here, though they need not be.) This makes the discount factor $\beta(t)$ a state variable with its own shadow price $\gamma(t)$. Consider the economy at date τ, some time beyond base-date t. Then the current-value Hamiltonian is:

$$H(\tau) = U[C(\tau)]\beta(\tau) + \lambda(\tau)\{F[K(\tau), N] - C(\tau)\}$$
$$- \gamma(\tau)\beta(\tau)\delta[C(\tau), K(\tau)].$$

The necessary conditions include

$$\frac{\partial H}{\partial C} = 0 \Rightarrow \beta(\tau)U_C(\tau) = \lambda(\tau)$$

$$-\frac{\partial H}{\partial K} \dot{\lambda}(\tau) \Rightarrow -\lambda(\tau)F_K(\tau) - \gamma(\tau)\beta(\tau)\delta_K(\tau) = \dot{\lambda}(\tau)$$

$$-\frac{\partial H}{\partial \beta} = \dot{\gamma}(\tau) \Rightarrow -U(\tau) + \gamma(\tau)\delta(\tau) = \dot{\gamma}(\tau)$$

and transversality conditions. The key step is taking the last condition and rewriting it as

$$[\dot{\gamma}(\tau) - \delta\gamma(\tau)] \exp\left[-\int_t^\tau \delta(s)ds\right] = -U[C(\tau)] \exp\left[-\int_t^\tau \delta(s)ds\right]$$

or

$$\frac{d}{d\tau}\left\{\gamma(\tau) \exp\left[-\int_t^\tau \delta(s)d(s)\right]\right\} = -U[C(\tau)] \exp\left[-\int_t^\tau \delta(s)ds\right]$$

which, given the transversality conditions, reduces to

$$\gamma(t) = \int_t^\infty U[C(\tau)] \exp\left[-\int_t^\tau \delta(s)ds\right]d\tau$$

$$= V[K(t), \beta(t)]$$

$$= V[K(t), 1]$$

for initial conditions $K(t) = K_0$ and $\beta(t) = 1$.

In this formulation the Hamiltonian happens to equal zero at each date τ. Hence the result, util-valued NNP equals interest on util-valued wealth at each date.[5] That is

$$U[C(\tau)] + \frac{\lambda(\tau)}{\beta(\tau)} = \delta[C(\tau), K(\tau)]\gamma(\tau).$$

A different approach to the question of non-constant discount rates (Asheim, 1997) is to ask what is the 'NNP(t)' equivalent, $h(t)$, given

$$\int_t^\infty \Lambda(s)h(t)ds = \int_t^\infty U[C^*(s)]\Lambda(s)ds$$

where $-\dot{\Lambda}(t)/\Lambda(t)$ constant, is the familiar constant discount rate case. One has

$$h(t) = \int_t^\infty U[C^*(s)]\Lambda(s)ds/\Gamma(t)$$

where $\Gamma(t) = \int_t^\infty \Lambda(s)ds$. Hence

$$h(t) = \theta(t) \int_t^\infty \frac{\Lambda(s)}{\Lambda(t)} U[C^*(s)]ds.$$

Obviously $\theta(t)$ functions as a long-term interest rate and $\Lambda(s)/\Lambda(t)$ operates like $e^{-\rho(s-t)}$ for the case of a short-term discount factor constant, at rate ρ. Now, it follows that

$$\dot{h}(t) = \theta(t)[h(t) - U(C^*(t)]$$

and $h(t)$ is the 'NNP(t)' equivalent for a non-constant discount rate. Since $h(t)$ is not defined in terms of current prices and quantities alone, it cannot function as a practical 'NNP(t)' equivalent.

3.10 DISCOUNT RATE VARYING WITH THE DATE ALONE

Recall that the present value of $1 paid in perpetuity, given constant discount rate δ, is $V(t) = \$1 \int_t^\infty e^{-\delta\tau} d\tau$. When δ varies with the calendar date, the corresponding expression is

$$V(t) = \$1 \int_t^\infty \exp\left[-\int_t^\tau \delta(s)ds\right] d\tau.$$

Hence $1/\int_t^\infty \exp\left[-\int_t^\tau \delta(s)ds\right] d\tau$ can be interpreted as an average interest rate over the long term while $\delta(t)$ is the short-term rate. Clearly $\int_t^\infty \exp\left[-\int_t^\tau \delta(s)ds\right] d\tau$ must be finite for all values of t to be functioning as a meaningful discounting operator. Alternatively the so-called long-term rate must itself be finite for all t.

Agents are generally assumed, in theory, to discount by taking account of the complete path of future rates in the familiar textbook, perfect foresight manner. They correctly anticipate the values of future rates, the familiar rather strong assumption. Asheim (1997) and Lozada (1997) have done interesting analyses[6] with such varying interest rates. Note that these rates are functions of the calendar date and not of the interval between a future date τ and the present. When discounting varies with the interval rather than calendar time, time-inconsistency issues of a Strotz (1956) type can arise quite naturally. As Lozada (1997) makes clear, when interest rates vary with calendar time, the nature of the non-autonomousness of the problems facing optimizing agents is quite tractable. This tractability is suggested by the relatively simple form of the expression for the $1 annuity problem above.

3.11 MULTIPLE CAPITAL GOODS AND ASSET PRICE CHANGES

The interest rate r_t and the discount rate have been a focus of attention to this point. Multiple capital goods imply multiple interest rates and it is this point we wish to develop here. From an accounting perspective, the multiplicity of capital goods, human-made and natural, involve a multiplicity of capital goods prices and relative price change terms. It is capital goods and their prices as well as capital goods relative price changes that end up in national income (NNI). The value of stock changes (economic depreciation terms) end up in NNP. We illustrate these points with a model with K-capital and knowledge capital, denoted $A(t)$.

Consumption and investment goods are produced under constant returns to scale

$$NC + \dot{K} = F[K, A(N - N_1)A] \qquad (3.22)$$

with K the stock of K-capital, N, a fixed number of workers and A the knowledge stock, 'attached' to workers. Knowledge production takes place under constant returns to scale in

$$\dot{A} = aAN_1. \qquad (3.23)$$

In the planning solution, $\int_0^\infty NU(C)e^{-\rho t}dt$ is maximized subject to (3.22), (3.23) and $A(0) = A_0$ and $K(0) = K_0$. This implies a current-value Hamiltonian

$$H = NU(C) + \lambda(t)\{F[K, (N - N_1)A] - NC\} + \mu(t)aN_1A. \qquad (3.24)$$

The necessary conditions are

$$\frac{\partial H}{\partial C} = 0 \text{ or } U_C(t) = \lambda(t) \qquad (3.25)$$

$$\frac{\partial H}{\partial N_1} = 0 \text{ or } \lambda F_z = \mu a \qquad (3.26)$$

$$-\frac{\partial H}{\partial K} = \dot{\lambda} - \rho\lambda \text{ or } \rho - \frac{\dot{\lambda}}{\lambda} = F_K \qquad (3.27)$$

$$-\frac{\partial H}{\partial A} = \dot{\mu} - \rho\mu \text{ or } -\lambda F_z(N - N_1) - \mu aN_1 = \dot{\mu} - \rho\mu$$

$$\text{or } \left(\rho - \frac{\dot{\mu}}{\mu}\right)\frac{\mu}{\lambda} = aN_1\frac{\mu}{\lambda} + (N - N_1)F_z \qquad (3.28)$$

where

$$Z = (N - N_1)A$$

and

$$\lim_{t \to \infty} \lambda(t)K(t)e^{-\rho t} = 0,$$

$$\lim_{t \to \infty} \mu(t)A(t)e^{-\rho t} = 0.$$

Now $\rho - \dot{\lambda}/\lambda$ is r_t, our market rate of interest. It combines the λ price change and the social rate of discount, ρ. $\rho - \dot{\mu}/\mu$ is r_t^A, the own rate of interest associated with stock A.

Constant returns to scale in $F(\cdot)$ yields the first row–column pair in Table 3.2. Equation (3.27) multiplied by K yields the second row–column pair in

Table 3.2. Equation (3.28) multiplied by A yields the third row-column pair. The households column is NNP, the linearized, dollar-valued current-value Hamiltonian. It comprises consumption goods plus values of stock change for K-capital and A-capital. Values of stock change are often labelled 'economic depreciation', the value of stock change under optimal use. Here $\dot{K}$ and $\dot{A}\mu/\lambda$ are values of stock accumulation.

Table 3.2   National accounting matrix (K-capital and knowledge capital)

Expenditures ↓ Receipts →	Goods production	K-capital	A-capital	Households
Goods production				$C + \dot{K}$
K-capital	KF_K			
A-capital	AZF_z			$aAN_1\mu/\lambda$
Households		$r_t K$	$Ar_t^A\mu/\lambda$	

The households row is net national income or value-added or the value of primary inputs. Labor is attached to the A-stock and thus does not make a separate appearance. Own interest rate r_t^A is a theoretical concept, not observable in the market. We can re-express $r_t A$ as

$$\rho - \frac{\dot{\lambda}}{\lambda} + \frac{\dot{\lambda}}{\lambda} - \frac{\dot{\mu}}{\mu} = r_t - \frac{\lambda}{\mu} \, d\left(\frac{\mu}{\lambda}\right)/dt.$$

Then NNI becomes

$$r_t K + r_t A\mu/\lambda - Ad\left(\frac{\mu}{\lambda}\right)/dt.$$

Each of the first two terms is interest on the value of a capital stock. Such terms are 'stationary equivalents' or the perpetual flow value of a dollar-valued stock. The last term is stock A multiplied by its change in price relative to the price of K-capital. *Such asset price changes are an integral part of national income and re-appear in the accounts throughout this volume because we are dealing always with more than one capital good.* In balanced growth, a dynamic steady state, the ratio K/A is unchanging and the price ratio μ/λ will be unchanging. Then asset price change will be zero. However, balanced growth is a textbook concept and in practice asset price changes will be non-zero and must be entered in the income side of the accounts.

3.12 CAPITAL GAINS IN THE NATIONAL ACCOUNTS

There is a long tradition of excluding 'capital gains' or terms associated with price changes from 'the national accounts'. Implicit is the idea that national accounting should be measuring the values of certain physical entities and not value attributable to simple price change. This approach does not make complete sense because if the price of a durable good jumped unexpectedly, one could sell the good, place the capital gain in the bank and enjoy a new perpetual income stream. Hence unanticipated capital gains and losses are components of 'sustainable income'. Unexpected price changes of durable goods are often associated with unanticipated technical change. If NNP is supposed to be measuring 'sustainable income', the interest on unanticipated capital gains should be included in NNP.

Our capital gains are (a) anticipated and (b) placed on the income side of the national accounts. Thus we are conforming with accepted practice by excluding anticipated capital gains from the product side of the accounts.

3.13 *K*-CAPITAL AND OIL DEPOSIT CAPITAL

We turn now to a model with two capital goods: produced, *K*-capital and wasting or depleting oil capital, as stock $S(t)$. Our goal is to observe the own rate of interest for *S*-capital and the capital gains, which we will insert in the income side of the national accounts.

Current depletion $R(t)$ $(= -\dot{S}(t))$ will depend on labor, N_1 and the current stock size, $S(t)$ in

$$-\dot{S}(t) = g[S(t), N_1(t)] \tag{3.29}$$

where $g(\cdot)$ exhibits constant returns to scale in $S(t)$ and $N_1(t)$. This assumption makes our life easier when we do the accounts because there will be no residual income to allocate.

Goods production, $C(t) + \dot{K}(t)$, involves inputs from *K*-capital, labor, $N - N_1(t)$, and oil, $R(t)$. That is

$$\dot{K}(t) = F[K(t), N - N_1(t), R(t)] - C(t) \tag{13.30}$$

where $F(\cdot)$ exhibits constant returns to scale and $\dot{K}(t)$ is new *K*-capital and $C(t)$ is consumption. The market acts to maximize $\int_0^\infty U[C(t)]e^{-\rho t}dt$ subject to $K(0) = K_0$, $S(0) = S_0$ and (3.29) and (3.30) above. This leads to the current-value Hamiltonian

$$H = U(C) + \lambda(t)\{F[K, N - N_1, g(S, N_1)] - C\} - \mu(t)[g(S, N_1)].$$

The necessary conditions are

$$\frac{\partial H}{\partial C} = 0 \text{ or } U_C(t) = \lambda(t) \tag{3.31}$$

$$\frac{\partial H}{\partial N_1} = 0 \text{ or } -\lambda(t)F_z(t) + \lambda F_R g_{N_1} - \mu(t)g_{N_1}(t) = 0 \tag{3.32}$$

for $Z = N - N_1$,

$$-\frac{\partial H}{\partial K} = \dot{\lambda} - \rho\lambda \text{ or } \rho - \frac{\dot{\lambda}}{\lambda} = F_K(t) \tag{3.33}$$

$$-\frac{\partial H}{\partial S} = \dot{\mu} - \rho\mu \text{ or } \rho - \frac{\dot{\mu}}{\mu} = -gs(t) + \frac{\lambda}{\mu}F_{RgS} \tag{3.34}$$

and

$$\lim_{t\to\infty} e^{-\rho t}\lambda(t)K(t) = 0$$

$$\lim_{t\to\infty} e^{-\rho t}\mu(t)S(t) = 0.$$

Now $\rho - \dot{\lambda}/\lambda(= r_t)$ is the market rate of interest and is associated with K-capital. $\rho - \dot{\mu}/\mu(= r_t^S)$ is the own rate of interest associated with S-capital. Though r_t is observable in the marketplace, $\rho - \dot{\mu}/\mu$ is not observable directly. Since $\mu(t)$ and $\lambda(t)$ are capital goods prices, in utils, for a unit of $S(t)$ and $K(t)$, respectively, we turn to price changes $\mu(t)$ and $\lambda(t)$ in the national accounts.

The first row–column pair in Table 3.3, derives from constant returns to scale in goods production. The labor row–column pair derives from (3.32), multiplied by Z; the K-capital row–column pair derives from (3.33), multiplied by K; and the S-capital row–column pair derives from (3.34), multiplied by S.

The households column simplifies because $(R - Sg_S N_1 g_{N_1}) F_R = 0$ and $(-Sg_S - N_1 g_{N_1}) \mu/\lambda = \dot{S}_\lambda^\mu$. Hence the Households column reduces to the linearized, dollar-valued current-value Hamiltonian namely,

$$C + \dot{K} + \dot{S}\mu/\lambda.$$

This is NNP, here. The households row is net national income and appears straightforward except that r_t^S is unobservable. We can express r_t^S as $r_t(\dot{\lambda}/\lambda - \dot{\mu}/\mu) = rt - \mu/\lambda d(\mu/\lambda)dt$. Then $r_t^S S\mu/\lambda$ becomes $r_t S\mu/\lambda - Sd (\mu/\lambda)/dt$ where this latter is the change in the market price of S-capital relative to the numeraire. Then capital values K and $S\mu/\lambda$ show up in NNI as stationary equivalents (that is as $r_t K$ and $r_t S\mu/\lambda$) plus 'capital gains' or price change effects. Hence

Table 3.3 *National accounting matrix (K-capital and oil stock capital)*

Expenditure ↓ Receipts →	'Goods' production	K-capital	Labor	S-capital	Households
'Goods' production					$C + \dot{K}$
K-capital	KF_K				
Labor	ZF_z				$N_1 g_{N_1} F_R - N_1 g_{N_1}\, \mu/\lambda$
S-capital	RF_R				$Sg_S F_R - RF_R - Sg_S\, \mu/\lambda$
Households		K_{r_t}	NF_z	$S_{r_t}\, \mu/\lambda$	

$$NNI = NF_Z + Kr_t + S\frac{\mu}{\lambda}r_t - S_d\left(\frac{\mu}{\lambda}\right)/dt.$$

We have then observed the presence of own interest rates in the national accounts and price change terms in NNI. Once one moves to more than one capital good, one must deal with these terms.[7]

3.14 ON SUBSTITUTING K-CAPITAL FOR S-CAPITAL

NNP in Table 3.3 (the households column), would reduce to $C(t)$ if $\dot{K}(t)$ happened to equal $-S\mu/\lambda$ at a point in time. Since $\dot{S}(t)\mu(t)/\lambda(t)$ is economic depreciation of $S(t)$ at date t, one would be covering off this depreciation with investment in more K-capital. The open question is whether $C(t)$ is sustainable if $\dot{K}$ were set equal to $-\dot{S}(t)\mu(t)/\lambda(t)$ for an interval of time. Solow (1974) answered this affirmatively for the case of the elasticity of substitution between K and R in production equal to unity (his $F(\cdot)$ function was Cobb–Douglas as in $K^{\alpha}R^{\beta}(N-N_1)^{1-\alpha-\beta}$ with $\alpha > \beta$). Maintaining C constant was not only possible for an interval, it was possible for the infinite future. $K(t)$ would be getting larger indefinitely and $S(t)$ would be approaching zero asymptotically.

'Covering off oil stock depreciation' is then a strategy for maintaining $C(t)$ (here NNP) constant in the face of a seemingly insuperable scarcity and this idea figures prominently in the literature on sustainability and natural resource scarcity.[8] Consider $C + \dot{K} = F(K, R)$ with $R = -\dot{S}$ and $S(0) = S_0$ and $K(0) = K_0$. Dynamic efficiency requires that $\dot{F}R = F_K F_R$ (the so-called Hotelling Rule). Savings-investment is $\dot{K} = RF_R$. Then

$$\dot{C} = \dot{K}F_K + \dot{R}F_R - d\dot{K}/dt$$
$$= RF_R F_K + \dot{R}F_R - F_R\dot{R} - RF_R$$
$$= 0.$$

For this simple case, we observe that $C(t)$ is unchanging at a moment of time under (a) dynamic efficiency in oil use and (b) covering off the depreciation of S-capital with investment in K-capital.

The converse result was established by Dixit et al. (1980) and is proven more directly in Withagen and Asheim (1998). An infinite-horizon, optimal constant-utility path is assumed. For each subproblem with a finite horizon, it is shown that if at the end, current stocks achieve their optimal values, then the subproblem has the same solution as the original infinite horizon problem. Then since the Hamiltonian must equal zero at the end of each subproblem, one observes that the shadow prices for the original problem imply zero 'net investment' at each 'end' date. Thus, a constant utility optimal program must display zero net investment at each date or $\dot{K} + \dot{S}F_R = 0$ as in our example above. Economic depreciation of S-capital must be being covered off by investment in K-capital if a constant utility program is to be achieved. A constant consumption program is a special case of a constant utility program. Further details on constant consumption programs are presented in Appendix 3A1.

3.15 CONCLUDING REMARKS

We have explicated 'sustainable income' paths for an economy and how they related to NNP and NNI. Interest rates played a large role in our analysis. Multiple interest rates emerged when more than one capital good was being dealt with and these multiple rates could be collapsed to the market rate plus capital gains terms. Capital gains were associated with changing ratios of quantities of different types of capital. We placed these capital gains terms in the income side of the national accounts. The product side corresponded to the linearized, dollar-valued, current-value Hamiltonian and a key component of this entity was the value of the change in quantity of capital (economic depreciation of the stock) for each capital good. Netting out economic depreciation terms from gross product leaves net product or NNP.

APPENDIX 3A1   CONSTANT CONSUMPTION PROGRAMS

Introduction

The idea that the systematic depletion of a capital good need not spell disaster for the economy goes back a long way. For example, Malthus's model could be interpreted as the increase in population asymptotically depleting the fixed stock of arable land and driving per capita consumption ever downward, at least to 'subsistence'. Critics argued that the accumulation of person-made capital and technical progress could counter the seeming inexorable decline in per capita consumption, given steady population growth. Pigou (1935) was explicit about one form of capital being built up to counter the seeming negative effects on welfare from the decline in magnitude of another stock whose services were essential in production. The concept of a stationary economy has been reflected on at least since John Stuart Mill's *Principles of Political Economy* (1848) and was a lively topic among theorists in the UK in the 1930s. Among other motivations was the matter of incorporating capital into a national accounting framework, and a stationary economy was considered a good abstract environment in which to sort out issues. 'Maintaining capital intact' was a phrase that recurred in the debates. (Although the stationary state is a reasonable place to start in organizing one's thoughts, particularly about national accounting, results obtained in this context need much refinement when the economic environment is not stationary. Capital gains and losses become tricky central issues in non-stationary economic environments.)

But it was the article of Solow (1974) that put the matter of one form of capital accumulation compensating, in some sense, for the depletion of another stock in a precise framework. Inspired by John Rawls's famous *A Theory of Justice*, Solow inquired about the nature of a constant consumption path for an economy 'working with' an exhaustible essential stock, say oil. Suppose then that a constant consumption path is optimal, in the optimal economic growth sense, and this economy requires oil as an input as well as the services from produced stock $K(t)$. And let the labor force (population) be constant. Then

$$Q(t) = C(t) + \dot{K}(t) = F[K(t), R(t), N]$$

where $F(\cdot)$ displays constant returns to scale and substitutability among inputs. We inquire about cases in which $C(t)$ remains constant. One should distinguish between setting $C(t)$ constant and having $C(t)$ emerge as constant from an optimal savings program.

Constructing Constant Consumption Paths

Leonard and Long (1992, pp. 300-304) report a trick for obtaining constant consumption paths. (See also Stollery, 1998 and Long and Yang, 1998.) One can impose a constraint that utility be unchanging when one introduces a special and essentially artificial form of discounting. For an arbitrary positive δ, one defines bound b in

$$W \equiv \int_0^\infty b\delta e^{-\delta t}dt = b.$$

One obtains a utility constant (and consumption constant) program by maximizing W subject to

$$I + C = F(K, R, N)$$
$$\dot{S} = -R$$
$$F(K, R, N) - I \geq b$$

and $K(0) = K_0$ and $S(0) = S_0$.

One makes use of the Lagrangian

$$L = H + \lambda(t)[F(K, R, N) - I - b]$$

where $\lambda(t)$ is a Lagrangian multiplier and H is the current-value Hamiltonian in

$$H = \delta b - \mu(t)R(t) + \eta I(t).$$

The Lagrangian multiplier satisfies $\int_0^\infty \lambda(t)dt = 1$. We turn to the limiting approach, reported in Dasgupta and Heal (1979). Specific functional forms are made use of. The planning problem is:

$$\max_c \int_0^\infty (-C^{1-\eta})e^{-\rho t}dt$$

subject to

$$\dot{K} = K^{\alpha_1} R^{\alpha_2} N^{1-\alpha_1-\alpha_2} - C$$

$$K(0) = K_0$$

$$R(t) = -\dot{S}(t)$$

$$S(0) = S_0$$

$\eta > 1$, and $1 - \alpha_1 - \alpha_2 > 0$. We can set $N = 1$. The current-value Hamiltonian is

$$H = -C^{1-\eta} + \lambda_1(K^{\alpha_1}R^{\alpha_2} - C) - \lambda_2 R$$

and the necessary conditions include

$$U_C(C) = \lambda_1$$

$$\lambda_1 F_R = \lambda_2$$

$$-\lambda_1 F_K = \dot{\lambda}_1 - \rho\lambda_1$$

$$0 = \dot{\lambda}_2 - \rho\lambda_2$$

for $U(C) \equiv -C^{1-\eta}$, $F(K, R) = K^{\alpha_1}R^{\alpha_2} (= Y)$.

For the special case of $\rho = 0$, and $\eta \to \infty$, Dasgupta and Heal (1979, pp. 303–7) show that Solow's constant consumption case is optimal. A larger ρ makes the plan favor large C early and hence ρ set at zero in a specification which favors the future. A larger value of η tends to bring consecutive values of $U(C)$ closer together. In the limit, we have $U[C(t)] = U[C(t + dt)]$ or constant consumption as the optimal solution.

Dasgupta and Heal (1979, pp. 200–206) then show that the constant consumption program is characterized by a linear accumulation of K rule in

$$K(t) = K_0 + mt, m > 0$$

$$R(t) = (\bar{C} + m)^{\frac{1}{\alpha2}} (K_0 + mt) - \frac{\alpha1}{\alpha2}$$

$$C(t) = \bar{C}, \bar{C} > 0$$

and

$$m + \bar{C} = m^{\alpha_2} \left(\frac{\alpha_1 - \alpha_2}{\alpha_2}\right)^{\alpha_2} S_0^{\alpha_2} K_0^{\alpha_1 - \alpha_2}.$$

It follows that $\bar{C}$ is a maximum when m satisfies

$$m^{1-\alpha_2} = \alpha_2 \left(\frac{\alpha_1 - \alpha_2}{\alpha_2}\right)^{\alpha_2} S_0^{\alpha_2} K_0^{\alpha_1 - \alpha_2}.$$

Insert this optimal m above and we obtain

$$m = \alpha_2 (m + \bar{C}) = \alpha_2 Y.$$

Since $\dot{K}(t) = m$, we have the savings rule $\dot{K} = \alpha_2 Y$, which is an instance of the general rule: 'investing resource rents yields a constant consumption program'.

To see this general result (dynamic efficiency and investing resource rents implies constant consumption), consider the general expression

$$C = F(K, R, N, t) - \dot{K}$$

and the dynamic efficiency condition (Hotelling Rule):

$$\dot{F}_R = F_K F_R$$

and the invest resource rents rule:

$$\dot{K} = RF_R.$$

We consider $\dot{C}$ above in

$$\dot{C} = \dot{K}F_K + \dot{R}F_R + \dot{N}F_N + F_t - \ddot{K}$$

and

$$\ddot{K} = \dot{R}F_R + R\dot{F}_R.$$

In the expression for $\dot{C}$, treat $\dot{N} = 0 = F_t$ (no population growth or exogenous technical change) and substitute (using the expressions for $\dot{F}_R$, $\dot{K}$ and $\ddot{K}$). One obtains

$$\dot{C} = 0.$$

The converse ($\dot{C} = 0$ implies invest resource rents (zero net investment)) is trickier to establish (Dixit et al., 1980; Withagen and Asheim, 1998).

Net (Genuine) Savings

The bottom line in sustainability is sustaining consumption in the long run. The Cobb–Douglas model does indeed allow $\bar{C}$ positive forever, even with a finite stock of oil. The stock gets run down asymptotically in the long run, approaching but never hitting zero. Note that for this good news result to be possible, K must be built up sufficiently rapidly *and* must offset the inevitable productivity implied by the decline in $R(t)$, current oil use. That is, K must be accumulated sufficiently rapidly and the shrinking $R(t)$ must not drag down current aggregate output too rapidly. We know about how fast to build up K, namely fast enough so that the economic depreciation in oil stock $S(t)$ is exactly offset by the increase in value of $K(t)$. The drag imposed by $R(t)$ shrinking is less if α_2 is small, in the Cobb–Douglas case. Small turns out to be implied by $\alpha_1 > \alpha_2$ as one observes by inspection of the key equations above. And the ease of substituting one form of service from capital with another turns on the underlying 'flexibility' of the production function. For the Cobb–Douglas case, the elasticity of substitution between inputs is unity. Cass and Mitra (1991) establish that less substitutability than is inherent in the Cobb–Douglas will prevent the long-run constant consumption from obtaining.

It seems apparent that if $\dot{K}(t) - R(t)F_R(t)$ were positive, future consumption would be higher eventually, and this notion has been drawn on by Pearce and Atkinson (1993) to evaluate the current sustainability of a number of nations' 'development programs', broadly defined. Drawing on the general model of Dasgupta and Heal (1974, 1979), and outlined above (with $\rho > 0$, $1 < \eta < \infty$), Asheim (1994) establishes that $\dot{K}(t) - R(t)F_R(t)$ can be positive forever and $C(t)$ can decline indefinitely beyond some date. Consumption turns out to be humped in its time profile in this case. The humped consumption profile has been systematically explored by Pezzey and Withagen (1998).

Asheim (1994) observes that associated with any well-behaved planning problem of the form

$$\max_{C(t)} \int_0^\infty e^{-\rho t} U[C(t)] dt$$

subject to

$$\dot{K}(t) = F[K(t), R(t), N] - C(t)$$

$$\dot{S}(t) = -R(t)$$

$$K(0) = K_0$$

$$S(0) = \int_0^\infty R(t) dt,$$

is the current-value Hamiltonian

$$H(t) = U[C(t)] + \lambda(t)\, \dot{K}(t) + \lambda(t) \dot{S}(t).$$

One can obtain an expression for net savings $NS(t) \equiv \lambda^*(t)\, \dot{K}^*(t) + \lambda_1^*(t)\, \dot{S}^*(t)$, and *s indicate values along an optimal path in

$$NS(t) = \int_t^\infty e^{-\rho(z-t)} \frac{\dot{\overline{U[C^*(z)]}}}{} dz$$

$$= \int_t^\infty e^{-\rho(z-t)} \frac{U_C[C^*(z)]^2}{U_{CC}[C^*(z)]} [\rho - F^*_K(z)] dz$$

This indicates what net savings is representing, with regard to the future, quite generally.

Asheim's analysis circumscribes the usefulness of the net savings (genuine savings) criterion, sign $[\dot{K} - R(t)F_R(t)]$, as a practical indicator of sustainability. The central problem which Asheim's critique raises is that the description of a point on a curve generally says little about the whole curve. Net savings, evaluated at a single date, cannot serve as a shorthand description of the future path of the economy. And we must not forget that current asset prices reflect a particular future path of the economy. Specifically, net savings equal to zero at date $\hat{t}$ may reflect net savings from a future constant consumption 'economy' or from an economy whose net savings at $\hat{t}$ happens to be switching from positive to negative or vice versa. But Asheim's critique is somewhat deeper. Can a finite interval of net savings positive guarantee that consumption will be higher at a point in the future? His answer is no. He exhibited a counter-example to the seemingly plausible idea.

Dasgupta and Maler (1998) have recently argued for non-decliningness in $V(t)$ as a criterion for sustainability. Current net savings non-negative is sufficient and presumably necessary for sustainability in this case.

Constant Consumption in a Two-country Trading System

It is provocative to view Solow's closed constant consumption model as representing a system of distinct trading units, comprising the world system. One then asks (Asheim, 1986 and Hartwick, 1995) whether each nation, with distinct endowments, can achieve a constant consumption path. If it can, will the levels of consumption be the same? What investment strategy is required in each country to allow it to achieve a constant consumption program? Asheim's analysis revealed that an oil importer will be at a disadvantage to an oil exporter because world oil prices will be increasing and the importer will necessarily be experiencing a form of terms-of-trade deterioration over time (the price of imports will always be increasing relative to the price of exports). The implication is that oil importers will have to invest proportionately more than oil exporters in order to achieve a constant consumption path and 'in the end' the oil importer's level of constant consumption will be lower.

To see this, we shall split Solow's one-world economy into two almost identical trading units, one, country 2, with slightly larger holding of oil stocks than the other. Each has the same K-stock at the outset. Populations are assumed equal but will be suppressed so that $Q_1(t) = F[K_1(t), R_1(t) + \varepsilon(t)]$ is current output in country 1 and $Q_2(t) = F[K_2(t), R_2(t) - \varepsilon(t)]$ is current output in country 2. Oil exports $\varepsilon(t)$ flow from 2 to 1 in return for the produced good. There are no extraction costs for oil. World prices for oil satisfy the Hotelling Rule

$$\dot{F}_R(t) = F_K(t)F_R(t)$$

and $F_K(t)$ is the world interest rate, and $F_{R_1}(t) = F_{R_2}(t) = F_R(t)$, the world price of oil. Prices are treated as parametric by agents in each country.

The Oil Importer (CI)

We have the output balance

$$C_1(t) = F[K_1(t), R_1(t) + \varepsilon(t)] - \dot{K}_1(t) - \varepsilon F_{R_1}(t),$$

where $\varepsilon FR(t)$ is payment for oil imports, $\varepsilon(t)$, and $\dot{K}_1(t)$ is own investment in $K_1(t)$. In keeping with each country 'covering off' the economic depreciation of its own oil stock $S_i(t)$, we have

$$\dot{K}_1(t) = \gamma_1(t)R_1(t)F_{R_1}(t),$$

where $\gamma_1(t)$ is a fraction, endogenous and, presumably near unity for $\varepsilon(t)$, small. Our task is to characterize $\gamma_1(t)$ in the 'adjusted' invest-resource-rents rule. We also have $\dot{F}_{R_1} = F_K F_{R_1}$. We differentiate our two equations with respects to time and substitute. We obtain

$$\dot{C}(t) = \dot{\Delta}_1(R_1)F_R(t) - \varepsilon(t)\dot{F}_R(t),$$

where $\Delta_1(R_1) = [1 - \gamma_1(t)]R_1(t)$. It follows that $\dot{C}_1(t) = 0$ if

$$\dot{\Delta}_1(R_1)/\varepsilon(t) = F_K(t).$$

This condition for $\dot{C}_1 = 0$ is an r% rule in quantities, since $F_K(t)$ is the 'rate of interest' here and $\varepsilon(t)$ and $[1 - \gamma_1(t)]R_1(t)$ are quantities of oil. This r% rule defines the time path of $\gamma_1(t)$ and when inserted above becomes the adjusted invest-resource-rents rule. Observe that if $\gamma_1(t)$ were set at unity then we would have the unadjusted invest-resource-rents rule and we would have

$$\dot{C}_1 = - \varepsilon(t)\dot{F}_R(t).$$

This is a rendering of the result in Asheim (1986), namely, if country i invests exactly its resource rents, its $C_i(t)$ will not be constant. In this case, importer C1's $C_1(t)$ is declining because it is 'undersaving' in covering its own economic depreciation in its stock $S_1(t)$ and in paying for imports, $\varepsilon(t)$. Thus $\gamma_1(0)$ must be greater than 1 and decrease toward 1 as time passes. Observe that $\varepsilon(t)\dot{F}_R(t)$ is a quantity traded $\varepsilon(t)$ multiplied by a price change $\dot{F}_R(t)$ and is thus a terms-of-trade effect.

An implication of the above analysis is that NNP(t) for a nation is an inadequate measure of sustainability in the nation when that nation is subject to continually changing terms of trade. A favorable changing terms of trade functions like exogenous technical progress on the nation. We take this up again later in the trade chapter (Chapter 7). Sefton and Weale (1996) have probed these terms-of-trade issues in a model free of the constant consumption 'constraint'.

Market Realization as an Overlapping Generations Model

Following Solow (1974), we have been vague about the details of the mechanics of a constant population and who owns what stocks at what dates. Long et al. (1995) decided to be precise about these details. They introduced finite, two-period lives for people and specific ownership arrangements for stocks.

At each date there is a younger generation, laboring, investing in machine capital K and consuming, and an older generation, only consuming and with its consumption financed from income derived from capital rentals from K and rents from oil sales, R. Labor is treated as a pure flow and human capital is ignored. If one accepts a continuous time setting for the moment and a Cobb–Douglas constant returns production function, one simply separates aggregate output and expenditure into two parts, young and old. Then, consumption C^Y of the young is

$$C^Y = N(t)F_N(t) - \dot{K}(t)$$

and consumption C^E of the older is

$$C^E = K(t)F_K(t) + R(t)F_R(t).$$

We know that the combination of the two groups is an aggregate constant consumption scenario when $\dot{K} = R(t)F_R(t)$. A subtlety is that for C^Y positive, $N(t)F_N(t) - \dot{K}(t)$ must be positive or the share of labor in production must exceed the share of oil rents. This becomes a new feasibility condition for the existence of the overlapping generations realization. Long et al. investigated the implementation of such an equilibrium when the younger generation must *purchase* the stocks of machines $K(t)$ and remaining oil $S(t)$ from the older generation. Their result was that this is not possible. The cost of acquisition, namely $K(t) + F_R(t)S(t)$, eventually exceeds labor income, $N(t)F_N(t)$. (This is not hard to see for the Cobb–Douglas case, since $N(t)F_N(t)$ and $K(t)$ will both be constant shares of output, and $\dot{K}(t)$ grows without bound.)

One could tax the older generation for the full value of their wealth at the end of the period and hand the wealth to the younger generation. This is a high rate of 'inheritance tax'. Long et al. proposed a tax on the income of the older generation which would be transferred to the younger generation. They found an income tax that worked. The central result is that a 'market solution', one without transfers between generations, will not support a Solow (1974) solution.

Long et al. computed some illustrative examples in a discrete time framework. Discrete time raises technical difficulties for the constant consumption scenario to go through under 'investing resource rents'. This matter was explored in Dasgupta and Mitra (1983).

APPENDIX 3A2   THE CHILCHILNISKY CRITERION

It is well known that discounting *per se* implicitly makes the future less important to an agent, the person doing the discounting, than the present. Matters seem to come to a head when natural resources are being considered. Consider the hydro power case. A river is dammed and hydro power is produced. New electricity improves welfare. In the long term the river silts up, generates little power and becomes, in the extreme, permanently depleted of flora and fauna. Such a project, building a power facility, would generally count positively in net welfare under a criterion that favored the near term over the long run. Maximization of the Benthamite utility functional, $\int_0^\infty U[C(t)]e^{-\rho\,t}dt$, is such a criterion. The future is weighted too lightly it seems, with such a criterion. Chichilnisky (1994) and Heal (1994) have proposed replacing the present-oriented criterion or functional above with one that puts more weight today on events in the distant future.[9] They replace the above criterion with

$$\max_{C(t)} \left\{ \int_0^\infty U[C(t)]e^{-\rho\,t}dt + \lim_{t\to\infty} U[C(t)] \right\}.$$

The term on the right effectively makes future payoffs count more than they would in its absence.

To illustrate the use of this criterion, Heal (1994) takes up a simple problem, somewhat analogous to our river-damming illustration. We have a stock S_0 which we can run down and 'live on', and this stock can also be used as capital to create a durable facility which in turn generates 'living on' services in the future. Given exogenously fixed date T for the facility becoming productive, how much S_0 should we allocate to it, given that its capacity to generate services is positively related to the investment from S_0 we make. I is the investment we make. Hence in phase (i), up to T,

$$-\frac{dS(t)}{dt} = C(t),\ S(t) - I \geq 0\ \forall t \leq T$$

and beyond T, we have

$$C(t) = b(I) - \frac{dS(t)}{dt},\ S(t) \geq 0\ \forall t \geq T.$$

Eventually $S(t)$ goes to zero and $C(t) = b(I)$ where $b(I)$ is the service flow from the facility built with I. Let $V_3[b(I)]e^{-\delta T}$ be discounted welfare in this third phase, discounted in turn from T back to time 0. Let $V_2[b(I), S_T]e^{-\delta t}$ be discounted welfare from the second phase, again discounted in turn back from T to time 0. Given the Hotelling Rule for depleting the stock, after I has been removed, we have welfare up to T represented by

$$V_1(S_0 - I - S_T),$$

where $S_T = S_0 - \int_0^T C(t)dt - I$.

Heal asks how large I will be under three different criteria. First, with the future-oriented criterion

$$\max_{C(t)} \lim_{t \to \infty} U[C(t)]$$

the optimal policy is to put all S_0 into I and consume nothing up to T. With the Benthamite criterion,

$$\max_{C(t)} \int_0^\infty U[C(t)]e^{-\rho t}dt$$

if T is distant enough, it is optimal to set $I = 0$ or, roughly speaking, consume all the S_0 and leave none for 'future considerations'. A future facility counts too little in terms of welfare at time 0. Under the Chichilnisky criterion, set out above, one obtains $I > 0$ for any T or more investment goes to the future facility than goes under the Benthamite criterion. Hence the Chichilnisky criterion leads to less neglect of the future than does the Benthamite criterion.

A somewhat different problem, also from Heal, is reported in Aronsson et al. (1997).

APPENDIX 3A3   STOCHASTIC DISCOUNT RATE

Weitzman (1996) makes the discount *factor* $A(t)$ a fixed coefficient Wiener process of the form

$$dA = \rho A dt + \sigma A dz.$$

That is, the discount *factor* grows at a constant rate ρ plus an error term such that the variance of the percentage rate is constant. The discount *rate* is then ρ plus an error term, normally distributed with a unit variance unchanging over time.

Production and consumption (a scalar) satisfy the general relationship at date t

$$C = \theta(K, I)$$

where K can be a vector with each component having an investment term I, negative, for depleting stocks, or positive for traditional stocks of machine capital.

$$\dot{K}_j = I_j^*(K, A)$$

$$P_j^*(K, A) = -\frac{\partial \theta}{\partial I_j}[K, I^*(K, A)]$$

where *s indicate equilibrium values and $P_j(\cdot)$ is the price of the jth capital good.

$$E[\dot{P}_j^*(K, A)] + P_j^*(K, A)\,\frac{\dot{E}(A)}{A} = -\frac{\partial\theta}{\partial K_j}[K, I^*(K, A)]$$

defines asset price equilibrium in expectations. $E(\cdot)$ is the expectations operator.

$$\lim_{t\to\infty} E_t(AP_j^* K_j^*) = 0$$

is the transversality condition. $K(0)$ and $A(0)$ are given at time 0.

This general equilibrium system with its stochastic discount factor has its approximate net national product in

$$Y^* \equiv C^*[K(0), A(0)] + P^*[K(0), A(0)]I^*[K(0), A(0)].$$

The main task is to show that Y^* is interest on wealth

$$W = E\int_0^\infty C_\theta(t)A(t)dt$$

where $C_\theta(t)$ is a feasible value of consumption at time t with its implicit corresponding probability of being realized.

Given state-valuation function $V(K, A)$ as the maximized value of the optimal savings problem, forward in time, one has the fundamental (Bellman) equation

$$-\frac{\partial V}{\partial A}\,\alpha = \max_I \left[A\theta\,(K, I) + \frac{\partial V}{\partial K}\,I\right] + \frac{1}{2}\,\beta^2\,\frac{\partial^2 V}{\partial A^2}$$

where $\alpha = -\rho A$. For our problem, $V(K, A)$ 'separates' to $AF(K)$. Our 'solved' Bellman equation becomes

$$\rho F(K) = \theta - \frac{\partial\theta}{\partial I}\,\dot{K}$$

which is the result: current NNP is interest on current wealth.

Weitzman defines a stationary equivalent consumption level $\bar{C}$ in

$$E\left[\int_0^\infty \bar{C}A(t)dt\right] = E\left[\int_0^\infty C_\theta(t)A(t)dt\right].$$

Since, by direct calculation,

$$E\left[\int_0^\infty A(t)dt\right] = \frac{A(0)}{\rho},$$

one has

$$V[K(0), A(0)] = \frac{A(0)}{\rho}\bar{C}^*.$$

This allows us to express our approximate NNP at time 0 as

$$\bar{C} = Y^*.$$

Hence the initial approximate NNP is equal to an average of all future optimal contingent consumption levels. This is a sustainability result for the case of the discount rate stochastic in a stationary process.

NOTES

1. Kuznets (1948) and Samuelson (1950).
2. That the current-value Hamiltonian in an optimal growth framework was a measure of current performance in the economy, in particular of NNP, had been recognized by many researchers in the early 1070s. See, for example, Cass and Shell (1976, pp. 31–2). Kemp and Long (1982) extended Weitzman (1976) to non-autonomous cases, such as the case of exogenous technical change. See also Weitzman (1997).
3. There is a large literature on the matter of translating the actual current-value Hamiltonian, in units of units, into a NNP measure, in dollars. We report on some approaches below.
4. Non-autonomous cases were first taken up in Kemp and Long (1982). See also Weitzman (1997).
5. This is net national product, absent the capital gains terms.
6. We report on Lozada (1997) in detail in Chapter 4.
7. For the special case of $R(t)$ bubbling up from $S(t)$ costlessly, on command, $F_R = \mu$ and $r_t^S = 0$. Then the stock $S(t)$ makes no appearance in NNI. This formulation appears in many places in the literature on exhaustible resource use.
8. Note that we started by asking: what is a useful measure of how well off a person or nation is in the long run? We answered that NNP could be viewed as measuring sustainable consumption. A different topic is: what is sustainable economic development? Constant consumption seems like an excessively conservative answer and a popular alternative is: a path of consumption which does not decline over time. There are some remarks on this in Appendix 3A1.
9. No discounting, or making all periods count equally in the present is another approach, but it seems to slight the present excessively.

REFERENCES

Aronsson, T., P.-O. Johansson and K.-G. Löfgren (1997), *Welfare Measurement, Sustainability and Green National Accounting*, Cheltenham: Edward Elgar.

Asheim, G.B. (1986), 'Hartwick's Rule in open economies', *Canadian Journal of Economics*, **19**, 395–402.

Asheim, G.B. (1994), 'Net national product as an indicator of sustainability', *Scandinavian Journal of Economics*, **96** (2), 257–65.

Asheim, G.B. (1997), 'Adjusting green NNP to measure sustainability', *Scandinavian Journal of Economics*, **99** (3), 355–70.

Blanchard, O.J. and S. Fischer (1989), *Lectures on Macroeconomics*, Cambridge, MA: MIT Press.

Cass, D. and T. Mitra (1991), 'Infinitely sustained consumption despite exhaustible resources', *Economic Theory*, **1**, 119–46.

Cass, D. and K. Shell (1976), 'The structure and stability of competitive dynamical systems', *Journal of Economic Theory*, **12**, 31–70.

Chichilnisky, G. (1994), 'What is sustainable development?', Technical Report No. 65, Stanford Institute for Theoretical Economics.

Dasgupta, P. and G.M. Heal (1974), 'The optimal depletion of exhaustible resources', *Review of Economic Studies*, Symposium, 3–28.

Dasgupta, P. and G.M. Heal (1979), *Economic Theory and Exhaustible Resources*, Cambridge: Cambridge University Press.

Dasgupta, P. and K.-G. Maler (1998), 'Decentralization schemes, cost–benefit analysis and net national product as a measure of social well-being', typescript.

Dasgupta, S. and T. Mitra (1983), 'Intergenerational equity and efficient allocation of exhaustible resources', *International Economic Review*, **24** (1), 133–53.

Dixit, A., P. Hammond and M. Hoel (1980), 'On Hartwick's Rule for regular maximum paths of capital accumulation and resource depletion', *Review of Economic Studies*, **47**, 551–6.

Epstein, L.G. (1987), 'A simple dynamic general equilibrium model', *Journal of Economic Theory*, **41**, 68–95.

Hartwick, J.M. (1994), 'National wealth and net national product', *Scandinavian Journal of Economics*, **96** (2), 253–6.

Hartwick, J.M. (1995), 'Constant consumption paths in open economies with exhaustible resources', *Review of International Economics*, **3**, October, 275–83.

Heal, E.M. (1994), 'Valuing the very long run: discounting and the environment', Paine Webber Working Paper, PW-94-04.

Hicks, J.R. (1939), *Value and Capital*, Oxford: Clarendon Press.

Kemp, M.C. and N.V. Long (1982), 'On the evaluation of social income in a dynamic economy: variations on a Samuelsonian theme', in G.R. Feiwel (ed.), *Samuelson and Neoclassical Economics*, Boston: Kluwer-Nijhoff, pp. 185–9.

Kemp, M.C. and N.V. Long (1998), 'On the evaluation of social income in a dynamic economy: generalizations', in Karl-Josef Koch (ed.), *Essays in Honour of Hans-Juergen Vosgerau*, Berlin: Springer-Verlag, pp. 101–10.

Kuznets, Simon (1948), 'On the valuation of social income – reflections on Professor Hicks' article', *Economica*, February, 1–16 and May, 116–31.

Leonard, D. and N.V. Long (1992), *Optimal Control Theory and Static Optimization in Economics*, Cambridge: Cambridge University Press.

Long, N.V., T. Mitra and G. Sorger (1995), 'Equilibrium growth and sustained consumption with exhaustible resources', Cornell University Discussion Paper CAE-95-02.

Long, N.V. and Zhao Yang (1998), 'Consumption growth and intergenerational equity: a neo-Rawlsian approach', typescript.

Lozada, G. (1997), 'The micro foundation of sustainability', typescript.

Pearce, D. and Giles Atkinson (1993), 'Capital theory and the measurement of sustainable development: an indicator of weak sustainability', *Ecological Economics*, **8** (2), 103–8.

Pezzey, J. and C. Withagen (1998), 'The rise, fall and sustainability of capital-resource economies', *Scandinavian Journal of Economics*, **100** (2), 513–27.

Pigou, A.C. (1935), 'Net income and capital depletion', *Economic Journal*, **45**, 235–41.

Rawls, John (1971), *A Theory of Justice*, Cambridge, MA: Harvard University Press.

Samuelson, P.A. (1950), 'Evaluation of real national income', *Oxford Economic Papers* (New Series), 1–29.

Sefton, J.A. and M.R. Weale (1996), 'The net national product and exhaustible resources: the effects of foreign trade', *Journal of Public Economics*, **61**, 21–47.

Solow, R.M. (1974), 'Intergenerational equity and exhaustible resources', *Review of Economic Studies*, Symposium, 29–45.

Stollery, Kenneth R. (1998), 'Constant utility paths and irreversible global warming', *Canadian Journal of Economics*, **31** (3), August, 730–42.

Strotz, R.H. (1956), 'Myopia and inconsistency in dynamic utility maximization', *Review of Economic Studies*, **23** (3), 165–80.

Uzawa, H. (1968), 'Time preference, the consumption function, and optimum asset holdings', in J.N. Wolfe (ed.), *Value, Capital and Growth: Papers in Honour of Sir John Hicks*, Edinburgh: Edinburgh University Press, 485–504.

Weitzman, M.L. (1976), 'On the welfare significance of national product in a dynamic economy', *Quarterly Journal of Economics*, **90**, 156–62.

Weitzman, M.L. (1996), 'On the welfare significance of national product under interest-rate uncertainty', typescript.

Weitzman, M.L. (1997), 'Sustainability and technical progress', *Scandinavian Journal of Economics*, **99** (3), September, 355–70.

Weitzman, M.L. (1999a), 'The linearized Hamiltonian as comprehensive NDP', *Environment and Development Economics*, (forthcoming).

Weitzman, M.L. (1999b), 'A contribution to the theory of welfare comparisons', National Bureau of Economic Research Working Paper No. 6988.

Withagen, C. and G. Asheim (1998), 'Characterizing sustainability: the converse of the Hartwick Rule', *Journal of Economic Dynamics and Control*, **23** (1), October, 159–65.

4. Exhaustible resources

4.1 INTRODUCTION

Capital gains or natural resource stock price changes appear in the expressions for economic depreciation in this chapter. That is, NNP contains terms with pure asset price changes in them. This is a departure from the tradition of 'no capital gains in NNP', and must be attributed to natural capital 'working' differently in the national accounts than does person-made or produced capital. We arrive at this 'result' by following the same steps as we used to construct our accounts for an economy without natural capital. See Table 1.2 in Chapter 1. Thus the same steps lead to coherent accounts when natural capital is present but lead also to the result that capital gains on natural stocks must be part of NNP.

We also observe that the interest flow corresponding to the market value of natural stock reserves, underground, appears on the income side of the national accounts. This puts natural stocks on an identical footing in the accounts as person-made stocks. Each stock enters as an interest flow; one however as interest on the current stock *in use* and the other as interest on the current stock awaiting 'use' or extraction. But there is a deeper unity here. Capital goods have future productivity measured by discounted future earnings and as such have current market values. These market values enter the income side of the accounts as interest flows and these entries are symmetric for natural stocks or person-made stocks. The representation of a market value of a capital good as an interest flow is referred to as the *stationary equivalent* of the value of the stock. Hence stationary equivalents are an inherent part of the income side of the national accounts, under traditional accounting and under green national accounting. The logical and practical structure of the income side of the national accounts is the same, whether one is dealing with natural capital or person-made capital. However, on the product side of the accounts (NNP), one is forced to incorporate anticipated capital gains on natural stocks into the accounts through the depreciation terms. These anticipated capital gains do not arise when dealing with person-made capital alone, or in traditional national accounting.

After establishing the structure of the accounts with non-renewable natural capital, we consider constant consumption paths briefly and turn to durable non-renewable resources such as gold, copper and so on. In these cases, stocks accumulate above ground and this accumulation 'offsets' value-loss resulting from the depletion of such stocks below ground. There are terms for the 'depreciation' of two stocks, one above ground and one below ground, in NNP. We then consider the case of purposeful discovery of new stocks. Stocks get augmented, but at a cost. We see two stocks in this case also, the inventory of discovered reserves and the stock underground, being explored at a cost.

4.2 DEPLETING AN OIL DEPOSIT

A straightforward case has an agent (firm) owning a homogeneous stock S_0, facing a *constant* price p for output, and working with an extraction technology involving costs $C(q)$ for q tons currently extracted from the stock

$$\dot{S}(t) = -q(t).$$

$C(q)$ has $C(0) = 0, C'(0) = 0$, $C'(q)$ and $C''(q)$ positive for q positive. The agent faces a constant discount rate r into the indefinite future.[1] Optimal depletion here can be interpreted as a sequence of planned extractions into the future, including today's extraction, which make the capital value of S_0 a maximum. More colloquially, the correct sequence of extractions makes the present discounted value of profits at each date a maximum. That is, one maximizes

$$\int_0^T \pi[q(t)]e^{-rt}dt$$

subject to

$$\dot{S}(t) = -q(t)$$

and

$$\int_0^T q(t)dt \le S_0.$$

where $\pi[q(t)] = pq(t) - C[q(t)]$. The solution to this problem satisfies the Euler equation (r% rule)

$$\frac{d\pi_q[q(t)]}{dt} = \pi_q[q(t)]r$$

and end-point condition

$$q(T) \; \frac{d\pi[q(T)]}{dq(T)} = \pi[q(T)],$$

(average equals marginal profit at terminal date T). This end-point condition reduces to $q(T) = 0$ under our assumptions on $\pi[q(t)]$ (or on $C[q(t)]$). That is, optimal extraction involves $q(t)$ declining precisely to zero at the instant $S(t)$ declines to zero. See Figure 4.1.

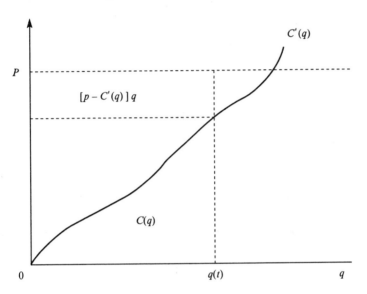

Figure 4.1 Optimal current extraction of oil deposits

Observe in Figure 4.1 that producer surplus is $qC_q(q) - C(q)$ which we denote by $\sigma(q)$. Since calendar dates are not relevant here, the extraction problem has the same form at each date. Only the stock size remaining has changed. Hence the terminal condition can be interpreted as: given a very small amount of stock remaining near the end, get the most profit from that stock. The most profit on a small amount of stock at the end is, of course, $p - C_q[q(T)]$, for $q(T)$ very small. Alternatively, the problem must solve correctly from terminal date T, back to initial date 0. From this perspective, it makes sense to get the most profit possible on the last quantity extracted, and this involves setting the last quantity extracted infinitesimally small when $(p - C_q(0))$ is large.

At date t, the remaining stock $S(t)$ is an asset with current value

$$V(t) = \int_t^{T^*} \pi[q^*(x)] e^{-r(x-t)} dx$$

where *s indicate optimal values. Now

$$\frac{dV(t)}{dt} = rV(t) - \pi[q^*(t)]$$

or the decline in asset value,[2] from optimal 'use' of the asset, is (a) current profit 'lost' because $S(t)$ has shrunk by $q^*(t)$ and (b) $rV(t)$, a positive term, indicating that residual value $V(t)$ has been moved forward in time, infinitesimally. $V(t)$ increases in value the less it is discounted.

From dynamic programming we have

$$rV(t) = \pi[q^*(t)] - q^*(t)\pi_q[q^*(t)].$$

Combining our two last relations yields the fundamental depreciation result

$$\frac{dV(t)}{dt} = -\{p - C_q[q^*(t)]\}q^*(t).$$

Asset value, $V(t)$, shrinks by resource rents or by current stock price $\{p - Cq[q^*(t)]\}$ multiplied by physical shrinkage in the stock size. And physical shrinkage is a planned or optimal value, not a value selected by rule of thumb. It was apparent that the decline in stock value must be related to physical stock shrinkage, $q(t)$. What we observe is that the decline in value is indeed physical shrinkage, valued at the current net price of a unit of stock.[3]

Our concept of depreciation dates back at least to Samuelson (1937). See also Samuelson (1964). Hicks (1939, Chapter 14) defines economic depreciation of an oil stock similarly and introduces the idea of a 'stationary equivalent' of the stocks value.[4] Hicks defines a stationary equivalent to rV_t in

$$\overline{\pi}_t = rV_t$$

yielding his expression for depreciation of an exhaustible stock (Hicks, 1939, p. 187):

$$\dot{V}_t = \overline{\pi}_t - \pi[q(t)].$$

Our specification involves $\dot{V}_t$ negative or current 'income' from the asset above its stationary equivalent. Note that this stationary equivalent declines over time, since $V(t)$ declines.

Although we viewed our problem as an extractive firm, mining its stock efficiently, we could be talking about a small open oil-exporting nation, one which imports all its consumption goods and pays for imports with revenues from oil exporting. We turn to the national accounts for such a small open economy. Static revenue equals expenditure in

$$pq(t) = \{p - C_q[q(t)]\}q(t) + C[q(t)] + \sigma[q(t)]$$

where $\sigma[q(t)]$ is producer surplus, accruing because oil extraction takes place under decreasing returns to scale (extraction costs are convex). Our accounts are in Table 4.1.

Table 4.1   *National accounting matrix (oil-exporting nation)*

Expenditures ↓ Receipts →	Oil flow	Primary inputs	Oil stock	Households
Oil flow				pq
Primary inputs	$C(q)$			
Oil stock	$(p - C_q)q$			$-(p - C_q)q$
Households	$\sigma(q)$	$C(q)$		

Gross national product is pq and NNP is $pq - (p - Cq)q$. We know that $-(p - Cq)q$ is the decline in market value of the oil stock as extraction, $q(t)$, occurs. Hence, zero profit intertemporal arbitrage (ZPIA) yields $-[p - C_q(q)]q$ as the loss in value of $S(t)$ over the 'period' of extraction. In calculating this depreciation, we made use of the Euler equation or arbitrage condition $d[p - C_q(q)]/dt = [p - C_q(q)]r$. Hence ZPIA implies economic depreciation, $-(p - C_q)q$. Observe here that there are no capital gains in NNP.

The households row seems to net national income. Of interest here is that oil stock, $S(t)$, makes no direct appearance. The stock *per se* is not 'productive' directly, only indirectly by being a reservoir of future flow. But this reservoir has a rental associated with it. Recall that $\dot{V}_t = rV_t - \pi_t$ and $\dot{V}_t = [p - C_q(t)]q_t$. Hence $rV_t = \pi_t - [p - C_q(t)]q_t$, which is our producer surplus, labelled $\sigma[q(t)]$. Hence $\sigma[q(t)]$ reflects rental flow, $rV(S_t)$ where $V(S_t)$ is the market value of the remaining stock. $rV(S_t)$ is the stationary equivalent income flow, represented by asset $V(S_t)$. It is a current-income representation of future income from the remaining stock.

It is instructive to compare the accounts for our simple K-capital economy (Table 1.2, Chapter 1) with those for our simple oil-exporting economy (Table 4.1). In each set of accounts, there are no asset price changes (capital gains or losses)[5] and economic depreciation is somewhat more complicated to arrive at for our oil economy. In each case, capital appears in the national *income* account as a stationary equivalent (capital value multiplied by the interest rate).

4.3   SUSTAINABLE INCOME IN THE OIL REPUBLIC

If the above oil-exporting nation chose to invest some of its oil sales revenue abroad and earn r% on the accumulated capital, it would have net oil profit left plus interest income in order to purchase consumption goods from abroad. It turns out that a permanently sustainable (constant) consumption stream, $G(q_0)$, is possible if (a) rent $\{p - C_q[q(t)]\}q(t)$ is invested abroad at each date and (b) interest $A(t)$ plus net profit, (producer surplus), $\sigma[q(t)]$ is used to pay for consumption goods. $A(t)$ is cumulative financial capital, held abroad at date t. When the oil stock is exhausted at T, $A(T)r$ will equal $G(q_0)$ and this net consumption can be sustained into the indefinite future. This 'investing-resource-rents' strategy is predicated on extraction taking place in a wealth-maximizing fashion, or as $d\{p - C_q[q(t)]\}/dt = \{p - C_q[q(t)]\}r$. To see this sustainable consumption strategy, define current consumption in

$$G(t) = rA(t) + \pi[q(t)] - \{p - C_q[q(t)]\}q(t),$$

where $\pi[q(t)] = pq(t) - C[q(t)]$ and $d\pi(q)/dq = p - C_q(q)$. Differentiating with respect to time yields

$$\frac{dG(t)}{dt} = \{p - C_q[q(t)]\}q(t)r + \frac{d\pi[q(t)]}{dq}\dot{q} - \frac{d\pi[q(t)]}{dq}\dot{q}$$

$$-q(t)\frac{d\{p - C_q[q(t)]\}}{dt}$$

which equals zero because $\{p - Cq[q(t)]\}r$ equals $d\{p - C_q[q(t)]\}/dt$. (Notice that $\dot{A}(t)$ is a net figure, equal to $\{p - Cq[q(t)]\}q(t)$.) Hence consumption $G(t)$ remains constant when resource rents are accumulated abroad and interest flow becomes part of the means to finance current consumption. The value loss in oil capital, from extraction, is covered off by the value 'gain' in financial capital, added to abroad.

4.4   TERMS-OF-TRADE EFFECTS

Suppose p, the world price of oil above, were rising exogenously through time. From dynamic programming[6] we obtain

$$rV(t) = \pi[q^*(t)] - q^*(t)\pi_q[q^*(t)] + \int_t^T q^*(v)\frac{dp(v)}{dt}e^{-p(v-t)}dv,$$

where $\pi[q(t)] = pq(t) - C[q(t)]$, a form of profit or surplus. Sustainable income includes the integral, the sum of future shift effects in the world price of oil. Sustainable income will be larger because of the positive future terms-of-trade effects. $V(t)$ continues to be the future optimal value, $\int_t^T e^{-r(v-t)} \pi[q^*(v)] dv$. Hence

$$\frac{dV(t)}{dt} = rV(t) - \pi[q^*(v)].$$

Substituting for $rV(t)$ yields the central result

$$\frac{dV(t)}{dt} = -q^*(t)\pi_q[q^*(t)] + \int_t^T q^*(v) \frac{dp(v)}{dt} e^{-r(v-t)} dv;$$

depreciation is smaller because of the positive future price shifts, terms-of-trade effects. Recall that Irving Fisher (1906) is primarily responsible for the modern idea of 'capital' being represented by its discounted future net earnings. Here we are observing change in current capital value 'capitalizing' future price-shift effects. This is, in a sense, an extension of the Irving Fisher argument. These price effects are embodied in capital value but show up most clearly when the change in capital value (macro-depreciation) is calculated.

The notion of sustainable development as a perpetually constant consumption level can be worked out for this case of future price shifts when the more general measure of macro-depreciation is used. It is this amount of macro-depreciation which must be covered off by investment abroad in order for the level of consumption to remain constant (see Vincent et al., 1997 and Hartwick and Long, 1999).

4.5 DATE-DEPENDENT INTEREST RATE

Suppose interest rate r is different on different dates into the infinite future and that agents know about the future time path. The optimization of oil extraction still satisfies the r% rule

$$\frac{d[p - C_q(t)]}{dt} = [p - C_q(t)]r(t)$$

but the time path of extraction ($q^*(t)$) will be affected by the varying $r(t)$. Corresponding to the optimal extraction program is the optimal initial value

$$V_o^* = \int_t^T \pi[q^*(t)]\exp\left[-\int_0^t r(z)dz\right]dt$$

where $\exp[-\int_0^t r(z)dz]$ is the date varying version, of $\exp[-(t-0)r]$ for r constant.

Since the oil stock S_0 could be sold at time 0 and V_0^* put in the bank, one could live on an interest flow indefinitely. What interest flow? Clearly the consumption level C^* satisfies

$$V_0^* = C^* \int_0^\infty \exp\left[\int_0^t -r(z)dz\right]dt.$$

Hence

$$\Delta_0 = \int_0^\infty \exp\left[-\int_0^t r(z)dz\right]dt$$

is an average discount operator for the interval 0 to ∞. This discount operator plays the exact role of $1/r$ for the case of a constant interest rate r. Hence $1/\Delta_0 = R_0$ is an average interest rate.

Suppose that part of current profit $\pi[q^*(t)]$ and interest income $r(t)A(t)$ from a sinking fund, built up from time 0, is invested in $A(t)$ each period, while consumption level C^* remains constant. At date t, the value of remaining oil is

$$V(t) = \int_t^T \pi[q^*(z)] \exp\left[\int_t^z -r(w)dw\right] dz$$

and the value of the sinking fund is $A(t)$. If the investing in the sinking fund strategy is correct, it must be the case that

$$V(t) + A(t) = C^* \int_0^\infty \exp\left[-\int_t^z r(w)dw\right]dz$$

$$= C^*/R(t)$$

for some date t, between 0 and T. (Recall that the remaining oil stock $S(t)$ could be sold for $V(t)$ and the $V(t)$ could be put in the bank, with the $A(t)$, to constitute a capital fund to live on.) Hence for $dC^*/dt = 0$, we obtain

$$\dot{A}(t) = -\dot{V}(t) + \frac{V(t) + A(t)}{\Delta(t)} [r(t)\Delta(t) - 1]$$

$$= (\text{depreciation}) + V_0 R(0) \left[\frac{r(t)}{R(t)} - 1\right]$$

as the formula for how much to invest in $A(t)$ at each date in order to keep consumption constant (Lozada, 1997, equation (6)). In the special case of $r(t)$ constant, we retrieve our familiar result: investing resource rent (equal to macro-depreciation) maintains consumption constant. Hence one invests more (less) than macro-depreciation when interest rates are on average declining (increasing). Declining interest rates can be interpreted here to mean that returns from the sinking fund will be marginally less and hence more current investment in the sinking fund is needed.

For the record, the derivative of $V(t)$ above takes the form (by Leibnitz's Rule)

$$\dot{V}(t) = r(t)V(t) - \pi[q^*(t)].$$

Although this looks familiar, it will not reduce to $-\pi_q[q^*(t)]q^*(t)$, given $r(t)$ not constant. Hence economic depreciation with the above date-varying interest rates will be a complicated variant of our earlier central result

$$\dot{V}(t) = -\pi_q[q^*(t)]q^*(t),$$

depreciation equals Hotelling Rent, for the autonomous case.

4.6   OIL AND LABOR PRODUCE COMPOSITE OUTPUT

We consider a simple economy, drawing on oil as an input in current production, the oil being taken from a known homogeneous stock. 'Preserving capital good j intact' is, we have noted, open to different interpretations. We suggest that 'preserving the value of the stock of natural capital good j intact' leads to a correct concept of NNP, one that belongs to the same family as our NANNP (National Accounts NNP, distinct for utility NNP) for the case of person-made capital alone. There are no extraction costs in the model here. S_t is the stock remaining at the end of period t. Our physical accounts are

$$C_1 = F(S_0 - S_1, N)$$

$$C_2 = F(S_1 - S_2, N)$$

$$C_3 = F(S_2 - S_3, N)$$

$$\cdot \quad \cdot$$

$$\cdot \quad \cdot$$

where $F(\cdot)$ exhibits constant returns to scale. There will be asymptotic depletion of the original stock for the case of $F(\cdot)$ Cobb–Douglas. We shall assume the depletion is asymptotic.

We require that goods producers purchase S_{t-1} at the end of period $t-1$, and sell $S_{t-1} - y_{t-1}(= S_t)$ at the end of t. That is, we have zero intertemporal profit in

$$F_y(t)S_t + F_y(t)y_{t-1} = F_y(t-1)S_{t-1}(1+r_t) \quad (t = 1, 2, \ldots)$$

or

$$F_y(t) = F_y(t-1)(1+r_t)$$

where r_t is the market rate of interest. This latter condition defines dynamic efficiency in extraction or wealth-maximizing extraction. The loss in value of S_{t-1} between the end of period $t-1$ and the end of period t is $S_t F_y(t) - S_{t-1}F_y(t-1)$. This combines price change $[F_y(t) - F_y(t-1)]S_t$ plus quantity change $-y_{t-1}F_y(t-1)$. Interest foregone is $r_t F_y(t-1)S_{t-1}$. Associated with the economy is the national accounting matrix in Table 4.2.

The households column is NNP. It comprises aggregate consumption, C_t and economic depreciation, $F_y(t)S_t - F_y(t-1)S_{t-1}$. The households row (net national income) comprises labor income and income, $r_t F_y(t-1)S_{t-1}$ on the stock S_{t-1}. The NNP (households column) in Table 4.2 is Hicks-consistent in the sense that if economic depreciation were covered off by investment, the value of the capital stock would be being preserved intact. The depreciation term $F_y(t)S_t - F_y(t-1)S_{t-1}$ is a natural idea of value loss in stock S_{t-1} over the accounting period. However, the appearance of $r_t F_y(t-1)S_{t-1}$ in the households row is somewhat novel. Given constant returns to scale here, $F_y(t-1)S_{t-1}$ can be viewed as the market price of stock S_{t-1}. It thus represents discounted future net income from S_{t-1}. The r_t transforms this stock value into a stationary equivalent flow value. Hence $r_t F_y(t-1)S_{t-1}$ is a proxy for future income from the remaining stock, S_{t-1}. Hence stock in the ground is showing up in the accounts as a stationary equivalent in the net national income. Recall that in Table 4.1, above, the $\sigma(q)$ term was reflecting this stationary equivalent value.

One might ask: why not move the capital gains term to the income side of the accounts instead of inserting it in the product side? Then NNP would be $C_t + (S_{t-1} - S_t)Fy(t-1)$ and net national income (NNI) would be $NF_N + r_t F_y(t-1)S_{t-1} - [F_y(t) - F_y(t-1)]S_t$. NNP now has no asset price change and NNI has acquired price change $-[F_y(t) - F_y(t-1)]S_t$. Such a change brings NNP in line with the dollar-valued, linearized current-value Hamiltonian favored by many (for example, Weitzman, 1999) but moves asset price change to the national income side of the accounts. As we noted in Chapter 3, the asset price change term is somewhat of an orphan and it is not clear-cut as to where the term should be placed.

Table 4.2 *National accounting matrix (exhaustible resources)*

Expenditures ↓ / Receipts →	Consumption goods	Labor	S-capital	Households
Consumption goods				C_t
Labor	NF_N			
S-capital	$y_{t-1}F_y(t)$			$F_y(t)S_t - F_y(t-1)S_{t-1}$
Households		NF_N	$r_t F_y(t-1)S_{t-1}$	

4.7 ECONOMIC DEPRECIATION AND THE CURRENT-VALUE HAMILTONIAN

In continuous time our exhaustive resource problem is $\max_{(y_t)} \int_0^\infty U[F(y_t, N)]$ $e^{-\rho t} dt$ subject to $\dot{S}(t) = -y_t$ and $S(0) = \int_0^\infty y_t dt$. $F(y_t, N)$ is output, equal to consumption. N is the constant labor force and y_t is current oil use. Associated with this problem is the current-value Hamiltonian or 'utility NNP' (UNNP)

$$H = U[F(y_t, N)] - \mu y_t$$

$$= U[F(y_t, N)] - U_c(t) F_y(t) y_t$$

given necessary condition $\mu(t) = U_c(t) F_y(t)$. Also, associated with this problem is the value function

$$V(t) = \int_0^\infty U[C^*(z)] e^{-\rho(z-t)} dz$$

where * indicates an optimal value. Hence it follows that

$$\dot{V}(t) = \rho V(t) - U[C^*(t)]$$

$$= -U_c(t) F_y(t) y_t$$

because $\rho V(t) = U[C^*(t)] - U_c(t) F_y(t) y_t$ from dynamic programming. Hence the current-value Hamiltonian captures the loss in value of the program, $\dot{V}(t)$, associated with stock decline $\dot{S}(t)$, equal to $-y_t$. Clearly $\dot{V}(t)$ (which might be labelled macroeconomic depreciation[7]) and our term for economic depreciation in NNP in Table 4.3 are measuring different things. $-\dot{V}(t)$ measures the output required as investment to keep the value, in utils, *of the optimal program* unchanged across periods.

The adjoint equation for this problem is $\dot{\mu}(t) = \rho \mu(t)$. This leads to

$$\frac{\dot{\mu}}{\mu} = \frac{\dot{U}_C}{U_C} + \frac{\dot{F}_y}{F_y}$$

$$= \rho$$

and suggests representing the *market* rate of interest r_t by $-\dot{U}_C / U_C + \rho$. That is, we obtain the familiar r% rule for extraction,

$$\frac{\dot{F}_y}{F_y} = r_{t'}$$

In discrete time our ZPIA condition is

$$S_t F_y(t) + F_y(t)y_{t-1} = S_{t-1}F_y(t-1)(1+r_t),$$

and in continuous time, this condition is

$$y_t F_y(t) + [S_t \dot{F}_y(t) - y_t F_y(t)] = S_t F_y(t)r_{t'}.$$

The term in square brackets is economic depreciation and comprises a quantity term and a price-change term. We observed this above in the discrete time version of this model. The term in square brackets can be written as $d[S_t F_y(t)]/dt$. The national accounts for this economy are set out in Table 4.3.

Table 4.3 *National accounting matrix (oil and labor produce output)*

Expenditures ↓ Receipts →	Consumption goods	Labor	Oil stock	Households
Consumption goods				C_t
Labor	$NF_N(t)$			
Oil stock	$y_t F_y(t)$			$d[S_t F_y(t)]/dt^*$
Households		$NF_N(t)$	$r_t F_y(t)S_t$	

Note: *This economic depreciation term comprises an oil price change term, $S_t\dot{F}_y(t)$ and a quantity term, $-y_t F_y(t)$.

The accounts in Table 4.3 are simply those for the continuous time version of the model economy, whose accounts are in Table 4.2. No novelties emerge in the switch from discrete time to continuous time. The central feature to note is the presence of a price change term in economic depreciation in the households column (NNP) and the presence of a stationary equivalent, $r_t F_y(t)S_t$, in national income in the households row.

4.8 ACCOUNTS FOR A CLOSED ECONOMY WITH OIL AS AN ESSENTIAL INPUT

We turn to a model of a closed economy using oil and the services of K-capital in production. Consumption C and new K-capital are produced in

$$C(t) + K(t) - K(t-1) = F[K(t-1), R(t-1), N]$$

where R is the input of oil and N the services of labor. N is constant and $F(\cdot)$ exhibits substitutability among inputs and constant returns to scale.[8] Oil resembles circulating capital because it gets used up in one period of goods production but it differs from circulating capital because the current oil is drawn off a stock that shrinks, irrevocably, after each draw-down. There is current oil use to consider as well as its impact on the rate of stock draw-down. The stock draw-down is signalled to the economy via an increase in the price of oil. A smaller stock implies increased scarcity and this shows up as a higher price for 'use' of the stock. A scarcer stock remaining 'translates' into a higher price per unit of oil in current use. These observations show up clearly in the ZPIA condition:

$$S(t)F_R(t) + R(t-1)F_R(t) = S(t-1)F_R(t-1)(1+r_t)$$

where $R(t-1)F_R(t)$ is rental income from the use of oil in period t and $F_R(t-1)$ $S(t-1)$ is the cost of the oil stock $S(t-1)$ one period earlier. r_t is the discount rate. Now $R(t-1)$ is drawn off a finite stock $S(t-1)$, so that

$$R(t-1) = S(t-1) - S(t)$$

or the stock shrinks as time passes or as oil is drawn off period by period. Substituting and cancelling $S(t-1)$ 'yields' the 'r% rule':

$$F_R(t) = F_R(t-1)(1+r_t).$$

The ZPIA condition associated with $K(t-1)$ is

$$K(t-1) + K(t-1)F_K(t) = K(t-1)(1+r_t),$$

which says that the sales value of $K(t-1)$ at the end of period t, namely $K(t-1)$, plus the rental income accruing to owners of $K(t-1)$ from its use in production in period t, equals the cost of $K(t-1)$, one period earlier, $K(t-1)$ $(1+r_t)$. This condition becomes the accounting relation: current rental income $K(t-1)F_K(t)$ equals interest foregone, $K(t-1)r_t$.

Table 4.4 *National accounting matrix (oil used in goods production)*

Expenditures ↓ / Receipts →	Consumption goods*	Investment goods*	Labor	M-capital	S-capital	Households
Consumption goods						$C(t)$
Investment goods						$K(t) - K(t-1)$
Labor	$N^1 F_N(t)$	$N^2 F_N(t)$				
M-capital	$K^1(t-1)F_K(t)$	$K^2(t-1)F_K(t)$				
S-capital	$R^1(t-1)F_R(t)$	$R^2(t-1)F_R(t)$				$S(t)F_R(t) - S(t-1)F_R(t-1)$
Households			$NF_N(t)$	$r_t K(t-1)$	$S(t-1)F_R(t-1)r_t$	

Note: *Consumption and investment goods are jointly produced with the constant returns to scale production function, $F(\cdot)$. Hence $N^1 + N^2 = N$, $K^1 + K^2 = K$, and $R^1 + R^2 = R$.

We combine these two ZPIA conditions with conditions of zero current profit in consumer goods (sector 1) production and investment goods (sector 2) production to obtain our national accounts matrix in Table 4.4.

In the households column in Table 4.4, $C(t) + K(t) - K(t - 1)$ is gross national product and the complete column sum is the national accounting net national product (NANNP). $S(t)F_R(t) - S(t - 1)F_R(t - 1)$ is the economic depreciation on the oil stock $S(t - 1)$. $R(t - 1)$ is physical shrinkage in the stock and $-R(t - 1)F_R(t)$ is the dollar value of the shrinkage. The depreciation term, when resigned, is a dollar sum, which if invested at the end of period t, will restore $S(t)$ to their respective values at the end of period $t - 1$.

In the households row in Table 4.4, $NF_N(t)$ is labor income, and $K(t - 1)r_t$ and $S(t - 1)F_R(t - 1)r_t$ are stationary equivalents for the capital values of $K(t - 1)$ and $S(t - 1)$, respectively, over the period of use (production). The row sum is net national income or aggregate value-added. To make NNP the dollar-valued, linearized current-value Hamiltonian, we must remove asset price change from the term $S(t)F_R(t) - S(t - 1)F_R(t - 1)$. To do this we simply added and subtract $S(t - 1)F_R(t)$. Then economic depreciation is $-[S(t - 1) - S(t)]F_R(t)$ and asset price change is $[F_R(t) - F_R(t - 1)]S(t - 1)$. The NNP is now $C + K(t) - K(t - 1) - [S(t - 1) - S(t)]F_R(t)$ and NNI inherits the asset price revaluation term to become $NF_N(t) + r_tK(t - 1) + S(t - 1)F_R(t - 1)r_t - [F_R(t) - F_R(t - 1)]S(t - 1)$.

4.9   COVERING OFF OIL STOCK DEPRECIATION IN GENERAL EQUILIBRIUM

The idea of maintaining consumption constant by compensating for the decline in the 'productivity' of one shrinking input with investment in a separate productive capital good originates in its modern form in Solow (1974) and Hartwick (1977). The analysis was undertaken in a model of a closed, general equilibrium system, a continuous-time version of the model in the previous section. We report on this 'covering off depreciation of the oil stock' here, in brief. (See also Appendix 3A1, Chapter 3.)

We consider a closed growing economy with two types of capital, namely machine capital K and oil stocks S. We consider an optimal growth path, a representation of a path of growth under competitive market conditions. Current oil use is

$$R(t) = -\dot{S}(t)$$

and the current growth of $K(t)$ is

$$\dot{K}(t) = F[K(t), N, R(t)] - C(t)$$

where $C(t)$ is aggregate consumption, N is the constant labor force, and $F(\cdot)$ is the constant returns to scale, neoclassical aggregate production function. Savings and use of $S(t)$ satisfy

$$\max_{C(t)} \int_0^\infty U[C(t)]e^{-\rho t}dt$$

subject to the above equations of motion and

$$K(0) = K_0$$

$$\int_0^\infty R(t)dt = S_0.$$

The 'solved' Bellman equation for our problem is

$$\rho V(t) = U[C^*(t)] + \dot{K}(t)U_c[C^*(t)] + \dot{S}(t)F_R(t)U_c[C^*(t)].$$

where

$$V(t) = \int_t^\infty U[C^*(v)]e^{-\rho(v-t)}dv$$

and

$$\dot{V}(t) = \rho V(t) - U[C^*(t)].$$

*s indicate values along the optimal path. Hence

$$\dot{V}(t) = [\dot{K}(t) + \dot{S}(t)F_R(t)]U_c[C^*(t)]$$

which is our generalized depreciation relation. (Dixit et al., 1980 labelled the term, $\dot{K}(t) + \dot{S}(t)F_R(t)$, 'net savings'.) Generalized depreciation or net savings might be zero if $\dot{K}(t)$ happened to equal $\dot{S}F_R(t)$. It would be highly coincidental for the optimal solution to exhibit $\dot{K}(t)$ equal to $\dot{S}(t)F_R(t)$ at every date. We do, in any case, have an expression for depreciation. The ZPIA conditions for this model reduce to $KF_K = Kr_t$ and $\dot{F}_R = F_R r_t$, where $-\dot{U}_C/U_C + \rho = r_t = F_K(t)$.

Solow (1974) constructed an optimal growth model along the lines above such that $C^*(t)$ constant and maximal was the optimal solution (Appendix 3A1, Chapter 3, above). Solow's path satisfied $\dot{K}(t) = -\dot{S}(t)F_R(t)$ at each date or satisfied the 'investing of resource rents' savings rule. It is important to note that it is a very particular optimal growth solution which implies that $\dot{K}(t)$ equals $-\dot{S}(t)F_R(t)$ at every date. And as Asheim (1994) has emphasized, although net savings or generalized economic depreciation may be zero *at an* *instant* in an actual economy, the asset prices used in the calculation will not in general derive from an economy moving along a Solow-type, constant consumption, optimal growth path. An observation of zero net investment at date *t* does not imply that the economy is on a long-run constant consumption path. The prices used in the calculation of economic depreciation (net savings) may or may not be those corresponding to a long-run constant consumption program. For example, current net savings could be zero at date *t* in two distinct economies. One might be an economy on an optimal constant consumption path and the other might be for an economy with consumption currently switching from increasing to decreasing.

NNP comprises gross product, $C + \dot{K}$ plus economic depreciation terms for K-capital and S-capital. Most of current oil use, in value, ends up as economic depreciation of the stock. The oil stock shrinks by current 'use' R and oil prices change, $-RF_R + S\dot{F}_R$. Net national income comprises labor income, NF_N, and stationary equivalents, Kr_t, and $S_t F_R(t) r_t$. There is a strong case implicit here for leaving asset price change out of NNP. If 'net investment' is zero, that is $\dot{K} = -\dot{S}F_R$, then under special but not incredible conditions, aggregate consumption remains constant. Hence NNP equal to $C + \dot{K} + \dot{S}F_R$ is sustainable. This would suggest moving asset price change, $S\dot{F}_R$, to the income side of the national accounts.

4.10   IS HICKSIAN NET NATIONAL PRODUCT (NANNP) SUSTAINABLE?

Our definition of Hicksian net national product is the value gross current product net of *n* separate terms, each of which is the value of resources which would maintain the value of current capital input *j*, intact, *j* = 1,...,*n*. Intuitively, with a constant labor force, the capacity of the economy to produce appears to remain unchanged if current consumption is the Hicksian net national product. In this sense 'maintaining capital intact' makes current Hicksian net national product sustainable. In other words, we should be able to recover the current Hicksian net national product one period later. That is, current Hicksian net national product should be locally-in-time sustainable. This proposition is difficult to establish in general because it requires information about the current magnitudes of inputs. (One needs a completely solved program.) Solow's (1974) model path provides the necessary information on magnitudes of inputs and so we work with this special but instructive case.

A Solow path is defined by C_t, R_t and K_t in

$$\dot{K}_t = F(K_t, R_t, N) - C_t$$

$$\dot{F}_R(t) = F_R(t)F_K(t)$$

$$\dot{K}_t = R_t F_R(t)$$

and

$$S_t = \int_t^\infty R_z dz.$$

N is assumed to be constant, $F(\cdot)$ exhibits substitutability among inputs and constant returns to scale. For the case of $F(\cdot) \equiv K^\alpha R^\beta N^{1-\alpha-\beta}$, α, β, $1 - \alpha - \beta > 0$ and $\alpha > \beta$, C_t will be positive, constant and maximal with respect to K_t and S_t. This level of C_t will be sustainable over infinite time. S_t will be depleted asymptotically.

One obtains net national income as $NF_N(t) + K_t F_K(t)$ and our net national product as $C_t + \dot{K}_t - R_t F_R(t) + S_t F_R(t)(\dot{F}_R/F_R) = F(K_t, R_t, N) - R_t F_R(t) + S_t F_R(t)(\dot{F}_R/F_R)$. On the Solow path, $d[F(K_t, R_t, N) - RF_R(t)]/dt = 0^9$ and $\dot{F}_R(t) > 0$. S_t declines over time. Hence Hicksian net national product is increasing (decreasing) on a Solow path as $d[S_t \dot{F}_R(t)]/dt > 0(< 0)$. In this model, $d(NANNP)/dt$ does not have one sign for all dates.

The Solow model provides one well-known benchmark for the concept of an economy evolving sustainably and yet it fails to exhibit the sustainability of Hicksian NNP. Capital gains appear to 'prevent' sustainability of Hicksian NNP from 'emerging'. Capital gains can be said to reflect changes in current input proportions and these changes can be independent of changes in the capacity of the economy to produce output. Thus the Hicksian notion here of maintaining the value of each current capital input intact confounds the maintaining of input proportions unchanged with productive capacity unchanged. There is another way to think about 'maintaining the value of capital input j intact'. Owners of a unit of capital good j will demand a market return, which comprises a gross income or return plus compensation for losses associated with the capital good over the period. An owner is indifferent between the loss associated with wear and tear or value loss associated with predictable changes in asset prices. Hence our economic depreciation in NANNP (Hicksian NNP) is a *market* concept, one associated with a decentralized economy. On the other hand the link between changes in inputs and change in productive capacity *of the economy* is a planning concept, one associated with central direction of the economy. Economic depreciation in UNNP captures the changes in productive capacity of the economy. It resembles a planning indicator rather than traditional market-oriented economic depreciation.

4.11 DURABLE EXHAUSTIBLE RESOURCES

A natural resource such as gold or diamonds is mined and *accumulated* above ground. There is little or no decay or depletion once extracted. We refer to such resources as durable. Copper and other metals deteriorate slowly over time above ground and are thus semi-durable. We shall set out the accounts for the case of imperfect durability. The central result is that as extraction proceeds there is a simultaneous decline in the value of the stock below ground and increase in the value of the stock above ground. We end up with two 'depreciation' terms in NNP, one for stock below ground and one for the stock above ground. The 'textbook' treatment of this matter, without accounts, is Levhari and Pindyck (1981). As they note, under competitive conditions, accumulation above ground puts downward pressure on market prices. In the extreme case of perfect durability (no 'rusting', once extracted), this downward pressure on price can lead to a spike in extraction at the initial date of extraction. This may be an important effect in real-world mineral markets and is certainly a large departure from the smooth or gradual extraction we have come to associate with, say, oil extraction. Oil is a non-durable resource in the sense that once extracted, it is usually consumed immediately and the services provided last only one period.

$R(t)$ equal to $g(H, S)$ is current extraction, where N is labor and S is the current stock below ground. Production function $g(\cdot)$ exhibits constant returns to scale:

$$\dot{S}(t) = -g[N(t), S(t)].$$

We can imagine that our competitive extractors belong to a small, open exporting nation, facing world demand $p(R)$.[10] Above ground we have stock $A(t)$ and

$$\dot{A}(t) = g(N, S) - \delta A$$

where δ is the exogenous, constant rate of decay ('rusting') of extracted material. When extraction ceases, at date T, the remaining stock $A(T)$ decays at exogenous rate δ and price rises to a terminal maximum value, $\bar{p}$. Hence for any value $A(T)$ we can calculate, working backwards, a $p(T^*)$ for price just after extraction. Price must move smoothly across this regime shift. This provides us with specific end-point conditions for extraction at date T.

Competitive extraction is wealth-maximizing for the economy and satisfies

$$\max_{[N(t)]} \int_0^T \{B[A(t)] - wN(t)\}e^{-rt}dt$$

subject to

$$\dot{A} = g(N, S) - \delta A,$$

$$\dot{S} = -g(N, S)$$

$$A(0) = A_0$$

and

$$\int_0^T g[N(t), S(t)]dt \le S_0$$

where $B(A)$ is consumer surplus or the area under the market demand schedule. The current-value Hamiltonian is

$$H = B(A) - wN + \mu(t)[g(N, S) - \delta A] - \eta(t)g(N, S).$$

The necessary conditions are

$$\frac{\partial H}{\partial N} = 0 \text{ or } [\mu(t) - \eta(t)]g_N(t) = w$$

$$\frac{\partial H}{\partial A} = \dot{\mu} - r\mu \text{ or } p(t) - \mu\delta + \dot{\mu} = r\mu$$

$$-\frac{\partial H}{\partial S} = \dot{\eta} - r\eta \text{ or } [\mu(t) - \eta(t)]gs(t) = r\eta(t)$$

and end-point condition, $p(T) = p(T^+)$, where $p(T^+)$ is defined by the stock $A(T)$ remaining above ground. The $A(T)$ decays at rate δ and $p(T^+)$ rises to an exogenously given maximum value.

Constant returns to scale implies that $g(N, S) = Ng_N + Sg_S$. This buys much simplification in setting out the accounts. Thus the first row and column in Table 4.5 is based on

$$\mu R = \mu g_N N + \mu g_S S.$$

The third row and column derives from the ZPIA condition

$$(\mu - \eta)g_S S + \dot{\eta}S = r\eta S$$

and the fifth row and column derives from the ZPIA condition

$$pA + \dot{\mu}A - \mu\delta A - r\mu A.$$

Table 4.5 *National accounting matrix (semi-durable exhaustible resources)*

Expenditures ↓ / Receipts →	Current extraction	Labor	Underground stock	Underground flow	Above ground stock	Households
Current extraction						μR
Labor	$(\mu-\eta)g_N N$					
Underground stock	$(\mu-\eta)g_S S$					$\dot{\mu} S$
Underground flow	ηR					$-\eta R$
Above ground stock						$pA + \dot{\mu}A - \mu\delta A$
Households		wN	ηS	0	$r\mu A$	

Note that in the households column of Table 4.5 $\mu R - \mu \delta A$ can be expressed as $\mu \dot{A}$. Hence the households column can be expressed as $pA + d(\eta S)/dt + d(\mu A)/dt$. And the integration of the expression for $\dot{\mu}(t)$ yields

$$\mu(t) = \int_t^\infty p(z)e^{-(r + \delta)(z - t)}dt$$
$$= P(t)$$

where $P(t)$ is the capital value of a unit of extracted $R(t)$. Hence NNP, the households column, is

$$pA(t) + \frac{d(\eta S)}{dt} + \frac{d[P(t)A(t)]}{dt},$$

the current value of services from the extracted $A(t)$ plus two stock revaluation terms, one for stock below ground and one for stock above ground. The households row is net national income (NNI) and comprises labor income wN plus $r\eta(t)S(t)$ and $rP(t)A(t)$, two stationary equivalents, representing the market value of stocks, as interest income. For non-durable non-renewable resources, there is no accumulation above ground. Hence pA reduces to pR and $d(PA)/dt$ is zero, in NNP. We have left asset price changes in the NNP in Table 4.5. If $\dot{\mu}S$ were moved to the income side, then we would have zero as the entry for underground stock in both NNP and NNI. There is much merit in this variant. For the aboveground stock, one would move $\dot{\mu}A$ to the households row, making the new entry $r\mu A - \dot{\mu}A$.

4.12 RECYCLING OF DURABLE EXTRACTED MATERIAL

We make costs of recycling above ground, extracted material explicit now. At the margin, the economy exhibits equal costs from getting a unit for current use from the recycling sector and from the extractive sector. Mining and recycling compete for the same market. In this setting, extractive activity does not dominate the economics narrative. The other curious valuation matter is that the value of a unit of extracted material has two positive components, rental in use per period and rental as input into the recycling sector.

We represent the recycled stock, from stock input A, by $R(A, N1)$ where N_1 is labor and $R(\cdot)$ exhibits constant returns to scale. (Clearly $R(\cdot)$ must be bounded above by A.) $X(S, N_2)$ is the amount currently extracted with labor N_2 and S in the ground. Then

$$\dot{A} = R(A, N_1) - A + X(S, N_2) \tag{4.1}$$

and

$$\dot{S} = -X(S, N_2) \tag{4.2}$$

and $N_1 = N - N_2$ for N fixed. We assume that $X(\cdot)$ exhibits constant returns to scale also. Consumers use the durable material for a period and derive surplus $B(Z)$ and then Z is recycled. Hence dB/dZ is a rental price denoted B_Z. $Z = X(N_2, S) + R(A, N_1)$.

The market maximizes $\int_0^\infty B[Z(t)]e^{-rt}dt$ subject to (4.1), (4.2) and $A(0) = A_0$ and $S(0) = S_0$. The current-value Hamiltonian is

$$H = B(Z) + \lambda[R(A, N_1) - A + X(S, N_2)] - \mu X(S, N_2).$$

The necessary conditions are

$$\frac{\partial H}{\partial N_1} = 0 \Rightarrow (B_Z + \lambda)R_{N1} = (B_Z + \lambda - \mu)X_{N2} \tag{4.3}$$

$$-\frac{\partial H}{\partial A} = \dot{\lambda} - r\lambda \Rightarrow (B_Z + \lambda)R_A - \lambda = r\lambda - \dot{\lambda} \tag{4.4}$$

$$-\frac{\partial H}{\partial S} = \dot{\mu} - r\mu \Rightarrow (B_Z + \lambda - \mu)X_S = r\mu - \dot{\mu} \tag{4.5}$$

$$\lim_{T \to \infty} e^{-rT}\lambda(T)A(T) = 0.$$

$$\lim_{T \to \infty} e^{-rT}\mu(T)A(T) = 0.$$

We multiply (4.3) by N_1 ($= N - N_2$) to obtain the fourth row–column pair in Table 4.6. We multiply (4.4) by A to obtain the fifth row–column pair in Table 4.6. And we multiply (4.5) by S to obtain the third row–column pair in Table 4.6.

The households column reduces to

$$(X + R)B_Z + \lambda\dot{A} + \mu\dot{S}$$

an NNP concept for this partial economy. This is the linearized current-value Hamiltonian. The corresponding NNI concept (the households row) includes labor value, at the prevailing wage, interest on capital values, $r\mu S$ and $r\lambda A$ (stationary equivalents) plus capital gains terms, $-\dot{\mu}S$ and $-\dot{\lambda}A$. Note that a unit of A has two concurrent values: B_Z value in use for a period and λ, value

Table 4.6   National accounting matrix (recycling durable extracted material)

Expenditures ↓ Receipts →	Extraction	Recycling	S-stock	Labor	A-stock	Households
Extraction						XB_Z
Recycling						RB_Z
S-stock	SX_SB_Z					$SX_S(\lambda - \mu)$
Labor	$N_2X_{N_2}B_Z$	$N_1R_{N_1}B_Z$				$N_1R_{N_1}\lambda + N_2X_{N_2}(\lambda - \mu)$
A-stock		AR_AB_Z				$\lambda AR_A - \lambda A$
Households			$S\mu(r - \dot\mu/\mu)$	$(B_Z + \lambda - \mu)X_{N_2}N$	$A\lambda(r - \dot\lambda/\lambda)$	

in recycling. Thus $(B_Z + \lambda)R_A - \lambda$ is price minus marginal cost in recycling and $(B_Z + \lambda)X_S - \mu X_S$ is price minus marginal cost in extraction. The so-called r% rule for extraction assumes the complicated form

$$\frac{(B_Z + \lambda - \mu)X_S + \dot{\mu}}{\mu} = r.$$

The pace of extraction is dependent on the costs of recycling. At each date labor is allocated between extraction and recycling so as to equalize the wage in the two sectors. $\mu - \lambda$ is net 'depletion' value on the stock, $S(t)$.

4.13   DURABLE GOODS EXTRACTION AND RECYCLING IN GENERAL EQUILIBRIUM

A general equilibrium version of the above model has stock A of durable capital an input into the production of $Q(= F(K, A, N - N_1 - N_2))$ with

$$\dot{K} = F(K, A, N - N_1 - N_2) - C \tag{4.6}$$

where K is machine capital and C is aggregate consumption. Then

$$\dot{A} = R(A, N_1) - A + X(S, N_2), \tag{4.7}$$

as above, and

$$\dot{S} = -X(S, N_2) \tag{4.8}$$

where $X(\cdot)$ is currently extracted durable material. We assume that $F(\cdot)$, $R(\cdot)$ and $X(\cdot)$ exhibit constant returns to scale.

   The market acts to maximize

$$\int_0^\infty U(C)e^{-\rho t}dt$$

subject to (4.6), (4.7), (4.8) and

$$K(0) = K_0$$

$$A(0) = A_0$$

$$S(0) = S_0.$$

The current-value Hamiltonian is

$$H = U(C) + \lambda[F(K, A, N - N_1 - N_2) - C] + \mu[R(A, N_1) - A$$

$$+ X(S, N_2)] - \gamma X(S, N_2).$$

The necessary conditions are

$$\frac{\partial H}{\partial C} = 0 \Rightarrow U_C = \lambda$$

$$\frac{\partial H}{\partial N_1} = 0 \Rightarrow -\lambda F_Z + \mu R_{N_1} = 0 \qquad (4.9)$$

$$\frac{\partial H}{\partial N_2} = 0 \Rightarrow -\lambda F_Z + \mu X_{N_2} - \gamma X_{N_2} = 0 \qquad (4.10)$$

$$\text{for } Z \equiv N - N_1 - N_2,$$

$$-\frac{\partial H}{\partial K} = \dot{\lambda} - \rho\lambda \Rightarrow -\lambda F_K = \dot{\lambda} - \rho\lambda$$

$$\text{or } r_t = F_K \text{ for } r_t \equiv \rho - \frac{\dot{\lambda}}{\lambda} \qquad (4.11)$$

$$-\frac{\partial H}{\partial A} = \dot{\mu} - \rho\mu \Rightarrow -\lambda F_A - \mu(R_A - 1) = \dot{\mu} - \rho\mu$$

$$\text{or } \frac{\mu}{\lambda} r_t^A = \frac{\mu}{\lambda} - (R_A - 1) + F_A \text{ for } r_t^A \equiv \rho - \frac{\dot{\mu}}{\mu} \qquad (4.12)$$

$$-\frac{\partial H}{\partial S} = \dot{\gamma} - \rho\gamma \Rightarrow -\mu X_S + \gamma X_S = \dot{\gamma} - \rho\gamma$$

$$\text{or } \frac{\gamma}{\lambda} r_t^S = \left(\frac{\mu - \gamma}{\lambda}\right) X_S \text{ for } r_t^S \equiv \rho - \frac{\dot{\gamma}}{\gamma} \qquad (4.13)$$

and transversality conditions: $\lambda(t)e^{-\rho t}K(t) = 0$ as $t \to \infty$, $\mu(t)e^{-\rho t}A(t) = 0$ as $t \to \infty$ and $\gamma(t)e^{-\rho t}S(t) = 0$ as $t \to \infty$.

Our national accounting matrix in Table 4.7 has the fourth row–column pair derived from (4.9) and (4.10). We multiply (4.9) by Z and proceed. Multiply (4.11) by K to get the second row–column pair and multiply (4.12) by A to get the third row–column pair and (4.13) by S to get the fifth row–column pair. The first row-column pair is based on constant returns to scale in $F(\cdot)$.

We rationalize the households column, invoking constant returns to scale in $R(\cdot)$ and $X(\cdot)$ to get

$$NNP(t) = C + \dot{K} + \frac{\mu}{\lambda}\dot{A} + \left(\frac{\mu - \gamma}{\lambda}\right)\dot{S},$$

the linearized, dollar-valued, current-value Hamiltonian. The net national income, the households row is

$$NNI(t) = Kr_t + \left(r_t + \frac{\dot{\lambda}}{\lambda} - \frac{\dot{\mu}}{\mu}\right)\frac{\mu}{\lambda}A + NF_z + \left(r_t + \frac{\dot{\lambda}}{\lambda} - \frac{\dot{\gamma}}{\gamma}\right)\frac{\gamma}{\lambda}S$$

$$= Kr_t + \frac{\mu}{\lambda}r_tA + d\left(\frac{\lambda}{\mu}\right)/dtA + NF_z + \frac{\gamma}{\lambda}r_tS + d\left(\frac{\lambda}{\gamma}\right)/dtS$$

where $d(\lambda/\mu)/dt$ and $d(\lambda/\gamma)/dt$ are capital goods price changes.

Somewhat novel here is that extractive material is intermediate. And 'depletion' value is the net figure, $(\gamma - \mu)$. With costless recycling ($R(\cdot) = A$), the model reduces to essentially the one in Levhari and Pindyck (1981).

4.14   EXPLORATION ACTIVITY

A valuation case that has provoked controversy is the accounting for discovery of new resource stock. Superficially, new stock $\dot{S}(t)$ would seem to be the opposite of stock depletion and hence would appear in the accounts as 'investment' rather than disinvestment (Hartwick, 1990). However, it makes sense to view new stock as being the product of purposeful and resource-using search. There is, of course, a large mineral exploration industry in the world. One would expect that the marginal cost of discovering another ton of deposits is approximately equal to the market value of another ton. Then D_t tons discovered at date t should show up in 'product' or investment as net of the discovery cost (Hartwick, 1993). Pindyck (1978) presented a formal model of an extractive firm, jointly extracting from 'discovered' stock and exploring for new stock under deterministic assumptions. His tractable model serves well for the larger task of getting exploration and discovered stock into the national accounts. Discoverable stock remains the fundamental scarcity. Once a portion is discovered, it enters an inventory, $Z(t)$, from which current sales of oil, $R(t)$, are withdrawn. Thus

Table 4.7   National accounting matrix (durable goods extraction and recycling)

Expenditures ↓ Receipts →	Goods production	K-capital	A-capital	Labor	S-capital	Households
Goods production						$C + \dot{K}$
K-capital	KF_K					
A-capital	AF_A					$(R_A - 1)\mu A/\lambda$
Labor	ZF_Z					
S-capital						$(\mu - \gamma)X_S S/\lambda$
Households		$r_t K$	$r_t\mu A/\lambda + Ad\,(\lambda/\mu)\,/dt$	NF_Z	$r_t\gamma S/\lambda + Sd\,(\lambda/\gamma)\,/dt$	

$$\dot{Z}(t) = D(t) - R(t)$$

where $D(t)$ is current discoveries. Meanwhile $S(t)$ underground shrinks by current discoveries

$$\dot{S}(t) - D(t).$$

We assume that both discovery and 'extraction' from inventory require labor and stock and take place under constant returns to scale. That is

$$D(t) = g(N_2, S)$$

and

$$R(t) = f(N_1, Z).$$

Labor is available at exogenous wage rate w. (We could easily endogenize the wage by having total labor fixed in supply.) We can view our economy as a small, open exporter, comprising many competitive extractive and exploring firms, facing a market demand schedule, $p(R)$. Firms are motivated to build up their inventories because it is cheaper to extract (takes less labor per unit) from a larger inventory.[11] Wealth maximization is formalized in

$$\max_{(N_1 N_2)} \int_0^\infty \{B[f(N_1 Z)] - w(N_1 + N_2)\} e^{-rt} dt$$

subject to

$$\dot{Z}(t) = g(N_2 S) - f(N_1 Z)$$

$$\dot{S}(t) = -g(N_2 S)$$

$$Z(0) = Z_0 > 0.$$

$$\int_0^\infty g(N_2, S) dt \le S_0 > 0$$

where $B(R)$ is consumer surplus corresponding to demand schedule $p(R)$. The current-value Hamiltonian for this problem is

$$H = B[f(N_1, z)] - w(N_1 + N_2) + \mu(t)[g(N_2, S) - f(N_1, Z)] - \eta(t)g(N_2, S)$$

and the necessary conditions are

$$\frac{\partial H}{\partial N_1} = 0 \text{ or } (p - \mu)f_{N_1} = w$$

$$\frac{\partial H}{\partial N_2} = 0 \text{ or } (\mu - \eta)g_{N_2} = w$$

$$-\frac{\partial H}{\partial Z} = \dot{\mu} - r\mu \text{ or } (p - \mu)f_Z + \dot{\mu} = r\mu$$

$$-\frac{\partial H}{\partial S} = \dot{\eta} - r\eta \text{ or } (\mu - \eta)g_S + \dot{\eta} = r\eta$$

and $R(t)$ can be zero at terminal date T if physical exhaustion occurs, or $R(t)$ can be positive at the end of extraction if marginal profits turn negative. (See Levhari and Leviatan, 1997.)

The assumption of constant returns to scale implies $f(N_1, Z) = N_1 f_{N_1} + Z f_Z$ and $g(N_2, S) = N_2 g_{N_2} + S g_S$. Hence the straightforward nature of the first row and column, and also the fifth row and column, in Table 4.8.

The third row and column reflect the ZPIA condition

$$(p - \mu)f_Z Z + \dot{\mu}Z = r\mu Z$$

and the seventh row and column reflects the ZPIA condition

$$(\mu - \eta)g_S S + \dot{\eta}S = r\eta S.$$

The complication in the accounts involves the 'extraction' firms purchasing discovered stock from the 'exploring' firms. 'Extractive' firms pay μ dollars for each unit of stock purchased from 'exploring' firms. This interdependence connects the 'depreciation' of the inventory stock to the depreciation of the stock below ground. Since $\dot{A} = D - R$ and $\dot{S} = -D$, the households column (NNP) in Table 4.8 can be expressed as

$$pR + \frac{d(\mu Z)}{dt} + \frac{d(\eta S)}{dt},$$

the value of current sales from inventory plus two depreciation terms, one for the inventory stock, $Z(t)$, and one for the stock underground, $S(t)$.

The households row is net national income and comprises the value of labor currently used in production plus two stationary equivalents, $r\mu Z(t)$ and $r\eta S(t)$, corresponding to the interest representation of stock values $\mu Z(t)$ and $\eta S(t)$. $r\mu Z(t)$ and $r\eta S(t)$ are stationary equivalent representations of market values

Table 4.8 *National accounting matrix (exploration and extraction activity)*

Expenditures ↓ / Receipts →	From inventory	Labor inventory	Inventory stock	*	From underground	Labor Exploration	Underground stock	**	Households
From inventory									pR
Labor inventory	$(p-\mu)f_{N_1}N_1$								0
Inventory stock	$(p-\mu)f_Z Z$								$\mu\dot{Z}$
*	$\mu R - \mu D$								$\mu D - \mu R$
From underground	μD								0
Labor exploration					$(\mu-\eta)g_{N_2}N_2$				0
Underground stock					$(\mu-\eta)g_S S$				$\eta\dot{S}$
**					ηD				$-\eta D$
Households	0	wN_1	$r\mu Z$	0	0	wN_2	$r\eta S$	0	

Notes
* Accounts balance relation.
** Accounts balance relation.

114

$\mu Z(t)$ and $\eta S(t)$. If asset price changes were moved from NNP to NNI, then we would have in our revised NNI, $r\mu Z - \dot{\mu} Z$ for inventory stock and $r\eta S - \dot{\eta} S$ for the underground stock. This latter term equals zero under efficient extraction.

4.15 CONCLUDING REMARKS

We considered extraction of oil in a small, open economy and derived the market value of stock decline or economic depreciation of the stock. With this depreciation value in hand, we appealed to the condition of zero profits from current *production* to complete our national accounts. The stationary equivalent of the value of the remaining stock, underground, turned up in net national income. Hence the principle: when NNP is correct, net national income contains a term for the flow value of the stock remaining underground. We then considered a more general model, with oil price endogenous, and arrived at our second principle: capital gains on the current stock must enter economic depreciation (and hence NNP) in order for net national income to be correct. These two principles constitute the capital-theoretic foundation of green national accounting. They can be interpreted as the outcome of the two equilibrium or market conditions: zero profits for producers of current 'product' and zero profits for arbitrageurs (dealers) in capital goods. These latter agents seek profits by buying and selling capital goods 'across' different dates.

We observed our two principles 'at work' in a variety of models in the remaining sections of the chapter. Of interest were the two stocks to keep track of when resources are durable, the stock above ground and the one below ground. Two depreciation terms appear in NNP. And when stock must be discovered at a cost, there are also two stocks to keep track of, the stock underground awaiting 'discovery' and the inventory of discovered stock from which current sales are drawn.

APPENDIX 4A1: ECONOMIC DEPRECIATION AND TAXING THE EXTRACTIVE FIRM

Samuelson (1964) invariance involves showing that a firm's action under Samuelson taxation and under no taxation is the same. The solution is invariant to the level of taxation τ. We shall use subscript τ for a variable under taxation and subscript $n\tau$ for a variable under no taxation.

No Taxation

The firm maximizes

$$\int_0^T \{pq(t) - C[q(t)]\}e^{-rt}dt$$

subject to

$$\dot{S}(t) = -q(t)$$

$$\int_0^T q(t)dt = S_0.$$

We assume $C(0) = 0$ and $C'(q)$ and $C''(q)$ are positive for q positive.

The solution satisfies boundary conditions, including $q(T) = 0$ and Euler equation (r% rule)

$$\frac{d\{p - C'[q(t)]\}}{dt} = \{p - C'[q(t)]\}r.$$

Taxation

Samuelson taxation allows deductible $D(t)$ from current profit before tax and 'interest payment deductibility' implying effective discount rate, $(1 - \tau)r$, for the firm. Net profit at each date is $pq(t) - C[q(t)] - \tau\{pq(t) - C[q(t)] - D(t)\}$ equal to $(1 - \tau)\{pq(t) - C[q(t)]\} + \tau D(t)$. To establish invariance, one must choose $D(t)$ correctly. We observe that $D(t) = V'[S(t)]_{n\tau}q(t)$ does the trick. This $D(t)$ is an expression for true economic depreciation, under no taxation. $V'[S(t)]_{n\tau}$ acts as a price and cannot be manipulated by the firm because it depends on the state vector $S(t)$. $V[S(t)]$ is the value of the firm under no taxation.

The firm maximizes, under Samuelson taxation,

$$\int_0^T [(1 - \tau)\{pq(t) - C[q(t)]\} + \tau V'[S(t)]_{n\tau}q(t)]e^{-(1 - \tau)rt}dt$$

subject to

$$\dot{S}(t) = -q(t)$$

$$S_0 = \int_0^T q(t)dt.$$

The current-value Hamiltonian is

$$H(t) = (1 - \tau)\{pq(t) - C[q(t)]\} + \tau V'[S(t)]_{n\tau}q(t) - \psi q(t).$$

Key necessary conditions are

$$(1 - \tau)[p - C'(q)] + \tau V'[S(t)]_{n\tau} = \psi(t)$$

$$\Rightarrow \dot{\psi}(t) = (1 - \tau)\frac{d[p - C'(q)]}{dt} + \tau V''(S)_{n\tau}\dot{S}(t)$$

and

$$\tau V''[S(t)]_{n\tau}q(t) = \dot{\psi}(t) - (1 - \tau)r\psi(t)$$

which, when combined, yield

$$\frac{d[p - C'(q)]}{dt} = r\psi(t).$$

We know $V'[S(t)]_{n\tau} = [p - C'(q)]_{n\tau}$. If $V'[S(t)]_{n\tau} = [p - C'(q)]_\tau$, we would have

$$\frac{d[p - C'(q)]_\tau}{dt} = r[p - C'(q)]_\tau,$$

that is, we would have the same Euler equation for each problem.

We now establish that $V(S)_\tau$, equal to $V(S)_{n\tau}$, solves the firm's problem under taxation. That is, $V(S)_\tau$, equal to $V(S)_{n\tau}$, solves the dynamic programming relation

$$(1 - \tau)rV(S)_\tau = \max_q \{(1 - \tau)[pq - C(q)] + \tau V'(S)_{n\tau}q - V'(S)_\tau q\}.$$

This reduces to

$$rV(S)_\tau = \max_q [pq - C(q) - V'(S)_\tau q]$$

which is the same problem as that for the firm with no taxation. Hence the [$q(t)$] paths which solve the firm's problem under no taxation and under Samuelson taxation, with $D(t) = V'(S)_{n\tau}q(t)$, are the same. The (a) value of the firm and (b) the action of the firm are invariant to tax rate τ, including τ set at zero.

APPENDIX 4A2:   INVENTORY DRAW-DOWN AS STOCK DEPLETION

A Formulation Under Certainty

Our firm's objective is the maximization of discounted profits to infinity. Its decision problem decomposes into (a) the choice of S, the stock-up level and (b) the speed of draw-down of S. We shall deal with the second problem first. There is an exogenous output price p and cost of selling from inventory, $C(q)$, independent of time. $C(0) = 0$ and $C(\cdot)$ is convex in q, the amount currently removed from inventory.[12] We assume that marginal cost is increasing in q. At each date t, $q(t)$ is removed from inventory and current profit is

$$\pi(t) = pq - C(q).$$

There are no costs of storage. Given S_0 the firm selects paths $[q(t)]$ and $[S(t)]$ to maximize

$$\Pi = \int_0^T [pq - C(q)]\ \exp(-rt)dt$$

where

$$dS/dt = -q(t),$$

and r is the discount (interest) rate. The solution to this problem is in part characterized by the Euler equation

$$d(p - C_q)/dt = (p - C_q)r$$

and the optimal end-point condition[13]

$$q(T)\{d[pq(T)] - C[q(T)]/dq(T)\} = pq(T) - C[q(T)].$$

There is the boundary condition, $\int_0^T q(t)dt = S_0$. Current rate, $p - C_q[q(t)]$, is just discounted terminal rent, $p - C_q[q(T)]$, and difficulties are avoided when $C_q(0)$ is assumed to be zero.[14] The essential output of our analysis above is that initial rent, $p - C_q[q(0)]$, is a single-valued function of stock, S_0, and this initial rent is declining in the value of S_0. Also the interval of inventory draw-down, T, is a single-valued function of S_0, and is increasing in S_0.

The second part of our certainty formulation of the problem involves the choice of stock-up level S_0 given the possibility of producing new 'inventory'. The simplest approach here, given our assumption of increasing returns to scale in production, is to treat stock S as producible with cost function

$$A + BS$$

where A and B are positive.[15] One then obtains the simple decision rule: stock up when current inventory, $S(t)$, 'hits' zero and choose the new inventory level such that the marginal value of a unit of stock equals the marginal cost, B. That is

$$p - C_q[q(0)] = B.$$

This is an instance of value-matching at a regime-switch.[16] Recall that $p - Cq[q(0)]$ is a decreasing function of the chosen stock, S_0. Given S_0, one has to have profits for the firm positive or else there will be no production and selling. Thus set-up cost A cannot be too large. Set-up cost, A, cannot be zero or else production will not be 'bunched' at distinct dates. All so-called Hotelling rents associated with stock S_0 are 'dissipated' in the cost BS_0 of producing the stock. There remains positive discounted producer surplus as net profit and this must exceed cost A for the firm to remain active.

Demand (Price) Uncertain

A simple approach to the case of uncertain demand is to make output price random as in a Wiener (stochastic) process. The price process is then

$$pd = \sigma dz$$

where σ^2 is the variance of a standard Wiener process and dz is the increment of the Wiener process z. There is no trend or drift in the price process.[17] Hence the best estimate of the price an instant later is the current value of price. The firm's objective function is expected discounted profit to infinity. The stationarity of the price process allows us to treat the producer's problem as a variant of the one solved above under certainty. Consider problem (b) above (inventory draw-down) first when price p is now Wiener-stochastic. The endowment of stock is given. The seller optimizes current sales from inventory under the assumption that current price will persist. This is an optimization problem under certainty. We solved such a problem above. Current output sold from inventory will be the result of the seller's calculation of drawing down the current stock $S(t)$ to exhaustion in the profit-maximizing fashion; the seller assumes that the current price will be the observed price to the end of the drawing down of the current stock. Given a new price an instant later, there will be a new optimal $q(t)$ to be drawn from inventory. A new draw-down program is solved for at each date and the program will change with each change in price $p(t)$. The path of $q(t)s$ will be stochastic, a function of current price and inventory size. When the stock in inventory is exhausted, the problem of optimal selling, given S_0, is complete.[18] We turn now to the question of the selection of stock level S_0, for the case of 'inventory' producible.

Our cost function is $A + BS$, the same as for the case with certainty. However, the marginal profit from having an additional unit of S, namely $p(t) - Cq[q(t)]$, is a function of the currently realized price. At exhaustion of the current inventory, there will be a particular realized price $p(t)$ which determines the current value of a marginal unit of new inventory, namely $p(t) - Cq[q(t;S_0)]$, where $q(t;S_0)$ is the optimal value of selling from a new inventory size S_0. The determination of the optimal stock-up level, S_0, at a particular date of exhaustion of current stock follows then from the value-matching condition

$$p(t) - C_q[q(t; S_0)] = B.$$

Value-matching is the condition that, at the transition from low stock (zero) to high stock, marginal cost B equals the marginal 'benefit' (marginal profit), $p(t) - Cq[q(0)]$. This is just a statement of the requirement that intertemporal profit across the date of stock-out to stock-up must be zero. Note that the level of the particular stock-up value S_0 depends on the realized level of price, $p(t)$, at the date of stock-out. In contrast with the familiar result in (S,s) theory, here we have an essentially autonomous problem and *there is no autonomous target level for stock-up*. Each stock-up level in our model will be a function of the current price realized at the date of exhaustion of the current inventory. This completes our statement of the problem of inventory production and draw-down for the case of output price stochasticity.

A number of difficulties remain. At some dates of stock-up, discounted profit may be negative because the fixed costs of inventory production cannot be covered, given current low output prices. The simplest approach here is to assume that capital is not firm-specific and can be returned at zero cost to the owners. The firm then disappears and can be reborn if profitability turns positive. If capital is firm-specific, one needs a model of shut-down which incorporates carrying costs in the short run and capital write-down and sell-off in the long run. (See, for example, Dixit, 1989 for the introduction to a theory of start-up and shut-down for a firm facing fixed costs of closing down and of reopening and a random output price.)[19] Our set-up costs of inventory or output production, namely A, could be viewed as the firm taking on a debt of *A* at each stock-up. In this interpretation, current profit of the firm could turn negative at low positive prices for output. Once this has occurred, the firm is forced to decide whether to shut down or keep producing in the hope that product price will move up soon. There is no positive trend or mean reversion in our price process, so it seems reasonable for the firm to liquidate when current profit turns negative. There are no grounds for a belief that current bad times are temporary. Profit will turn negative in our model before prices turn negative. Our price process admits negative price realizations. These negative realizations seem absurd from the perspective of an economics scenario, but really do not figure in our analysis. We could replace *ex post* each negative realization with a price of zero and nothing in our analysis would change.

NOTES

1. We take up date-varying interest rates below.
2. T^* needs to be differentiated with respect to t but the 'effect' washes out (equals zero) by the envelope theorem.
3. In Appendix 4A1 we report on the use of economic depreciation in taxation design, following Samuelson (1964).
4. The term 'stationary equivalent' is due to Weitzman (1970, 1976).
5. For the model with *K*-capital in Chapter 1, the price of a unit of investment goods is set to be the same as the price of a unit of consumption goods. Since the price of consumption goods is unity at all times, the price of investment goods gets locked in at unity. In our oil production model, output price is fixed and *net price* rises at the rate of interest. This keeps the present value of net price constant and we observe no set price changes in economic depreciation. In the model with oil below (see Table 4.2), oil price is endogenous and oil price changes *do* appear in the term for economic depreciation.
6. See Aronsson et al. (1997, Proposition 4.1) for a different approach.
7. With many capital goods, $V(t)$ measures 'net savings' (Dixit et al., 1980, Hartwick and Long, 1999). Aronsson et al. (1997, pp. 105–8) present a good exposition of 'net savings'. They use the term 'net investments'.
8. This model was the focus of attention in Dasgupta and Heal (1974) and has recently been re-analyzed by Pezzey and Withagen (1998).
9. This is the constant consumption property of the Solow model.
10. We could endow our economy with a fixed amount of labor and endogenize the wage rate but we will make matters slightly simpler by taking the wage as a parameter and assuming inflow and outflow of labor.
11. The drawing down of a given inventory is the same as the problem of depleting a known stock. We report on this in Appendix 4.A2 in more detail. Inventory accumulation is usually made in anticipation of uncertain future demand.
12. There are no direct costs, as in warehousing, associated with inventory holding in our model. Our costs of selling from inventory could include warehousing but one thinks here primarily of the management costs of operating the inventory. With stockpiles, there are costs of building up the stocks and then of disassembling them at selling time. The other cost of inventory holding in our model is the interest cost incurred by producing in advance of selling.
13. See for example Gelfand and Fomin (1963, p. 60).
14. If average selling costs were U-shaped then there would be some scale economies in selling and stock-out would occur with a strictly positive quantity. The scale economies associated with the U-shaped cost schedule raise problems with decentralizing the first-best solution.

See Eswaran et al. (1983). Our depletion problem was set out and solved with examples by L.C. Gray (1914).

15. See Dixit (1991) for a recent statement of the (S, s) approach to inventory management. He emphasizes the declining average costs in the process of producing new inventory. Bartmann and Beckmann (1992) provide more details on the (S, s) model and other classic models of inventory management, largely in the operations research tradition. There is considerable recent work on incorporating the (S, s) model into an economy-wide framework (for example, Cabellero and Engel, 1991). Aggregation issues are central to making use of the (S, s) model in macroeconomics. Note that we treat all production occurring in the form of periodic stocking-up. Stocking up is not peripheral to 'regular' production.

16. *Smooth-pasting* and *value-matching* are conditions which characterize a regime-switch or transition (boundary-hitting) along an optimal program. (See, for example, Dixit, 1989 or Dixit and Pindyck, 1994.) These optimality conditions characterize the zero profit arbitrage condition over the transition date.

17. Predictable upward trend in prices would create an option demand for inventory holding. That is, hold some stock back so that relatively large sales can be made when prices are relatively high. The same idea holds with mean reversion in prices. When prices are low, sales from inventory should be curtailed so that stock will be available when prices are relatively high.

18. This problem of the drawing down of a given stock under the assumption of a Wiener stochastic output price was analyzed first by Pindyck (1981). He side-stepped the problem of dealing with realizations of negative prices by (a) introducing a positive trend in output price and (b) by making price a geometric Wiener process.

19. The pioneering paper in this area is Brennan and Schwartz (1985) which in fact dealt with opening and closing a mine in response to random output price changes. Exhaustibility was not incorporated into their analysis.

REFERENCES

Aronsson, T., P.-O. Johansson and K.-G. Löfgren (1997), *Welfare Measurement, Sustainability and Green National Accounting*, Cheltenham: Edward Elgar.

Asheim, G.B. (1994), 'Net national product as an indicator of sustainability', *Scandinavian Journal of Economics*, **96** (2), 257–65.

Bartmann, Dieter and Martin J. Beckmann (1992), *Inventory Control: Models and Methods*, Berlin/Heidelberg: Springer–Verlag.

Brennan, M. and E. Schwartz (1985), 'Evaluating natural resource investments', *Journal of Business*, **58** (2), April, 135–57.

Caballero, R.J. and E.M.R.A. Engel (1991), 'Dynamic (S,s) Economies', *Econometrica*, **59** (6), November, 1659–86.

Dasgupta, P. and G.M. Heal (1974), 'The optimal depletion of exhaustible resources', *Review of Economic Studies*, Symposium, 3–28.

Dixit, A.K. (1989), 'Entry and exit decisions under uncertainty', *Journal of Political Economy*, **93** (3), June, 620–38.

Dixit, A.K. (1991), 'A simplified treatment of the theory of optimal regulation of Brownian motion', *Journal of Economic Dynamics and Control*, **15** (4), October, 657–73.

Dixit, A.K. and Robert S. Pindyck (1994), *Investment under Uncertainty*, Princeton, NJ: Princeton University Press.

Dixit, A., P. Hammond and M. Hoel (1980), 'On Hartwick's Rule for regular maximin paths of capital accumulation and resource depletion', *Review of Economic Studies*, **47**, 551–6.

Eswaran, M., T.R. Lewis and T. Heaps (1983), 'On the nonexistence of market equilibrium in exhaustible resource markets with decreasing costs', *Journal of Political Economy*, **91** (1), February, 154–67.

Fisher, Irving (1906), *The Nature of Capital and Income*, New York: Macmillan.

Gelfand, I.M. and S.V. Fomin (1963), *Calculus of Variations*, Englewood Cliffs, NJ: Prentice-Hall.

Gray, L.C. (1914), 'Rent under the assumption of exhaustibility', *Quarterly Journal of Economics*, **28**, May, 466–89.

Hartwick, J.M. (1977), 'Intergenerational equity and the investing of rents from exhaustible resources', *American Economic Review*, **66**, 972–4.

Hartwick, J. (1990), 'Natural resources, national accounting, and economic depreciation', *Journal of Public Economics*, **43**, 291–304.

Hartwick, J.M. (1993), 'Notes on economic depreciation of natural resource stocks and national accounting', in A. Franz and C. Stahmer (eds), *Approaches to Environmental Accounting*, New York: Springer-Verlag, 167–98.

Hartwick, J.M. and N.V. Long (1999), 'Constant consumption and the economic depreciation of natural capital: the non-autonomous case', *International Economic Review*, **40** (1), February, 53–62.

Hicks, John R. (1939), *Value and Capital*, Oxford: Clarendon Press.

Levhari, D. and D. Leviatan (1977), 'Notes on Hotelling's economics of exhaustible resources', *Canadian Journal of Economics*, **X** (2), May, 177–92.

Levhari, David and R.S. Pindyck (1981), 'The pricing of durable exhaustible resources', *Quarterly Journal of Economics*, **96** (3), August, 365–77.

Lozada, G. (1997), 'The micro foundation of sustainability', typescript.

Pezzey, J. and C. Withagen (1998), 'The rise, fall and sustainability of capital-resource economies', *Scandinavian Journal of Economics*, **100** (2), 513–27.

Pindyck, R. (1978), 'The optimal exploration and production of nonrenewable resources', *Journal of Political Economy*, **86** (5), October, 841–61.

Pindyck, Robert S. (1981), 'The optimal production of an exhaustible resource when price is exogenous and stochastic', *Scandinavian Journal of Economics*, **83** (2), 277–88.

Samuelson, P.A. (1937), 'Some aspects of the pure theory of capital', *Quarterly Journal of Economics*, May, 469–96.

Samuelson, P.A. (1964), 'Tax deductibility of economic depreciation to insure invariant valuations', *Journal of Political Economy*, **72**, 604–6.

Solow, R.M. (1974), 'Intergenerational equity and exhaustible resources', *Review of Economic Studies*, Symposium, 29–45.

Vincent, J., T. Panayotou and J. Hartwick (1997), 'Resource depletion and sustainability in small open economies', *Journal of Environmental Economics and Management*, **33**, 274–86.

Weitzman, M.L. (1907), 'Aggregation and disaggregation in the pure theory of capital and growth: a new parable', Yale University, Cowles Foundation Discussion Paper No. 292, April.

Weitzman, M.L. (1976), 'On the welfare significance of national product in a dynamic economy', *Quarterly Journal of Economics*, **90**, 156–62.

Weitzman, M.L. (1999), 'The linearized Hamiltonian as comprehensive NDP', *Environment and Development Economics*, (forthcoming).

5. Renewable resources

5.1 INTRODUCTION

A clear analysis of sustainable timber harvesting in 1849 by Faustmann is one reasonable point of departure in the history of modern capital theory. Faustmann understood that discounted future returns constituted capital value and he used this large insight to arrive at a present value maximizing harvest-plant strategy. We take up this analysis first and move on to consider various abstract economies in which harvesting from a naturally growing (renewing) stock plays a central role. In a steady state, nature replenishes the exact harvest drawn from the stock. It is quite standard to treat renewable natural resources as the central case, with non-renewable resources taken up as a sub-case. This approach is easily defended but one can also make a case for treating renewable and non-renewable cases separately. The analysis of renewable resources can often be done near a steady state. But inferences about the economy in a steady state are clearly very special. With non-renewable resources, there is no steady state and one cannot fall back on simple special cases. Of interest is that economic depreciation for the case of renewable resources is not easy to interpret, though the special case with non-renewable resources is quite straightforward.

Effluent dispersal is a service provided by environmental capital, objects such as airsheds and watersheds. Thus environmental capital can be viewed as a renewable resource, one that can be degraded by excess 'harvesting' of services. We take up environmental capital and observe the central role of Pigouvian pollution charges. And lastly, we take up deforestation, essentially a land use change problem. Here the revaluation of land as its changing use is a central topic.

5.2 PERIODIC TREE HARVESTING

A widely observed growth pattern has very young organisms growing slowly at first, exhibiting a rapid growth phase next, and then displaying a slow growth phase before expiration. Some actual shrinkage of the organism can occur in old age. The S-shaped path (slow–rapid–slow growth) has large effects on capital management. First, the manager is induced to lag, in an optimizing fashion, the delay between planting and harvesting. This was the focus of the brilliant analysis of Faustmann (1849), a forestry engineer. The S-shaped growth pattern introduces a non-concavity in the optimal management problem, a non-concavity which asks the maximizer to introduce an optimal lag into the planning problem. Second, once one has a framework with an optimal lag, one is confronted with the question of the stability of lag length, at the optimum. It turns out that typical S-shaped growth patterns can easily have unstable optimal lag lengths so that regular cycles can be optimal as well as irregular (non-repeating) cycles (chaotic dynamics). Faustmann (1849) was unaware of this instability but Robert May (1976) drew researchers' attention to it. In summary, S-shaped growth requires us to redo our analysis of circulating capital in order to incorporate an optimal lag between planting and harvesting. We illustrate this first in a variant of Faustmann's model and then we move to a complete, optimal saving framework.

We have an area of land L to plant with tree seeds, K_t, at dollar cost $C(K_t, L)$. At date τ in the future, we shall harvest the grown trees with a net profit $(p - c)g(K_t; \tau - t)$. $g(K_t; \tau - t)$ is the standing timber to harvest after the interval $\tau - t$ has elapsed. $(p - c)$ is unit revenue net of harvest cost, c. The S-shaped growth function can be parameterized as a simple quadratic:

$$\dot{K}(t) = aK(t) - bK(t)^2.$$

We can think of K_t growing, via this function, for interval $\tau - t$ to emerge as $g(K_t; \tau - t)$. Faustmann's problem was to maximize

$$V = e^{-r\tau_1}(p - c)g(K_0, \tau_1 - 0) - C(K_0, L)$$

$$+ e^{-r\tau_2}(p - c)g(K_1, \tau_2 - \tau_1) - e^{-r\tau_1} C(K_1, L)$$

$$+ e^{-r\tau_3}(p - c)g(K_2, \tau_3 - \tau_2) - e^{-r\tau_2} C(K_2, L)$$

by choice of $K_0, K_1, K_2, ...$, and intervals $\tau_1 - 0, \tau_2 - \tau_1, \tau_3 - \tau_2, ...$ Our growth function constrains the optimal solution to one with $\tau_{t+1} - \tau_t$ not increasing, in the limit. And the essentialness of positive K at the beginning of each cycle implies that an infinitesimal rotation interval is not an optimal solution. In fact, the optimal solution will have $\tau_{t+1} - \tau_t$ positive and constant. This means that the search for an optimal solution can be reduced to finding a K and interval T maximizing V in

$$V = e^{-rT}(p - c)g(K, T) - C(K, L) + e^{-rT}V$$

by choice of T and K. The necessary condition for K is

$$e^{-rT}(p-c)\frac{\partial g(K, T)}{\partial K} = \frac{\partial C(K, L)}{\partial K},$$

and for the rotation interval T:

$$\frac{\partial g(K, T)}{\partial T} - rg(K, T) = \frac{rV^*}{(p-c)}$$

where V^* can be viewed as the market value of the land being used for tree farming. An interpretation of this condition is that the optimal T is a date such that marginal delay yields a large harvest, worth $(p-c)\partial g/\partial T$, but at 'delay cost'

$$rV^* + rg(K, T)/(p-c).$$

The tree harvesting or optimal rotation problem is rather specialized because the harvest arrives at particular dates rather than in a flow, per unit time. We turn now to situations in which the harvest can be treated as a flow as in, for example, fishing or even selective timber harvesting over a large area.

5.3 HARVESTING TIMBER FOR FUEL

Renewable resources have some biological renewal each period so that stock change is $\dot{S} = \theta(S) - R$ where R is harvest and $\theta(S)$ is some renewal given by nature. With non-renewable resources we had $\dot{S} = -R$ or 'harvesting' simply depleted the stock. This suggests that non-renewable resources should operate as a special case of the functioning of renewable resources, and this is correct. We should then look for our earlier results in Chapter 4 in the analysis of these renewable resource models in this chapter. We proceed then to take up two of our early models from Chapter 4 with $\dot{S} = -R$ replaced by $\dot{S} = \theta(S) - R$ and $R = f(N_1, S)$. That is, harvesting requires labor and stock. We assume that production function $f(\cdot)$ exhibits constant returns to scale and $f(\cdot)$ is increasing in labor, N_1 and in stock size, S. A larger stock means a given harvest requires less labor or effort. Renewal or natural growth, represented by the current net increment function $\theta(S)$, introduces a residual income flow $\theta(S) - S\theta_S$ in national income, 'caused by' the concavity of $\theta(S)$. The natural growth in the stock, from zero, is S-shaped, non-linear, and this makes the natural increment concave. Hence $\theta(S) - S\psi_S$ is positive and ends up as income, like producer surplus, in national income. Let us turn to detail.

We then have harvest, say as fuel, combine with labor to produce final consumption, C in

$$C = F(R, N - N_1)$$

where N is total labor in the economy. Planning or competition maximizes

$$\int_0^\infty U[C(t)]e^{-\rho t}dt$$

subject to

$$\dot{S} = \theta(S) - f(N_1, S) \text{ and } S(0) = S_0.$$

The current-value Hamiltonian for this problem is

$$H = U\{F[f(N_1, S), N - N_1]\} + \mu(t)[\theta(S) - f(N_1, S)].$$

The necessary conditions are

$$\frac{\partial H}{\partial N_1} = 0 \text{ or } F_R f_{N_1} - F_Z - \mu f_{N_1}/U_C = 0$$

where $Z = N - N_1$, and

$$-\frac{\partial H}{\partial S} = \dot{\mu} - \mu \text{ or } F_R f_S + \mu\theta S/U_C - \mu f_S/U_C + (\dot{\mu} - \rho\mu)U_C = 0,$$

and

$$\lim_{t\to\infty} \mu(t)S(t)e^{-\rho t} = 0.$$

If we multiply the first condition by Z, we get

$$ZF_Z + \left(F_R - \frac{\mu}{U_C}\right)N_1 f_{N_1} = \left(FR - \frac{\mu}{U_C}\right)Nf_{N_1}$$

and the second by S, we get

$$Sf_S\left(F_R - \frac{\mu}{U_C}\right) + \frac{\mu S\theta_S}{U_C} = \frac{Sr_t^S \mu}{U_C}.$$

These two equations form the second and third row–column pairs in Table 5.1, our national accounting matrix. The households column (prospective NNP) needs cleaning up or the collecting of terms. Harvest is an intermediate good in this economy. Recall that $f(\cdot) = N_1 f_{N_1} + S f_S = R$. Hence the households column becomes

$$C + \theta(S)\frac{\mu}{U_C} - f(\cdot)\frac{\mu}{U_C} + [S\theta_S - \theta(S)]\frac{\mu}{U_C} = C + \frac{\dot{S}\mu}{U_C} + [S\theta_S - \theta(S)]\frac{\mu}{U_C}.$$

The first two terms are the dollar-valued, linearized current-value Hamiltonian, a good version of NNP. The last term, with a sign change, is a residual income category, analogous to producer surplus, emerging because $\theta(S)$ is not linear in S. This term resides most naturally in national income and when moved, we have NNI as

$$\left(F_R - \frac{\mu}{U_C}\right)Nf_{N_1} + \frac{\mu S r_t^S}{U_C} + [\theta(S) - S\theta_S]\frac{\mu}{U_C}.$$

Each term here is novel. The labor endowment is being valued, not at the market dollar wage f_{N_1} in harvesting, but at a 'total' value which reflects the fact that labor in harvesting actually depletes the natural stock, $S(t)$. The second entry is unusual because the stock $S(t)$ is valued at its own rate of interest r_t^S not a market rate on produced capital goods. And the last term is the residual income, emerging because of 'non-constant returns to scale' in stock growth.

Observe that if harvesting activity were 'non-linear' as with, say, $f(N_1, S)$ becoming, say, $f(N_1)$, concave in labor, N_1, then a new residual surplus term would emerge in national income, a term analogous to $\theta(S) - S\theta_S$ discussed above. Such a term is in Table 5.5 below. A concave clearing function yields the surplus. In general, non-linearities of these sorts result in residual surpluses as incomes in NNI. Although we are familiar with such residuals for the case of 'production' taking place with non-constant returns to scale, such residual incomes emerge quite generally when other functions in the economy exhibit 'non-constant returns to scale'.

5.4   HARVESTING ECONOMY WITH *K*-CAPITAL

We observe a new phenomenon with renewable resources, one associated with the concavity of the net increment in the stock from natural growth, with respect to current stock size. This net increment function (births over deaths of standard-sized units such as fish or trees) is typically expressed as $\theta(S)$

Table 5.1 National accounting matrix (harvesting timber for fuel)

Expenditures ↓ Receipts →	'Goods' production	Labor	S-capital	Households
'Goods' production				C
Labor	ZF_Z			$(F_R - \mu/U_C)\, N_1 f_{N_1}$
S-capital	RF_R			$(F_R - \mu/U_C)\, Sf_S + \mu S\theta s/U_C - RF_R$
Households		$(F_R - \mu/U_C)\, Nf_{N_1}$	$\mu r^s S/U_C$	

with $\theta(S) - S\theta_S > 0$. This difference shows up as a residual income in the national accounts in a way similar to residual income appearing when returns to scale in production are not constant.

Production of goods has an input of harvest $f(N_1, S)$ from the stock S. We have then

$$\dot{K} = F[K, f(N_1, S), N - N_1] - C \tag{5.1}$$

as 'goods' production. $F(\cdot)$, under constant returns to scale yields investment goods k and consumption goods, C. Inputs are the services of stock K, harvest from stock S, $f(N_1, S)$, and labor services $N - N_1$ where N is the fixed endowment of labor in the economy and N_1 is taken up in harvesting activity. The natural stock S responds to harvesting in

$$\dot{S} = \theta(S) - f(N_1, S) \tag{5.2}$$

where $f(\cdot)$ exhibits constant returns to scale and $\theta(S)$, the natural increment, is inverted U-shaped with $\theta(0) = 0$.

Competition or planning acts to maximize

$$\int_0^\infty U[C(t)]e^{-\rho t}dt$$

subject to (5.1), (5.2), and $K(0) = K_0$ and $S(0) = S_0$. ρ is the constant social rate of discount. The current-value Hamiltonian is

$$H = U(C) + \lambda(t)\{F[K, f(N_1, S), N - N_1] - C\} + \mu(t)\{[S(t)] - f[N_1(t), S(t)]\}$$

where $\lambda(t)$ and $\mu(t)$ are util-valued shadow prices (co-state variables on K and S, respectively). The necessary conditions are

$$\frac{\partial H}{\partial C} = 0 \text{ or } U_C = \lambda$$

$$\frac{\partial H}{\partial N_1} = 0 \text{ or } (\lambda F_R - \mu)f_{N_1} = \lambda F_Z \tag{5.3}$$

where $Z = N - N_1$ and $R = f(N_1, S)$

$$-\frac{\partial H}{\partial K} = \dot{\lambda} - \rho\lambda \text{ or } \rho - \frac{\dot{\lambda}}{\lambda} = F_K$$

where

Table 5.2 *National accounting matrix (harvest used in goods production)*

Expenditures ↓ Receipts →	'Goods'	Labor	K-capital	Harvest	Labor	S-capital	Households
'Goods'							$C + \dot{K}$
Labor	ZF_Z						
K-capital	KF_K						
Harvest	RF_R						
Labor				$N_1 f_{N_1} F_R$			
S-capital				$Sf_S F_R$			$[S\theta_S - \theta(S)]B + d(SB)/dt$
Households		$(N-N_1)F_Z$	$r_t K$		$N_1 F_Z$	SBr_t	

131

$$\rho - \frac{\dot{\lambda}}{\lambda} = r_t \qquad (5.4)$$

$$-\frac{\partial H}{\partial S} = \dot{\mu} - \rho\mu \quad \text{or} \quad -\lambda F_R f_S - \mu\theta_S + \mu f_S = \dot{\mu} - \rho\mu \qquad (5.5)$$

and transversality conditions for stocks S and K.

Our national accounts are set out in Table 5.2. Constant returns to scale (or Euler's Theorem) yields the first row–column pair in Table 5.2 for 'goods' production, and again constant returns to scale in $f(\cdot)$ yields the third row–column pair in Table 5.2. Equation (5.4) above yields row–column pair, four and equation (5.3) yields row–column pair, five.

Equation (5.5) is the basis of row–column pair six in Table 5.2. However, some re-writing is done to (5.5) to get it into the appropriate form for the table. First the equation is multiplied by S/λ. Second $\theta(S)\mu/\lambda$ is added and subtracted in the last term in the row. And third, r_t is made to 'replace' ρ in equation (4.5).

This latter involves taking μ/λ from (5.5) and obtaining

$$\frac{\dot{\mu}}{\mu} - \rho = \frac{\dot{B}}{B} + \frac{\dot{\lambda}}{\lambda} - \rho = \frac{\dot{B}}{B} - r_t$$

where $B = \mu/\lambda = (fN_1 F_R - F_Z)/f_{N_1}$. Hence (5.5) becomes

$$Sf_S F_R + S\theta_S \mu/\lambda - Sf_S \mu/\lambda + \left(\frac{\dot{B}}{B} - r_t\right)\mu S/\lambda = 0,$$

before $\theta(S)\mu/\lambda$ is added and subtracted. Hence the last two entries in the final column of Table 5.2 are

$$\frac{d(SB)}{dt} + [S\theta_S - \theta(S)]B.$$

Net national income (the households row) is

$$NF_Z + Kr_t + SBr_t$$

wage payments plus the flow value of capital in use, expressed as interest foregone, with r_t the explicit market rate. It is apparent that $\theta(S) - S\theta_S$ is a residual income category emerging because the net increment function is concave in S. One should place this in national income. Also $S\dot{B}$ is an asset price change term that could be placed on the income side of the accounts. Hence revised NNI becomes

$$NF_Z + Kr_t + SBr_t - S\dot{B} + [\theta(S) - S\theta_S]B.$$

The novelty here is the presence of the residual income term. NNP becomes its dollar-valued, linearized curent-value Hamiltonian representation:

$$C + \dot{K} + \dot{S}B.$$

We now move on to allow harvesting to cause pollution. If the harvest is fuel for energy generation, then fuel use in production will cause pollution of some form.

5.5 POLLUTION ASSOCIATED WITH USE OF THE NATURAL RESOURCE

We extend the previous model, along the lines of Brock (1977), so that extraction or harvesting is linked to pollution. Harvested timber might be used for fuel and the burning of the fuel could cause pollution from particulates, for example. We limit attention to a first-best case in which the externality, pollution, is charged for by 'the government' via Pigouvian taxes. Such solutions are taken up in more detail in the next chapter. Our attention here is on the accounts. We observe that the price of the natural underline *stock*, gross of the pollution charge, plays a central role in the analysis. Given this gross stock price for the natural resource, we observe that economic depreciation involves the linked change in value of the natural stock and the stock of pollution. The resulting accounts indicate that the economic depreciation term emerges as a qualitative new entity when pollution, with a stock representation, enters the analysis. I can think of no analogue to our new economic depreciation term. The conventional wisdom of adjusting the accounts with Pigouvian taxes, given pollution, to achieve an approximate first-best set of accounts, overlooks the complicated task of adjusting the term for economic depreciation of capital in order to capture pollution stock effects, of both a price and quantity nature.

The pollution stock, X, shows up as an entry in current utility, yielding negative 'vibrations'. We have utility in $U(C, X)$. Net pollution generation, $\dot{X}$ occurs in

$$\dot{X} = f(N_1, S) - \gamma X \tag{5.6}$$

where γ is the constant rate of natural abatement and $f(N_1, S)$ is current harvest from stock S. (N_1 is labor in harvesting and $f(\cdot)$ exhibits constant returns to scale.) That is,

$$\dot{S} = \theta(S) - f(N_1, S) \tag{5.7}$$

where $\theta(S)$ is the natural increment with $\theta(0) = 0$ and $\theta(\cdot)$ increasing and concave in S. Consumption and investment goods production occurs in

$$\dot{K} = F[K, f(N_1, S), N - N_1] - C \tag{5.8}$$

where $N - N_1$ is labor in 'goods' production, N is fixed, and C is consumption goods production. $\dot{K}$ is investment goods production. K is produced 'machine' capital. $F(\cdot)$ exhibits constant returns to scale.

The market or planning maximizes

$$\int_0^\infty U(C, X) e^{-\rho t} dt$$

subject to (5.6), (5.7), (5.8) and $K(0) = K_0$, $S(0) = S_0$, and $X(0) = X_0$. ρ is the constant rate of discount of utility. The current-value Hamiltonian is

$$H = U(C, X) + \lambda \{ F[K, f(N_1, S), N - N_1] - C \}$$

$$+ \mu[\theta(S) - f(N_1, S)] + \eta[f(N_1, S) - \gamma X]$$

where λ, μ, and η are co-state variables (shadow prices in utils for K, S and X). Note that η will be negative because more X contributes negatively to current utility. $\mu - \eta$, the gross price of a unit of S, emerges below as a central piece in the analysis of valuation in this economy. The necessary conditions are

$$\frac{\partial H}{\partial C} = 0 \text{ or } U_C = \lambda \tag{5.9}$$

$$\frac{\partial H}{\partial N_1} = 0 \text{ or } \lambda(F_R f_{N_1} - F_Z) = (\mu - \eta) f_{N_1} \tag{5.10}$$

where $R = f(N_1, S)$ and $Z = N - N_1$,

$$-\frac{\partial H}{\partial K} = \dot{\lambda} - \rho \lambda \text{ or } \rho - \frac{\dot{\lambda}}{\lambda} = F_K \tag{5.11}$$

and $r_t \equiv \rho - \dot{\lambda}/\lambda$ is the market interest rate,

$$-\frac{\partial H}{\partial S} = \dot{\mu} - \rho\mu \text{ or } \dot{\mu} - \rho\mu + \lambda F_R f_S + \mu\theta_S - (\mu - \eta) f_S = 0 \tag{5.12}$$

$$-\frac{\partial H}{\partial X} = \dot{\eta} - \rho\eta \text{ or } \dot{\eta} - \rho\eta + U_X - \eta\gamma = 0 \tag{5.13}$$

and

$$\lim_{t\to\infty} \lambda(t)K(t)e^{-\rho t} = 0,$$

$$\lim_{t\to\infty} \mu(t)S(t)e^{-\rho t} = 0,$$

$$\lim_{t\to\infty} \eta(t)X(t)e^{-\rho t} = 0.$$

We multiply (5.10) by Z/λ and rearrange to get

$$ZF_Z + \left[F_R - \left(\frac{\mu - \eta}{\lambda}\right)\right]N_1 f_{N_1} = \left[F_R - \left(\frac{\mu - \eta}{\lambda}\right)\right]Nf_{N_1}$$

which is the fourth row–column pair in Table 5.3. We multiply (5.12) by S/λ, represent $(\rho - \dot\mu/\mu)$ by r_t^S, to get

$$\left[F_R - \left(\frac{\mu - \eta}{\lambda}\right)\right]Sf_S + S\theta_S \frac{\mu}{\lambda} = Sr_t^S \frac{\mu}{\lambda}.$$

This becomes the third row–column pair in Table 5.3. And we multiply (5.13), represent $(\rho - \dot\eta/\eta)$ by r_t^X, to get

$$\frac{XU_X}{\lambda} - \frac{\gamma X\eta}{\lambda} = \frac{Xr_t^X\eta}{\lambda},$$

which becomes the fifth row–column pair in Table 5.3. We need to rationalize or collect and cancel terms in the households column in Table 5.3. Central is $f(\cdot) = Sf_S + N_1 f_{N_1} = R$. Hence the households column becomes

$$C + \dot K + \theta(S)\frac{\mu}{\lambda} - f\frac{\mu}{\lambda} + [S\theta_S - \theta(S)]\frac{\mu}{\lambda} + \frac{f\eta}{\lambda} - \frac{\gamma X\eta}{\lambda} + \frac{XU_X}{\lambda}$$

$$= C + \dot K + \dot S\frac{\mu}{\lambda} + \frac{\dot X\eta}{\lambda} + \frac{XU_X}{\lambda} + [S\theta_S - \theta(S)]\frac{\mu}{\lambda}.$$

The first five terms are the dollar-valued, linearized current-value Hamiltonian. Somewhat novel is the stock of pollution as a consumption 'good' in XU_X/λ. U_X is negative because the stock is assumed to be a dis-amenity or a bad. The final entry is the residual income category emerging because $\theta(S)$ is concave or net linear. This term should be moved to the income side of the accounts where it will enter as a positive, residual income flow. Then NNI (the adjusted households row) becomes

Table 5.3   *National accounting matrix (harvesting contributes to a pollution stock)*

Expenditures ↓ / Receipts →	'Goods' production	K-capital	S-capital	Labor	X-capital	Households
'Goods' production						$C + K$
K-capital	KF_K					0
S-capital	RF_R					$-RF_R + S\theta_{S_t}\mu/\lambda + [FR - (\mu-\eta/\lambda)]Sf_S$
Labor	ZF_Z					$[F_R - (\mu-\eta/\lambda)]N_1 f_{N_1}$
X-capital						$-\gamma X\eta/\lambda + XU_X/\lambda$
Households		Kr_t	$\mu Sr_t^S/\lambda$	$[F_R - (\mu-\eta/U_C)]Nf_{N_1}$	$\eta Xr_t^X/\lambda$	

$$Kr_t + \frac{\mu Sr_t^S}{\lambda} + \left[F_R - \left(\frac{\mu - \eta}{\lambda}\right)\right]Nf_{N_1} + \frac{\eta Xr_t^X}{\lambda} + [\theta(S) - S\theta_S]\frac{\mu}{\lambda}.$$

The central novelty here is labor N being valued at the market wage f_{N_1}, weighted by $F_R - (\mu - \eta)/\lambda$. The weight reflects the fact that labor is directly productive in goods production and harvesting and indirectly unproductive in running down stock S and in augmenting the pollution stock X. Certainly in practice this 'total' or 'social' wage, $F_R - (\mu - \eta)/\lambda f_{N_1}$ would be difficult to estimate. Finally, we note that r_t^S and r_t^X are own interest rates, not observable in the marketplace. These rates embody asset price changes of μ and η relative to λ. Recall from Chapter 3 that $r_t - r_t^S = \mu/\mu - \dot\lambda/\lambda$ and $r_t - r_t^X = \dot\eta/\eta - \dot\lambda/\lambda$. Thus account of these asset price changes would have to be taken because r_t^S and r_t^X are not market rates of interest.

Our formulation was first best or implicit was a regime of Pigouvian pollution taxes. Harvesting causes pollution and thus users of harvest must pay a mark-up or Pigouvian tax $(\eta - \mu)/\lambda$ per unit of harvest.

5.6 LAND IN A STATIONARY OVERLAPPING GENERATIONS MODEL

Land is a durable asset and is associated with a sustainable stream of harvests. Its role as an asset makes it a convenient vehicle for transferring claims on income from one generation to the next. Here we set out a simple overlapping generations model for a stationary economy with 'income' derived from land worked by N workers. In each period there are N retired workers as well, deriving income from land rents and, at their death, land sales. Each person lives for two periods, a laboring period (young) and a retired period (old). There is a fixed amount of land L and current output is $F(N, L)$ with $F(\cdot)$ exhibiting constant returns to scale. Current product, wheat, sustains the $2N$ people as 'consumption' goods.

Adjacent periods are linked by two equilibrium conditions: (a) the cost of the land to the purchaser at the end of period $t - 1$ equals its discounted value (rentals plus sales value) at the end of period t

$$[LF_L(t) + L]U_c(C^0) = LU_c(C^y)(1 + \rho),$$

and (b) the current savings S of the young purchases the land being sold by the old for L dollars. That is, $S = L$, and $C^y(t) = NF_N(t) + B - S$, where B is a bequest from old to young, and $C^0(t) = LF_L(t) + L - B$. Recall that total current output $F(N, L)$ $(= NF_N + LF_N)$ equals $C^y(t) + C^0(t)$.

Our national accounts are set out in Table 5.4, where the households column is net national product. $[1-U_c(C^y)/U_c(C^0)]L$ is capital gains on land. Since N and L are fixed, bequests B will be non-zero in general. It must be non-zero in order for the consumptions, C^y and C^0, to satisfy

$$\frac{U_c(C^y)}{U_c(C^0)} = \frac{[1+F_L(t)]}{(1+\rho)}.$$

Hence our somewhat rigid, stationary model represents a theory of non-zero bequests.

If machine capital were the durable input, instead of land, its magnitude could be varied via investment and there would be no need for bequests. Labor income of the young would then purchase the current stock, K, plus new produced K and the remainder would be current consumption of the young. The old would finance their consumption from accrued rentals to K_t plus its sales value. The young would select their savings (investment) to maximize the present value of lifetime utility and this decision would yield the zero arbitrage profit condition (see, for example, Romer, 1996; pp. 73–4). With the number of working people N fixed, there would be no balanced growth, simply the accumulation of K_t, given N constant.

5.7   CLEARING LAND OF FORESTS TO OBTAIN LAND FOR AGRICULTURE

We take up deforestation or land clearing for a small open economy being settled by immigrants. Canada in the eighteenth and nineteenth centuries comes to mind. Deforestation here is land-use adjustment, adjustment of a sticky and purposeful sort. The economy begins with a shortage of land open for agricultural use. We are interested in the time path of adjustment to what will be a steady state. Roughly speaking, land price differences drive the clearing process.

There are two commodities produced under constant returns to scale with land and labor, namely (sustainable) forestry products, with production function $f(N^F, L)$ and (sustainable) agricultural products, with production function $g(N^A, L - L^F)$, where L is the endowment of land in the economy, L^F is the area in forest, N^F is labor in forestry harvesting, and N^A is labor in agricultural (farming) activity. The world price for forestry product is ψ and for agricultural product is unity.

$N(t)$ is the current labor supply in the economy and is growing quickly up to an upper bound. (We can discuss a steady-state outcome when labor approaches a constant value.)

Table 5.4 *National accounting matrix (stationary OLG (overlapping generations) model with land)*

Expenditures ↓ Receipts →	Young	Old	Labor	Land	'Transfer'	Households
Young					$S-B$	C^y
Old						C^0
Labor	$NF_N(t)$					
Land		$LF_L(t)$				$[1 - U_c(C^y)/U_c(C^0)]L$
'Transfer'		$L-B$				
Households			$NF_N(t)$	$\rho L U_c(C^y)/U_c(C^0)$		

139

$$N(t) = N^A(t) + N^F(t) + N^C(t)$$

where $N^C(t)$ is labor employed in clearing forested land. Land-use change is costly and sticky and this is modelled as

$$R(t) = h[N^C(t)]$$

where $R(t) = -\dot{L}^F$ is hectares currently cleared. We assume that $h(0) = 0$ and $h'(\cdot) > 0$ and $h''(\cdot) < 0$ for N^C positive. Here current clearing cost is $w(t)N^C(t)$ for wage $w(t)$. However, there will be a scarcity value $\lambda(t)$ on land in forest. Hence

$$[p - \lambda(t)]h'(t) = w(t) \qquad (5.14)$$

where p is the world price for the 'harvest' from the cleared land. Harvested product is assumed proportional to land cleared, with unity being the factor of proportionality.

The allocation of activity to land and the pace of clearing is governed by the wealth-maximization problem for the small open economy: maximize by choice of N^A, N^F and N^C

$$\int_0^\infty \{\psi f(N^F, L^F) + g(N^A, L - L^F) + ph[N^C(t)]\}e^{-rt}dt$$

subject to

$$\dot{L}^F(t) = -h[N^C(t)]$$

$$N(0) = N_C$$

$$L^F(0) = L_0^F$$

$$N(t) = N^F(t) + N^A(t) + N^C(t).$$

The necessary conditions are

$$\psi f_{N^F} = g_{N^A} = [p - \lambda(t))h'(t) = w(t)$$

where $w(t)$ is the Lagrangian multiplier corresponding to the labor constraint and $\lambda(t)$ is the co-state variable corresponding to L^F. We also have

$$g_{L-L^F}(t) - \psi f_{L^F}(t) = \dot{\lambda}(t) - r\lambda(t) \qquad (5.15)$$

and the transversality condition

$$\lim_{T \to \infty} e^{-rT} \lambda(T) L^F(T) = 0.$$

We write $L - L^F = L^A$, this being land currently in agriculture. (5.15) multiplied by L^F yields the fifth row–column pair in Table 5.5, our national accounting matrix. The fourth row–column pair captures current labor, N, allocation at equal value of marginal products across our three competing activities, sustainable forestry, agriculture and clearing. The first three row–column pairs capture value of inputs equal value of product for our three activities.

The households column in Table 5.5 is a sum of current product and $\lambda N^C h_{N^C}$ and needs adjusting or rationalization. We add and substract $\lambda h(N^C)$ and obtain a new households column

$$\psi f + g + ph + \lambda \dot{L}^F - [h(N^C) - N^C h_{N^C}]\lambda.$$

The first four terms comprise the dollar-valued linearized current-value Hamiltonian and is our NNP. The last term is a surplus which should be on the income side of the accounts. Hence NNP is the value of the three current products plus a 'depreciation' term for land. For λ positive, this 'depreciation' term is positive. The income side (NNI), the revised households row is

$$(h - N^C h_{N^C})p + Nw + L g_{L^A} + \lambda\left(r - \frac{\dot{\lambda}}{\lambda}\right)L^F + (h - N^C h_{N^C})\lambda.$$

There are two surpluses arising from $h(N^C)$ being concave, one flow valued and one valued at the stock price, $\lambda(t)$. Then there is labor value Nw plus total land L valued at its value of marginal product in agriculture plus λL^F valued at an own interest rate. $L g_{L^A} + (r - \dot{\lambda}/\lambda)\lambda L^F = L^A g_{L^A} + L^F \psi f_{L^F}$. Hence

$$NNI = (h - N^C h_{N^C})(p + \lambda) + Nw + L^A g_{L^A} + L^F \psi f_{L^F},$$

a fairly straightforward expression.

We define a regular solution as one with $L_0^F \cong L$, forest abundant, and $R(t)$ positive and declining toward zero, and $\lambda(t)$ increasing toward p in the limit. We impose the Inada-like condition

$$\lim_{N^C \to 0} h'(N^C) = \infty.$$

For the limiting solution to be a 'steady state', we assume that $N(t)$ is at or very close to an upper bound as $R(t) \to 0$. We assume that $L^F(\infty) > 0$ so that there is some sustainable forestry activity remaining as clearing ends. This will occur if the world price of timber or product from the cleared land, p, is not too large.

Table 5.5   *National accounting matrix (forest clearing for agriculture)*

Expenditures ↓ / Receipts →	Forestry	Agriculture	Clearing	Labor	Land	Households
Forestry						ψf
Agriculture						g
Clearing						ph
Labor	$\psi N^F f_{N^F}$	$N^A g_{N^A}$	$p N^C h_{N^C}$			$\lambda N^C h_{N^C}$
Land	$\psi L^F f_{L^F}$	$L^A g_{L^A}$				
Households			$ph - p N^C h_{N^C}$	Nw	$\lambda(r - \dot{\lambda}/\eta)\, L^F + L g_{L^A}$	

One can label

$$[\psi f_{L^F}(t) - g_{L-L^F}(t)]/r$$

as the static gap between the price of land in sustainable forestry and in sustainable agriculture. In our regular solution, we envisage this as being negative at the initial date of clearing and equal to $-p$ at the end of phase of clearing. We envisage $\lambda(0)$ negative and increasing to zero in the first phase of clearing. Then $\lambda(T_1)$ increases from zero at T_1 to date T_2 when

$$\psi f_{L^F}(T_2) - g_{L-L^F}(T_2) = 0,$$

and

$$\dot{\lambda}(T_2) = r\lambda(T_2).$$

Beyond T_2, $g_{L-L^F} - \psi f_{L^F}$ is positive rising to p as $R(t) \to 0$. Roughly speaking, timber is a nuisance in the first phase and land is cleared at a loss on the marginal hectare. In the final phase, forested land has become scarce and valuable, but clearing is driven by the profitability of clearing *per se*. In the intermediate phase, both clearing and land-use change are profitable.

Capital gains $\lambda(t)/r$ are positive in our regular case and represent a wedge in the static difference of land price on land in sustainable forestry and agriculture. Roughly speaking, the land price gap 'drives' the clearing process up to the steady state. $\lambda(t)$ declines to zero in the steady state. When sticky stock adjustment declines to zero, capital gains decline to zero also. At each date, labor and land in, say, agriculture, are different as well as the wage prevailing in the economy. It is tricky to isolate conditions that guarantee that $g_{L-L^F} - \psi f_{L^F}$, $1/\lambda(t)$ and $R(t)$ decline uniformly over time as clearing proceeds. But this characterizes our regular case. An irregular case would have an interval of increasingness in one of these key variables. For the special case of $N(t)$ constant, $N^C(t)$ will be declining as clearing, $R(t)$, declines. But the behavior of $\lambda(t)$ and $w(t)$ cannot be nailed down without more information on the time path of relative input proportions in sustainable forestry and agriculture.

The clearing activity involves dynamic rent, $\lambda(t)R(t)$ which we might consider being allocated to a fund $A(t)$ abroad earning r% per 'period'. Then net earnings from abroad, under the exporting of all current product, are

$$Z(t) = (p - \lambda)h(N^C) + \psi f(N^F, L^F) + g(N^A, L - L^F) + rA$$

where $\lambda h(N^C)$ is the rent invested abroad, rA is interest income flowing from abroad, and $\dot{A}(t) = \lambda h(N^C)$. Now

$$\dot{Z}(t) = -(\psi f_{L^F} - g_{L-LF})h(N^C) - \dot{\lambda}h(N^C) + r\lambda h(N^C) + w(t)\dot{N}(t)$$

$$= w(t)\dot{N}(t)$$

using (5.15) above.

Hence earnings from abroad will be increasing for the case of positive immigration and will be constant under no immigration. If all export earnings are used to support the importing of consumables from abroad, we have the result that aggregate consumption increases over time, given positive immigration. The current level of increase is $w(t)\dot{N}(t)$.

Given $\lambda(t)$ negative in the early phase of clearing, the small open economy would be dis-investing in $A(t)$ early in its development, or importing capital from abroad in order to, roughly speaking, support the clearing of forests.

5.8 CONCLUDING REMARKS

Renewable capital includes fish stocks, timber stands, and watersheds and airsheds. Services (harvests) can be drawn off and nature will replenish some of the stock drawn-down. In a steady state the exact current draw-down gets replaced by nature's natural increment. The accounting anomaly we observed in this chapter was a negative term for economic depreciation of renewable capital, in a steady state in the NANNP. In contrast, in the UNNP the economic depreciation term was zero.

After considering fairly standard harvesting issues, we turned to utilization of environmental capital. Here Pigouvian pollution taxes figured prominently. Our environmental use charge showed up in asset price and this made the expressions for the economic depreciation of natural capital very complicated. In our investigation of deforestation, land value change figured prominently.

REFERENCES

Brock, W. (1977), 'A polluted golden age' in V.K. Smith (ed.), *Economics of Natural and Environmental Resources*, New York: Gordon & Breach, pp. 441–61.

Faustmann, M. (1849), 'On the determination of the value which forest land and immature stands possess of foresting', reprinted in M. Gane (ed.), *Martin Faustmann and the Evolution of Discounted Cash Flow*, Oxford Institute Paper, No. 42, Oxford: Oxford University Press, 1968.

May, Robert (1976), 'Simple mathematical models with very complicated dynamics', *Nature*, **261**, 459–67.

Romer, David (1996), *Advanced Macroeconomics*, New York: McGraw-Hill.

6. Green national accounting for an economy with a free access distortion

6.1 INTRODUCTION

There seem to be two distinct reasons for developing and doing green national accounting. One is to arrive at a better measure of truly sustainable 'income' for a nation. The concept of NNP (net national product) that was developed in the 1930s was a concept of 'income' or of potential current consumption compatible with preserving capital intact. Thus NNP was an expression for a sustainable consumption flow. The greening of national accounting can be viewed, then, from one perspective, as the development of 'procedures' for expanding the concept of capital in the notion of 'maintaining capital intact'. Alternatively, green national accounting involves expanding the notion of 'decline in the value of capital' over the accounting period. This decline separates GNP from NNP. Thus there is a basic reason why the greeners of the accounts seldom stray far from the concept of NNP. The other reason to green the national accounts is to attempt to come up with a first-best reference point, a state in which negative environmental externalities are fully charged for. The reference point becomes a benchmark to be used to evaluate the current, distorted state of the economy. Part of this program is the analysis of revenues that would accrue under a program of full Pigouvian taxation and whether these revenues could be used to replace those currently collected with obvious distorting taxes. This is an analysis of the nature of the 'double dividend' that might await bold tax reformers. The large question of taxation, distortions and valuation (shadow pricing) preoccupied public economics theorists in the 1970s. They appear to have been overwhelmed by the complexity of the task of coming up with a proxy for a first-best national income, given a distorted second-best current state. Issues in incentives moved quickly to center-stage. The shadow pricing research program seemed to shrink from view fairly rapidly. Perhaps the incentive issues that emerged simply chastened researchers into putting the original task aside until a future decade. The possibility of reaping a double dividend from greening the tax system has rekindled interest in doing accounting or valuation in second-best economies. Our 'program' here does not ascend to the complexity of double-dividend analysis.

We simply consider a second-best economy, burdened with underpriced access to a fish stock[1] and compare a set of green national accounts for an abstract economy devoted to fishing under a planning or first-best and under a free access regime. Roughly speaking, entries for the natural stock wash out in the accounts for the free access solution, creating an impression that one is dealing with ordinary, non-greened accounts. We note that multiple equilibria will be a standard outcome under a free access solution and the accounts fail to signal which equilibrium has been arrived at. In the accounts for the first-best, we observe the stationary equivalent or flow value of the stock in the income side of the accounts and we observe the economic depreciation of the stock in the product side of the accounts. The model we make use of treats the free access problem as one of an absence of Pigouvian taxes, rationing entry to the fishery.[2] We treat the case of a large number of identical fishers and so we rule out strategic interactions among agents.[3] We observe the generic stock rent dissipation under free access which Gordon (1954) emphasized. Our model possesses a steady state and this makes analyzing its equilibria fairly straightforward. It is the accounts for the model which we wish to focus on. We have a very simple general equilibrium model, 'turning on' an agent's labor leisure choice, with which we can exhibit key aspects of a free access equilibrium and its associated national accounts. One aspect which seems new in our analysis is the question of a firm 'satiating' itself with an input, here the stock of fish, when the price drops to zero. We pay attention to this matter below. It seems to be a generic problem associated with defining equilibria with zero charges or equilibria without Pigouvian taxes.

We turn first to the model and the planning or first-best solution. We then treat the free access or no Pigouvian tax case. In each instance we set out the national accounts corresponding to the equilibrium in the economy.

6.2 THE MODEL AND THE FIRST-BEST (THE PLANNING SOLUTION)

There are N (large and fixed exogenously) fishers who live by fishing and live on the fish they harvest. Each individual puts out labor at an explicit sacrifice of leisure. In our first formulation, a planner sets a charge (Pigouvian tax) for access to the fish stock and an agent collects the fees and returns them as a lump sum to the fishers, in equal allotments. Each fisher harvests according to a constant returns to scale production function, with substitutability between inputs. We have

$$h = f(L, S)$$

where L is individual labor supply, S is the current stock of fish in the water, and h is the current harvest for the individual. This production function exhibits 'satiation' with respect to S, as indicated in Figures 6.1a and 6.1b.

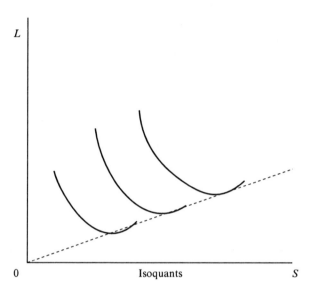

Figure 6.1a Isoquant map with satiation of input S

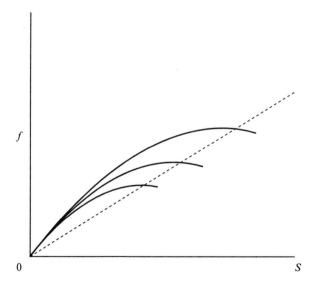

Figure 6.1b Outputs with satiation of input S

Figure 6.1a indicates an isoquant map with satiation of input S and Figure 6.1b is the companion sketch with output on the horizontal axis. 'Satiation' implies that there is always an interior point at which $\partial f(L, S)/\partial S = 0$. We require this property in our free access equilibrium.[4] To get ahead of ourselves, $\partial f(L, S)/\partial S > 0$ plays a central role in our planning equilibrium and $\partial f(L, S)/\partial S = 0$ plays a central role in our free access equilibrium. Since this sort of satiation creates awkward technical problems for isolating a well-behaved equilibrium, we suggest proceeding by substituting $\partial f(L, S)/\partial S = \varepsilon$, with ε a small positive number, for $\partial f(L, S)/\partial S = 0$. For many production functions, one will end up with a finite value of S in equilibrium, under this approximate solution.[5]

An individual's current utility is $U(h, z)$ where z is leisure time, equal to $E - L$, where E is the endowment of time. We assume $U(\cdot)$ to be increasing and concave in its arguments and to satisfy Inada conditions for the case of an argument tending to zero. L is time devoted to fishing. The planner's maximand is

$$\int_0^\infty NU[h(t), z(t)]\,\exp(-\rho t)dt$$

where ρ is the social rate of discount.

The stock grows by net amount in $\dot{S}$ equal to $\psi[S(t)]$, in nature and by

$$\dot{S} = \phi[S(t)] - Nf[L(t), S(t)]$$

while it is being fished by our N fishers. $\phi(\cdot)$ is strictly concave with $\phi(0) = \phi(K) = 0$, and $\phi(S) > 0$, for $0 < S < K$. We assume that the derivative $\phi_S(S) \to \infty$ as $S \to 0$ from above.[6] Note that S is a public input in the sense that it enters 'equally' in each fisher's production function. The intuition is of course that with a given L, it is easier to catch a specific harvest when the stock, S, is larger. A larger stock makes fishing effort more productive.

The planning problem is to maximize, by choice of path, $[L(t)]$,

$$\int_0^\infty NU\{f[L(t), S(t)], E - L(t)\}\,\exp(-\rho t)dt$$

subject to

$$\dot{S}(t) = \phi[S(t)] - Nf[L(t), S(t)]$$

and

$$S(0) = S_0.$$

The current-value Hamiltonian is

$$H(t) = NU[f(L, S), E - L] + \mu(t)[\phi(S) - Nf(L, S)].$$

The necessary conditions are

$$\frac{\partial H}{\partial L} = 0, \Rightarrow (U_h - \mu)f_L = U_z \tag{6.1}$$

where $(U_h - \mu)$ is the net price of a unit of harvest,

$$-\frac{\partial H}{\partial S}\,\dot{\mu} - \rho\mu, \Rightarrow (U_h - \mu)f_S N + \dot{\mu} = (\rho - \phi_S)\mu \tag{6.2}$$

(when μ and $\dot{\mu}$ are substituted for, we have our Euler equation, which we refer to below) and

$$\lim_{t \to \infty} \mu(t)S(t)\exp(-\rho t) = 0.$$

The only capital here is the S-stock and its own rate is $\rho - \dot{\mu}/\mu = r_t^S$. To derive our national accounting matrix, we multiply (6.1) by $Z = E - L$ to get

$$NLf_L U_h + U_Z ZN - \mu NLf_L = (U_h - \mu)NEf_L.$$

This equation becomes the second row–column pair in Table 6.1. We multiply equation (6.2) by S, add and subtract $\mu\theta(S)$, and substitute for $\rho - \dot{\mu}/\mu = r_t^S$. This yields

$$NSf_S U_h + \mu\theta(S) - \mu NSf_S = \mu Sr_t^S + [\theta(S) - S\theta_S]\mu.$$

This equation becomes the third row–column pair in Table 6.1. The households column is NNP in utils. We substitute $\mu Nf + \dot{S}\mu$ for $\mu\theta(S)$ and divide by U_h. Then NNP is the familiar-looking

$$Nf + NZU_Z/U_h + \dot{S}\mu/U_h$$

dollar-valued linearized current-value Hamiltonian. The two outputs are harvest, Nf, and leisure, NZU_Z/U_h. Economic depreciation of S-capital is $\dot{S}\mu/U_h$.

The households row is NNI in utils. Recall that $\theta(S) - S\theta_S$ is a 'residual' income flow arising because $\theta(S)$ is concave. Somewhat novel is the 'labor' entry, comprising the E units going to harvesting as labor and to leisure. f_L is the dollar-valued wage for working in the harvesting sector. But total 'labor' endowment NE gets valued at dollar value $f_L(U_h - \mu)/Uh$ per unit. This is a wage net of the 'damage' which labor does to the stock S, via harvesting. This net valuation term is new to our accounting analysis.

Table 6.1   National accounting matrix (labor/leisure and harvesting)

Expenditures ↓ / Receipts →	Harvest production	Labor	S-capital	Households
Harvest production				$U_h Nf$
Labor	$NLf_L U_h$			$NZU_z - \mu NLf_L$
S-capital				$\mu\theta(S) - \mu NSf_S$
Households		$(U_h - \mu)NEf_L$	$\mu Sr_t^S + [\theta(S) - S\theta_S]\mu$	

Of central importance is the presence of leisure in the product side of the accounts. Leisure is, of course, not normally included in national product and this is presumably for reasons of practicality, not logical coherence. An increase in average hours of leisure to society is an important 'byproduct' of modern economic growth.

The first-best for our economy requires rationing of entry to the stock of fish. This is achieved by charge Sf_S per harvesting firm. All harvesters contribute NSf_S dollars to the owners of S while they engage in harvesting activity. The total value of harvest Nf gets allocated back to the labor input as NLf_L and to the S-capital access charges as NSf_S. A steady state with $\dot{S} = 0$ and $\dot{\mu} = 0$ is illustrated in Figure 6.2.

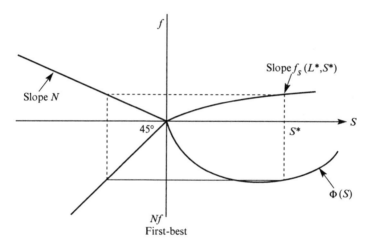

Figure 6.2 The steady-state first-best solution (no satiation of S)

Dynamics involve movement in the economy from an abundant initial stock S_0 to the steady-state value or from a scarce initial stock to S_0 (see Long, 1977).

6.3   FREE ACCESS EQUILIBRIA

The key aspect of a free access equilibrium is the zero charge to a fisher for
accessing the fish stock. This takes the form of a fisher making use of stock S
to the point that $f_S = 0$ or $f_S = \varepsilon$ in an approximate equilibrium. Given labor
paid the value of its marginal product, there will be a residual profit $\pi(t)$
accruing to the fisher. Hence a fisher's income will comprise labor income
wL plus profit, $\pi(t)$. This latter is treated as a parameter by the fisher. w is the
equilibrium wage. Income will be spent on harvest, h. Residual time becomes
leisure, z. Each fisher acts to yield

$$U_h w = U_z$$

and w equals $\partial f[L, S(t)]/\partial L$. There is no controller of access to the stock and
no obvious mechanism around which to construct a dynamics of stock evolu-
tion. We proceed to treat the stock as being in a steady state. The model
becomes essentially stationary or static. An equilibrium is sketched in Figure
6.3, the companion diagram to Figure 6.2.
    The salient difference in the equilibria, planning versus free access, is in
the place of f_S. User charge or Pigouvian tax f_S is positive in the planning

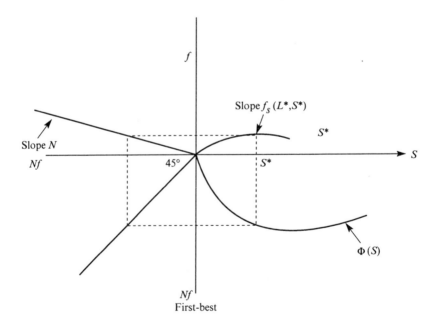

Figure 6.3   The steady-state free access solution (satiation of S)

solution and zero for the free access solution. NNP is now simply $Nh + (E - L)U_z/U_h$. There is no entry for natural capital. Net national income is simply Ef_L. The complete accounts are set out in Table 6.2.

Table 6.2   National accounting matrix (free access)

Expenditures ↓ Receipts →	Harvest	Leisure	Labor	Households
Harvest				Nh
Leisure				$N(E - L)U_z/U_h$
Labor	NLf_L			
Households	$N\pi$	$N(E - L)f_L$	NLf_L	

Observe that the accounts appear to be un-green because there is no entry for natural capital. One could easily get confused, then, between an accounts for a free access equilibrium and a traditional un-green set of accounts.

6.4   TWO EQUILIBRIA

An aspect of free access is the possibility of multiple equilibria.[7] The steady-state free access approximate equilibrium is defined by

$$wU_h(wL + \varepsilon S, E - L) = U_z(wL + \varepsilon S, E - L),$$

$$\frac{f_L(L, S)}{f_S(L, S)} = \frac{w}{\varepsilon}$$

and

$$f(L, S) = \phi(S)/N.$$

For f, Cobb–Douglas, $L^\alpha S^{(1-\alpha)}$ and $\phi(S) \equiv aS(1 - S/K)$, a and K positive parameters, the last equation defining the equilibrium can have, given L, two points of intersection as in Figure 6.4. We can express these two intersections[8] as $S = \hat{g}(L)$, and $S = \tilde{g}(L)$. If one substitutes for S in the first two equations, using $S = \hat{g}(L)$, one ends up with an approximate free access equilibrium (L^*, S^*, w^*). If one repeats with $S = \tilde{g}(L)$ one obtains a different approximate free access equilibrium. One will be a low-stock, low-labor, low-harvest, low-utility equilibrium and the other will be a high-stock, high-labor, high-harvest, high-utility equilibrium. This multiplicity phenomenon does not turn on approximateness or on ε being positive but, as we noted earlier, treating ε as positive in the free access equilibrium allows us to use familiar neoclassical production functions.

The multiplicity phenomenon destroys the often-made 'prediction' that, in the move from a first-best to a free access equilibrium, the equilibrium stock size will increase because the stock becomes underpriced or a free input. This is the basis of Chichilnisky's (1994) argument that free trade and free access lead to environmental degradation. Her position has been disputed by Karp et al. (1998), with an argument turning on a multiplicity of equilibria. In our case, a tragedy of the commons is the fact that only collective action will move the economy from an inefficient, low-stock equilibrium to the high-stock counterpart. Decentralized action will not work to effect this transition.

The implications of multiple equilibria for green national accounting are worth reflecting on. Two equilibria, such as those related to Figure 6.4, will have qualitatively identical national accounts. A reader of the accounts will get no signal about which equilibrium the economy is at. And the equilibria are rankable in a welfare sense but, again the accounts cannot indicate which

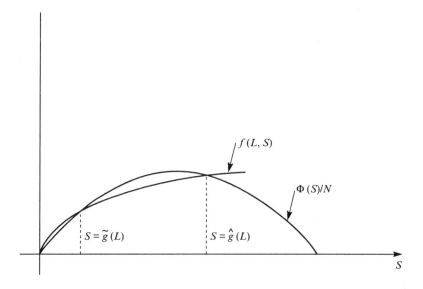

Figure 6.4 Two equilibria in free access

is the better equilibrium. This raises the question of the function of national accounts. Currently, it is popular to think that the accounts, suitably greened, can signal something about the level of sustainable income in the society. With a free access distortion, the accounts seem quite disconnected from a notion of Hicksian income or sustainable income. The free access accounts are not close proxies for the accounts for the first-best equilibrium. The accounts for the free access equilibria are simply accounts of dollar flows, with no obvious welfare meaning. A welfare economist might wish to compare the NNP measure of a free access solution with that for the first-best economy. A measure of the welfare cost of the free access distortion would emerge but it may not be the best measure one could come up with.

6.5   CONCLUDING REMARKS

We set out a simple general equilibrium model, considered its first-best and the associated national accounts, and then turned to its free access representation. For the first-best, we noted the optimal charge for access to the stock and how economic depreciation figured in the expression for NNP. We also observed the stationary equivalent representation for the value of the fish stock in national income or value-added. The free access solution had a zero charge for access to the stock. This raised technical issues for the nature of production functions required to make the model and related models work. Pigouvian taxes, set at zero, can be linked to zero marginal products and these are not standard for interior solutions for economic models. We suggested detouring around the technical problems by making use of an approximate zero charge for access. Our free access equilibrium was not unique and multiple equilibria raise the question of the ranking of the equilibria and whether the national accounts can contribute to resolving which is a better equilibrium. On this last question, we were negative. And we noted that the accounts for the two equilibria will be qualitatively the same. Moreover, a set of free access accounts has a distinctly un-green quality because the stock of fish does not make an appearance. There is no entry for current use of or disinvestment in the stock. In the accounts for the first-best there is in fact a positive depreciation entry representing natural growth in the stock.

It seems that 'positive' aspects of a program for greening the national accounts are linked to first-best situations. These elements of a program do not appear relevant to the issue of interpreting the information in accounts with natural capital and a free access distortion. There appears to be a general problem here. Accounts for a second-best equilibrium give almost no guidance as to (a) what a first-best equilibrium might look like or (b) what should be done to move the economy in question closer to its, or possibly a, first-best.

NOTES

1. Aronsson (1997) and Aronsson and Löfgren (1996) consider an economy burdened with underpriced pollution charges (or underpriced charges for accessing the abatement services of the environment) and inquire about valuation in the process to moving toward a first best.
2. Aronsson et al. (1997, Chapter 4) provides a good analysis of an underpricing problem in a dynamic economy. They deal with the question of excess pollution resulting from an absence of Pigouvian taxes. Lecomber (1979, pp. 45–50) explains free access to a fishery with the analogy of traffic congestion under a regime of zero charge for access.
3. Levhari and Mirman (1980) is the classic analysis of strategy and subgame perfection in the fishery. Hartwick and Yeung (1997) is a similar model except distinct clans compete for area on the commons by varying their birth rates or population sizes. Mason and Polasky (1994) consider the strategy of incumbents striving to limit entry to the commons by overexploiting the stock.
4. It also plays a key role in Aronsson et al. (1997, Chapter 4), but these authors do not comment when they invoke $\partial f(L, S)/\partial S = 0$.
5. A very small positive charge for access creates a distortion relative to the case of a presumably higher charge under the first-best regime. There is then useful economics to be elicited for this 'small charge' case. As we noted earlier, Aronsson and Löfgren have been analyzing valuation issues associated with moving an 'access charge' from an arbitrary low level toward its first-best level. Free access should, however, be associated with the case of a zero charge for access and it is our view that this case raises tricky technical issues associated with 'satiation'.
6. The classic quadratic $\phi \equiv aS(1 - S/K)$ is a well-behaved candidate for ϕ.
7. Copes (1970) alerted us to this phenomenon. See also Clark (1976, pp. 155–7). Dynamics in the neighborhood of each equilibrium is a separate topic. Our central point is that it is perfectly possible for an economy to get 'stuck' at either equilibrium and only collective action will move the economy to the other equilibrium.
8. The quadratic ϕ function is convenient because ϕ_S does not tend to infinity as $S \to 0$ from above. And a standard neoclassical production function can have $f_S(L, S) \to \infty$, as $S \to 0$ from above, L constant. This leads to two intersections in Figure 6.2. Two equilibria can occur quite generally, if an equilibrium exists. But a single equilibrium is also a possibility. This latter would correspond to a single intersection in the analogue of Figure 6.2.

REFERENCES

Aronsson, T. (1997), 'Welfare measurement, green accounting and distortionary taxes', typescript.

Aronsson, T., P.-O. Johansson and K.-G. Löfgren (1997), *Welfare Measurement, Sustainability and Green National Accounting*, Cheltenham: Edward Elgar.

Aronsson, T. and K.-G. Löfgren (1996), 'An almost practical step towards "green" accounting', *Umea Economic Studies*, no. 415.

Chilchilnisky, G. (1994), 'North–South trade and the global environment', *American Economic Review*, **84** (4), September, 851–74.

Clark, Colin (1976), *Mathematical Bioeconomics: The Optimal Management of Renewable Resources*, New York: John Wiley.

Copes, P. (1970), 'The backward bending supply curve of the fishing industry', *Scottish Journal of Political Economy*, **17**, 69–77.

Gordon, H. Scott (1954), 'Economic theory of a common property resource: the fishery', *Journal of Political Economy*, **62** (2), April, 124–42.

Hartwick, J.M. and D. Yeung (1997), 'The tragedy of the commons revisited', *Pacific Journal of Economics*, **2** (1), February, 45–62.

Karp, L., S. Sacheti and J. Zhao (1998), 'Common ground between free traders and environmentalists', Agricultural and Resource Economics, Berkeley, Discussion Paper no. 817.

Lecomber, Richard (1979), *The Economics of Natural Resources*, London: Macmillan.

Levhari, David and Leonard J. Mirman, (1980), 'The great fish war: an example using a dynamic Cournot–Nash solution', *Bell Journal of Economics*, **11** (1), Spring, 322–34.

Long, N.V. (1977), 'Optimal exploitation and replenishment of a natural resource', in J.D. Pitchford and S.J. Turnovsky (eds), *Applications of Control Theory to Economic Analysis*, New York: North-Holland, 81–106.

Mason, Charles and Stephen Polasky (1994), 'Entry deterrence in the commons', *International Economic Review*, **35** (2), May, 507–25.

7. International trade

7.1 INTRODUCTION

Classical trade theory detours around exchange rate issues by having commodity flows in trade balance in value across pairs of countries. It is as if all countries were using the same currency and no current balance of payments deficits or surpluses occurred. We consider two cases below along these lines. The first involves the accounts for one country exporting some of its consumption goods in return for some of 'the world's' investment goods. The second case involves oil imports to a small open economy. First we consider world prices unchanging, a stationary case, and then we consider world oil prices having a predictable upward trend. This latter is an unfavorable terms-of-trade effect to the importer of oil. These terms-of-trade effects affect the sustainability of a country's course of development (Asheim, 1986; Hartwick, 1995; Sefton and Weale, 1996; Vincent et al., 1997). Current net national product (NNP) of the oil importer becomes an over estimate of sustainable income when the country is facing a world of rising oil prices. And current NNP under estimates sustainable income to an oil importer facing declining world oil prices.

We then move to the more realistic case of currently unbalanced commodity trade. In this case financial claims abroad are built up (run down) when commodity exports exceed (fall short of) commodity imports in value. Tricky matters of exchange rate formation and revaluation arise here, but turn out not to show up in the annual accounts. These matters would show up in the changes in the accounts from one year to the next. The general principle that price changes should not be included in NNP is relevant here. Exchange rate re-valuations do not show up as capital gains or losses in the annual accounts. There is another notion of value here. Foreign trade can be viewed as a production process: exports, broadly defined, are the inputs to the process, and commodity and capital imports are the outputs of the process. Recall that the basis for trade is: intramarginally the exporter can produce x cheaper than can the importer. Trade under diversification is pursued until the cost at the margin of producing x is the same for the importer and exporter. But intramarginally, production cost savings have been capitalized upon. Hence, under diversification, importing can be seen as an alternative 'process' for producing commodity x by the importing country.

7.2 NATIONAL ACCOUNTS WITH EXPORTATION OF THE CONSUMPTION GOOD

For specificity we have the consumer good exported and the investment good imported. Exports are of course produced with domestic factors (labor and machine capital). Hence the imports are in a sense financed by sending some of domestic labor and capital services abroad, embodied in the exports. The services of inputs, embodied in the exports, that would otherwise produce output for local consumption are sent abroad and imports flow in, in return. The commodities imported end up being cheaper to acquire by this route than by the local production route.

The national accounting matrix is shown in Table 7.1. Column 'Trade-X' and row 'Trade-M' are new. $C^1 + X$ is domestic production of consumption goods (good 1) and Q^2 is domestic production of investment goods (good 2). Under balanced trade, the value of exports, pX, equals the value of imports, qM. Imports are paid for, indirectly, by the domestic 'consumption' foregone by the value of inputs used to produce exports, pX. A superficial look at Table 7.1 would suggest that national expenditure (the households column) has expanded by qM and there is no counter 'expansion' in the national income value (households row). In fact part of wN and rqK is embodied in pX and qM is imported 'to balance' the accounts.

7.3 OIL IMPORTING

A small change in our accounts allows for oil importation, where oil is an essential input into production, in return for the export of, say, consumer goods. A preliminary adjustment is the introduction of oil as an input into local production of the consumer and investment good. That is, in aggregate, we have

$$Q^1 = F^1(K^1, N^1, R^1)$$

and

$$Q^2 = F^2(K^2, N^2, R^2)$$

where R^i is the oil used in current production of good i. We continue to assume constant returns to scale and substitutability among inputs in production. Below, total output of good 1 includes domestically consumed goods and exports. The accounts are set out in the national accounting matrix in Table 7.2.

Table 7.1 *National accounting matrix (consumer goods exported)*

Expenditures ↓ Receipts →	Consumption goods	Investment goods	Labor	M-capital	Trade-X	Households
Consumption goods					pX	pC^1
Investment goods						qQ^2
Labor	wN^1	wN^2				
M-capital	rqK^1	rqK^2				
Trade-M						qM
Households			wN	rqK		

Table 7.2   National accounting matrix (oil importation)

Expenditures ↓ Receipts →	Consumption goods	Investment goods	Labor	M-capital	Trade-X	Households
Consumption goods					pX	pC^1
Investment goods						qQ^2
Labor	wN^1	wN^2				
M-capital	rqK^1	rqK^2				
Trade-M (oil)	sR^1	sR^2				
Households			wN	rqK		

In the case set out in Table 7.2, the value of oil imports, $s(R^1 + R^2)$, equals the value of exports, pX. $C^1 + X$ is the quantity of good 1 produced domestically. This nation is said to be diversified on the export side because it consumes some of its export goods domestically. It is said to be specialized on the import side because it is not simultaneously producing and importing oil. All domestic oil use is covered off by imports.

National income continues to be defined by the value of services provided by domestic primary factors over the accounting period. And national expenditure is what is expended on final product by local citizens. The extent to which trade can be said to expand 'national income' is represented by domestic expenditure being larger because something (oil here) was produced abroad more cheaply than it could have been locally, and thus the acquisition of oil from abroad ended up 'consuming' fewer domestic resources than it would have, had the foreign source not been available.

7.4 NNP AND SUSTAINABLE INCOME

The economy in Table 7.2 can be viewed as representing a snap-shot at date t of a competitive economy satisfying the following optimal savings problem. Maximize by choice of $C(t)$ and $R(t)$

$$\int_0^\infty e^{-\rho t} U[C(t)] dt$$

subject to

$$\dot{K}(t) = F[K(t), N, R(t)] - C(t) - X(t)$$

$$X(t) = s(t)R(t)$$

$$K(0) = K_0$$

$$s(0) = s_0.$$

The *autonomous* case has labor N and oil price $s(t)$ constant. This case has its util-valued NNP satisfying the dynamic programing conditioning

$$\rho V[K(t)] = U[C(t)] + \dot{K}(t) U_C[C(t)].$$

The right-hand side is util-NNP and the left-hand side is discount rate ρ multiplied by capital value $V[K(t)] = \int_t^\infty e^{-\rho(v-t)} U[C^*(v)] dv$, where $C^*(v)$ is the optimal path of future values of C. We have util-NNP as interest on a capital value or util-NNP as sustainable income (a flow of potential consumption which leaves capital value unchanged).

A *non-autonomous* case has oil price $s(t)$ rising over time along some 'independent' path. In this case the above dynamic programming condition becomes

$$\rho V[K(t), s(t)] - \frac{\partial V}{\partial t} = U[C(t)] + \dot{K}(t)U_C[C(t)]$$

where $\partial V/\partial t$ is negative because $s(t)$ is increasing. Hence the util-NNP on the right overestimates sustainable income, $V[K(t)]$. This country is experiencing a continuous negative terms-of-trade 'shock' as its import price rises relative to its export price. It is this sequence of future negative 'shocks' which are not 'capitalized' in the current value of NNP(t). Hence the util-NNP here is not a good measure of sustainable income.[1]

7.5 TRADE CURRENTLY UNBALANCED

If the export of goods exceeds import of goods, dollars 'pile up' abroad and end up invested in foreign banks, broadly defined, yielding an interest flow $rA(t)$ for $A(t)$ the current size of assets held abroad. rA is interest flows from abroad. The trade surplus can be viewed as a form of savings, since assets accumulate abroad. Formally, our accounts have a new capital good to deal with. The conceptual trick here, given $A(t)$ positive, is to think of exports, $pX(t)$, and $rA(t)$ as 'inputs' into a 'production process' called 'trade' and imports, qM, and stock growth $\dot{A}$ as 'outputs' from the 'production process'. One ends up with dollar flow $rA(t)$ as part of value-added and $\dot{A}$ entering national expenditure or net product as economic depreciation. The external flow account for the country is

$$\dot{A} = rA + pX - qM.$$

The complete accounts are shown in Table 7.3.

Domestic production is $X + C + \dot{K} = F(K, N)$. The 'trade' account has $pX - qM + rA = \dot{A}$, for A positive. $\dot{A}$ negative corresponds to 'economic depreciation' of the stock and $\dot{A}$ positive corresponds to net 'investment' in asset A. Asset A is treated completely symmetrically with other natural assets below. There is an interest flow rA in value-added from the stock and this flow is an input into trade 'production'.

There are two ways to think about the matter of domestic and 'abroad' currencies here. In a world of unchanging currency values (unchanging exchange rates), prices p and q in pX and qM can be thought of as already denominated by the 'abroad' exchange rate (price of the foreign currency). And in $\dot{A}$, with unchanging exchange rates, $\dot{A}$ would be stock change corresponding to a value in domestic currency units. Alternatively, we could be dealing with two regions of a country with one currency. The accounts in Table 7.3 reflect the single-currency scenario.

Table 7.3 *National accounting matrix (unbalanced commodity trade)*

Expenditures ↓ Receipts →	Consumption goods	Investment goods	Labor	M-capital	A-capital	Trade	Households
Consumption goods						pX	pC
Investment goods							$q\dot{K}$
Labor	N^1F_N	N^2F_N					
M-capital	K^1F_K	K^2F_K					
A-capital							$\dot{A}$
Trade					$\dot{A}$		qM
Households			NF_N	KF_K		rA	

164

Consider the case of the exchange rate changing between periods.[2] In this case the p and q would have to reflect foreign currency in a standard way. However, asset stock change would involve a price change $z\dot{A}$ and a size change $z\dot{A}$. We dealt with the anticipated price change for a commodity, such as oil, in Chapter 4.

7.6 THE SPECIALIZED OIL EXPORTER

A central case of unbalanced trade was our Oil Republic model in Chapter 4, with the nation specialized in oil exporting while exporting oil rents for investment. Residual income was spent on consumables imported from abroad. Oil income pq plus interest income rA on assets A held abroad financed imports and investment $\dot{A}$. That is,

$$pq + rA = M + \dot{A},$$

where M is imports of consumer goods. We had total cost $C(q)$ in dollars for extracting oil with $C(0) = 0$ and $C_q(q)$ positive and increasing. $C_q(0) = 0$. Current rent was $[p - C_q(t)]q(t)$. $\sigma[q(t)]$ is producer surplus, equal to $rV(S)$ where $V(S)$ is the market value of the stock (discounted future profit), given optimal extraction. The open economy accounts are shown in Table 7.4. Net depreciation is $\dot{A} - (p - C_q)q$. In the special case of $\dot{A} - (p - C_q)q = 0$, imports M equal the value of input, $C(q)$, plus the stationary equivalent value of stocks A and S. Recall that $\sigma(q)$ equals $V[S(t)]$.

It is instructive to replace oil 'production' with an explicit production function as in

$$R(t) = g(K_1, N), \tag{7.1}$$

where $R(t)$ is oil flow from stock $S(t)$ (that is, $-\dot{S}(t) = R(t)$), $g(\cdot)$ is a constant returns to scale production function, and N is a fixed input of labor. As $R(t)$ approaches zero, we have K_1 approaching zero and N remaining active under asymptotic depletion. The wage rate is endogenous and will decline as K_1 becomes smaller. Hence the wage will tend to zero as extraction declines to a small flow. The oil exporter owns capital K and $K - K_1$ is rented out abroad. rq is rent per unit of K and q is the price of a unit of K. Interest income $(K - K_1)rq$ flows in from abroad.

A wealth-maximizing extraction program satisfies

$$\max_{K_1} \int_0^\infty [pg(K_1, N) + (K - K_1)rq]e^{-rt}dt \tag{7.2}$$

Table 7.4   National accounting matrix (specialized oil exporter)

Expenditures ↓ / Receipts →	Oil flow	Input costs	Rent	A-stock	Currency inflow	Households
Oil flow					pq	
Input costs	$C(q)$					
Rent	$(p - C_q)q$					$-(p - C_q)q$
A-stock						$\dot{A}$
Currency outflow				$\dot{A}$		M
Households	$\sigma(q)$	$C(q)$			rA	

subject to

$$\dot{S}(t) = -g(K_1, N) \tag{7.3}$$

$$S_0 = \int_0^\infty g(K_1, N)dt$$

$$K_1(0) = \overline{K}_1.$$

The current-value Hamiltonian for this problem is

$$H = pg(K_1, N) + (K - K_1)rq - \mu(t)g(K_1, N). \tag{7.4}$$

The necessary conditions are

$$\frac{\partial H}{\partial K_1} = 0 \text{ or } [p - \mu(t)]g_{K_1} = rq \tag{7.5}$$

$$-\frac{\partial H}{\partial S} = \dot{\mu} - r\mu \text{ or } \dot{\mu} = r\mu. \tag{7.6}$$

and

$$\lim_{t\to\infty} \mu(t)S(t)e^{-rt} = 0.$$

We multiply (7.5) by K to get

$$(p - \mu)g_{K_1}K_1 + (K - K_1)rq = (p - \mu)g_{K_1}K$$

which is our second row–column entry in Table 7.5. We multiply (7.6) by S to get our fourth row–column entry in Table 7.5. Labor, in fixed supply, is our third row–column entry in Table 7.5.

In the households column, $-\mu g(\cdot)$ is $\mu\dot{S}$. Hence the households column is

$$NNP = pg(\cdot) + (K - K_1)rq + \mu\dot{S}$$

which is the current-value Hamiltonian. And the households row is net national income, comprising the value of K, of N and of S. The latter has a value, zero, because $r = \dot{\mu}/\mu$.

In this economy, μ increases as extraction proceeds. The N workers are locked into extraction activity. As μ rises $(p - \mu)$ declines and g_{K_1} must increase, since $(p - \mu)g_{K_1} = rq$, a constant. Hence K_1 steadily declines as

Table 7.5 *National accounting matrix (an oil-exporting nation)*

Expenditures ↓ / Receipts →	Oil flow	K-capital	Labor	S-capital	Households
Oil flow					$(p-\mu)g(\cdot)$
K-capital	$(p-\mu)g_{K_1}K_1$				$(K-K_1)rq$
Labor	$(p-\mu)g_N N$				
S-capital					
Households		$(p-\mu)g_{K_1}K$	wN	$(r-\dot{\mu}/\mu)S$	

extraction proceeds and the wage declines, with labor in extraction becoming more and more abundant relative to K_1. It is a straightforward exercise to obtain a constant import stream under investing rents on $S(t)$ abroad in a fund. We do this below for the somewhat more complicated 'Norwegian model'. In that two-sector model, the time path of the wage is a focus of attention.

7.7   A NORWEGIAN MODEL OF OIL EXPORTING

Our model of a stylized Norwegian economy has all output, including oil currently extracted, exported at world prices in return for consumption goods. The latter have a world price of unity. There is a traditional export (TE) sector earning foreign exchange, as well as the oil-exporting sector. The TE sector employs labor and machine capital K, under constant returns to scale, to produce quantity $X(t)$ of traditional exports.[3] This sector does not consume oil.[4] Oil has an extraction technology, requiring labor and machine capital, also combined under constant returns to scale. The known homogeneous stock $S(t)$ of oil has current depletion, $R(t)$, equal to $-\dot{S}(t)$. (The oil stock can be viewed as a third factor.) The standard case would have $R(t)$ declining over time so that current revenue to the exporter is declining and inputs are flowing out of the sector as it shrinks. Here things depart from the familiar. First we require movement in the world price of traditional exports in order that that sector can 'tolerate' a changing wage in the economy. If this movement in the export price is downward and relatively gradual, then this sector absorbs the labor shed by the shrinking oil sector. However, if the downward exogenous price trend is relatively steep, this sector will be 'exporting' labor and capital to the oil sector. Hence we obtain the novel result that the oil sector need not be shrinking continuously over time. Its domestic price, net of rent, will be declining. Thus in our Hotelling world, oil extraction may or may not coexist with an expanding traditional export sector. Given the ultimate exhaustibility of the oil stock, we assume that the world price of traditional exports remains positive[5] in order to retain some productive activity. This is reasonable since there is a productive labor force in place at all times.

We then consider the case of the world price for TEs increasing and we observe the possibility of a rising wage in the Norwegian economy. The economy opens with some durable capital $K - K_1 - K_2$ held abroad, earning current income $(K - K_1 - K_2)rq$, where r is the world interest rate and q is the world price of a unit of K. K_1 is employed in oil extraction and K_2 is employed in producing traditional exports. K_1 and K_2 will be changing as oil extraction proceeds and any 'excess' K will be rented out abroad.[6]

The Oil Extraction Sector

$R(t)$ tons are extracted with production function $g(K_1, N_1)$, and $g(\cdot) = R(t)$, where K_1 represents flows of services from machine stock, K_1, and N_1, is labor services from N_1 workers. $g(\cdot)$ exhibits constant returns to scale. Current rent $\mu(t)$ from oil extraction and selling satisfies

$$[p_1 - \mu(t)]g_{K_1} = rq$$

$$[p_1 - \mu(t)]g_{N_1} = w(t),$$

where p_1 is the world price of oil, $w(t)$ is the local or domestic wage rate, g_{K_1} is the marginal product of K_1, and g_{N_1} is the marginal product of N_1. Rent $\mu(t)$ is the shadow price of a unit of stock of oil $S(t)$, along a wealth-maximizing extraction program. Recall the physical 'constraint', $R(t) = -\dot{S}(t)$.

The Traditional Export Sector

$X(t)$ tons of traditional exports are produced with the production function, $f(K_2, N_2)$ under constant returns to scale, where K_2 represents the services of durable machine capital and N_2 represents the services of N_2 workers. Input levels satisfy

$$p_2 f_{K_2} = rq,$$

$$p_2 f_{N_2} = w(t).$$

The world price of traditional exports is p_2.

Input Constraints

The labor force is constant at N and there is full employment:

$$N_1(t) + N_2(t) = N.$$

The wage will be the shadow price of labor and is endogenous to this economy. We are capturing the idea that there is not free migration into and out of Norway. Norwegians own K of machine capital with $K - K_1(t) - K_2(t)$ rented out in world markets at rental rate rq.

$p_1 - \mu(t)$ is the net price of oil and since $\mu(t)$ rises at r% under efficient extraction, this net price will be declining over time. Recall that $R(t)$, equal to $g[K_1(t), N_1(t)]$, is the current extraction from current stock, $S(t)$.

Wealth Maximization

We assume that 'the market' acts to maximize the wealth of the country,[7] by choice of K_1, K_2, N_1 and N_2, in

$$V = \int_0^\infty [p_1 g(K_1, N_1) + p_2(t)f(K_2, N_2) + (K - K_1 - K_2)rq]e^{-rt}dt$$

Subject to

$$\dot{S}(t) = -g(K_1, N_1),$$

$$S(0) = S_0,$$

$$S(t) = \int_0^\infty g[K_1(z), N_1(z)]dz,$$

$$N = N_1(t) + N_2(t).$$

The current-value Hamiltonian for this optimization problem is

$$H(t) = p_1 g(K_1, N_1) + p_2(t)f(K_2, N_2) + (K - K_1 - K_2)rq - \mu(t)g(K_1, N_1)$$

and the Lagrangian is

$$L(t) = p_1 g(K_1, N_1) + p_2(t)f(K_2, N_2) + (K - K_1 - K_2)rq$$

$$-\mu(t)g(K_1, N_1) + w(t)(N - N_1 - N_2).$$

The necessary conditions are

$$[p_1 - \mu(t)]g_{K_1} = rq,$$

$$[p_1 - \mu(t)]g_{N_1} = w(t),$$

$$p_2 f_{K_2} = rq,$$

$$p_2 f_{N_2} = w(t),$$

$$\dot{\mu}(t) = r\mu(t),$$

$$\lim_{t \to \infty} e^{-rt}\mu(t)S(t) = 0.$$

For declining oil extraction to be choked off in the limit we make marginal extraction costs tend to zero as $R(t)$ approaches zero, from above. This condition on extraction costs is satisfied if

$$\lim_{N_1 \to 0} \lim_{K_1 \to 0} g_{K_1}(K_1, N_1) = \infty$$

and

$$\lim_{N_1 \to 0} \lim_{K_1 \to 0} g_{N_1}(K_1, N_1) = \infty$$

The accounts are set out in Table 7.6 and are similar to those in Table 7.5. We now have two producing sectors, the oil-extraction sector (row–column pair 1) and the traditional goods sector (row–column pair 2). The households column is NNP. Note that $-\mu g(\cdot) = \mu \dot{S}$, which is the economic depreciation of the oil stock. And the households row is net national income.

This economy will evolve like the one above (Table 7.5). The rising shadow price of oil, μ, will cause $p_1 - \mu$ to decline and this will 'result in' g_{K_1} increasing, given rq constant. Hence K_1 will tend to decline. This freed-up capital can enter the TE sector or be let out abroad. Net of rent on oil, the local price of oil is declining relative to that of traditional exports and this results in factors in the oil sector being driven from the oil-extraction sector. This can be labelled a negative terms-of-trade effect for the oil sector, causing a steady decline in that sector.

The time path of wages is easy to work out. When oil is exhausted, all labor will be in the traditional export sector. Given world prices fixed, including rental rq on K, the wage will be determined in Norway by the factor intensity of the traditional export sector. This wage can be compared to the one prevailing when the oil-extraction sector is active. Hence whether wages rise or fall over time depends on the relative factor intensities of the two sectors. If oil extraction uses much capital relative to labor, then the wage will rise over time and vice versa. These results will remain valid when the economy is experiencing a gradual increase in the world price of either good. However, the simplicity of prediction, based on factor intensities, breaks down when, say, oil is used in the production of traditional exports and/or the oil becomes more costly to extract as the stock is depleted.

A nation can smooth its consumption stream by investing some of its current oil income in assets that will be available in the future as sources of income. If surpluses from oil will be smaller or non-existent in the future, then a replacement could be interest and dividend flows from assets accumulated and possibly held abroad.[8] Our model above exhibits the constant consumption property of earlier models, under the strategy of currently

Table 7.6   National accounting matrix (Norwegian model)

Expenditures ↓ Receipts →	Oil flow	TE goods	K-capital	Labor	S-capital	Households
Oil flow						$(p_1 - \mu)g(\cdot)$
TE goods						$p_2 f(\cdot)$
K-capital	$(p_1 - \mu)g_{K_1}K_1$	$p_2 f_{K_2}K_2$				$(K - K_1 - K_2)rq$
Labor	$(p_1 - \mu)g_{N_1}N_1$	$p_2 f_{N_2}N_2$				
S-capital						
Households			rqK	wN	$(r - \dot{\mu}/\mu)S$	

investing to compensate for current capital value decline in the economy. We address the particular case of a declining world price for traditional exports. Here capital value decline is the sum of two components: the decline in the value of the oil stock because of draw-down for exporting and the decline in the long-term value of traditional exports because the world price is on a downward trend.[9] The current change in capital value from this latter effect is a negative terms-of-trade effect. We proceed to calculate this decline in capital value.[10]

Capital value for the economy at date t is

$$V(t) = \int_t^\infty [p_1 g(K_1, N_1) + p_2(z) f(K_2, N_2) + (K - K_1 - K_2) rq] e^{-r(z-t)} dt$$

under optimal extraction of oil. Hence

$$\dot{V}(t) = rV(t) - [p_1 g(K_1, N_1) + p_2(t) f(K_2, N_2) + (K - K_1 - K_2) rq].$$

For this economy, we have (see Aronsson et al., 1997, pp. 49–54)

$$rV(t) = H(t) + \int_t^\infty \dot{p}_2(x) f[K_2(z), N_2(z)] \exp[-r(z-t)] dz,$$

where $H(t)$ is the current-value Hamiltonian for our wealth-maximization problem above. Substitution for $rV(t)$ above yields

$$\dot{V}(t) = -\lambda(t) R(t) + \int_t^\infty \dot{p}_2(z) f[K_2(z), N_2(z)] \exp[-r(z-t)] dz.$$

Hence the change in capital value of the economy comprises the oil value decline and the negative terms-of-trade effect. If Norway invests abroad to compensate for this decline in capital value, its income from abroad will remain constant and its consumption, financed by income from abroad, will remain constant. We turn to this proposition.[11]

Under a strategy of investing an amount equal to the current decline in capital value in the economy in a fund $qK(t)$ abroad, our economy has current export plus capital rental income, net of investment abroad, in

$$Z(t) = [p_1 - \lambda(t)] g(K_1, N_1) + p_2(t) f(K_2, N_2) + [K(t) - K_1 - K_2] rq$$

$$+ \int_t^\infty \dot{p}_2(z) f[K_2(z), N_2(z)] \exp[-r(z-t)] dz,$$

where

$$q\dot{K}(t) = \lambda(t) R(t) - \int_t^\infty \dot{p}_2(z) f[K_2(z), N_2(z)] \exp[-r(z-t)] dz.$$

The time derivative of $Z(t)$ is

$$\dot{Z} = (p_1 - \lambda)g_{N_1}\dot{N}_1 + p_2 f_{N_2}\dot{N}_2 + [(p_1 - \lambda)g_{K_1} - rq]\dot{K}_1$$

$$+ [p_2 f_{K_2} - rq]\dot{K}_2 - \lambda R(t) + rq\dot{K}(t) + f(K_2, N_2)\dot{p}_2$$

$$-f(K_2, N_2)\dot{p}_2 + r\int_t^\infty \dot{p}_2(z)f[K_2(z), N_2(z)]\exp[-r(z-t)]dz$$

$$= 0,$$

because $\dot{N}_1 + \dot{N}_2 = 0$ and $(p_1 - \lambda)g_{N_1} = p_2 f_{N_2} = w(t)$, and $(p_1 - \lambda)g_{K_1} - rq = p_2 f_{K_2} - rq = 0$, and $r\lambda - \dot{\lambda} = 0$. Hence income from abroad is constant under the strategy of covering off the decline in 'capital value' of the economy at each date. Note that this strategy involves covering off the decline in capital value of the oil stock and the negative terms-of-trade effect resulting from the declining world prices for the exports from the traditional exporting sector. Since income from abroad finances the expenditure on imported consumables, we have aggregate consumption, in Norway, constant. We have then: under the strategy of investing abroad to cover off the decline in current capital value, aggregate consumption (the value of income from abroad) is constant along the wealth-maximizing path of extraction and production.

Constant consumption is occurring while $w(t)$, $N_1(t)$, $K_1(t)$ and $K_2(t)$ are changing over time. This represents an extension of earlier results because now the wage in the economy is endogenous and is changing systematically over time.[12] The general idea is that income from oil sales is substituted for by income from other assets as the oil stock is depleted. The traditional export sector may or may not be expanding while oil extraction is occurring and income from foreign funds is replacing income earned from oil sales. To 'make room' for the declining wage, the world price of traditional exports must be declining. Otherwise, we lose the neoclassical structure of our model with its constant returns to scale, substitutability among inputs, and zero profits.

7.8 CONCLUDING REMARKS

This chapter contains relatively simple accounts for a country in trade and takes us into two complicated and controversial areas, namely national accounting with essential terms-of-trade effects entering the valuations and exchange rate change effects entering the valuations. The latter complications get assumed away by convention and we see no reason to dispute that practice. However, revaluations arising from terms-of-trade effects raise large questions about the measurement of sustainable income, in a sense the goal of

NNP, and thus about the appropriateness of current practices. Difficult adjustments in approach may have to be dealt with if the measurement of 'Hicksian income' continues to be the goal of national accounting. We returned to our analysis in Chapter 4 concerning a small open economy specialized in oil exporting. We were able to extend this basic model to a larger economy exporting both oil and 'traditional' products. We examined some dimensions of 'Dutch Disease' in this expanded (Norway) model.

NOTES

1. This point was made by Asheim (1986) for a multi-country trade system within a constant consumption framework. Hartwick (1995) is a reformulation of Asheim's argument. See Appendix 3A1, Chapter 3. See also Vincent et al. (1997) for a small, open economy formulation. This was reported on in Chapter 4. Sefton and Weale (1996) make the point in a two-country model, with time-varying consumption.
2. Asea and Corden (1994) survey the matter of the quality of exchange rates reflecting some basic 'purchasing power parity' between countries.
3. Recall that in Appendix 3A1, Chapter 3, we considered a two-country trade framework with oil as one of the traded goods. That was the analysis of trade for large open economies.
4. In contrast with Corden–Neary models of 'Dutch disease' for a small open economy, we have no non-traded goods sector. See Corden and Neary (1982) and Corden (1984).
5. The net price of oil, equal to the value of labor and capital in the extraction of a unit, declines to zero since oil rent always increases.
6. The fixed stock K can be thought of as being augmented by the current oil rents being invested abroad when we take up the allocation of oil income.
7. Firms in the traditional export sector are in a zero current profit equilibrium. There are no capital gains to be reaped from changes in the price of K-capital.
8. It was only in 1991 that Norway's Petroleum Fund was formally set up to park abroad surpluses from oil sales and funds were actually first put into the fund in May 1996. In its 1995 budget, the Norwegian government states that the Petroleum Fund '(i) should absorb the currency inflows associated with the government's petroleum receipts from abroad (and hence contribute to containing upward pressure on the Krone exchange rate); and (ii) to diversify away from the risk of a combined fall in oil prices and the market value of domestic assets' (OECD, 1997, p. 37).
9. For concreteness we are dealing with the case of declining world price of traditional exports. The analysis goes through with this price, p_2, increasing over time. Then Norway enjoys a terms-of-trade windfall at each date. In this case less current income needs to be invested in order to sustain constant consumption.
10. Our decline in capital value is in principle the same as the one taken up in Samuelson (1937, 1964).
11. Since there is perfect foresight and certainty, consumption expenditure can be separated from current income via lending and borrowing, a result referred to as the Irving Fisher Separation Theorem. Under uncertainty or market distortions, this separation phenomenon would not go through.
12. The above constant consumption result goes through when either p_2 is increasing and/or the world price of oil is changing.

REFERENCES

Aronsson, T., P.-O. Johansson and K.-G. Löfgren (1997), *Welfare Measurement, Sustainability and Green National Accounting*, Cheltenham: Edward Elgar.

Asea, P.K. and W.M. Corden (1994), 'The Balassa–Samuelson model: an overview', *Review of International Economics*, **2** (3), October, 191–200.

Asheim, G.B. (1986), 'Hartwick's Rule in open economies', *Canadian Journal of Economics*, **19**, 395–402.

Corden, W.M. (1984), 'Booming sector and Dutch disease economics: survey and consolidation', *Oxford Economic Papers*, **36**, 359–80.

Corden, W.M. and J.P. Neary (1982), 'Booming sector and de-industrialization in a small open economy', *Economic Journal*, **92**, 825–48.

Hartwick, J.M. (1995), 'Constant consumption paths in open economies with exhaustible resources', *Review of International Economics*, **3** (3), October, 275–83.

Organization for Economic Cooperation and Development (OECD) (1997), *OECD Economic Surveys, Norway 1997*, Paris: OECD.

Samuelson, Paul A. (1937), 'Some aspects of the pure theory of capital', *Quarterly Journal of Economics*, May, 469–96.

Samuelson, Paul A. (1964), 'Tax deductibility of economic depreciation to insure invariant valuations', *Journal of Political Economy*, **72**, 604–6.

Sefton, J.A. and M.R. Weale (1996), 'The net national product and exhaustible resources: the effects of foreign trade', *Journal of Public Economics*, **61**, 21–47.

Vincent, J., T. Panayotou and J. Hartwick (1997), 'Resource depletion and sustainability in small open economies', *Journal of Environmental Economics and Management*, **33**, 274–86.

8. Labor, leisure and human capital

8.1 INTRODUCTION

A person, as worker, shows up in the national accounts as a *flow* of labor services into marketed production and as a flow of wage income in marketed national income. Labor services such as the services of home-makers do not appear. And leisure time, equal in value at the margin to labor time, does not appear in the accounts. These are two large omissions from the accounts and current practice presumably proceeds the way it does because these items, currently omitted, are difficult to estimate accurately. We comment on these two omissions below.

We then take up labor services as flowing from an explicit stock of human capital. 'Between periods' there is a flow of labor services, and 'across periods' there is a change in the stock of human capital. The stock of human capital has a quantity dimension (number of workers of a particular skill type) and a quality dimension (two workers can differ in skill by age and training). In our first model there is a produced stock of knowledge which gets attached or embodied in workers. In the next model the death of a worker, demographic change, shows up as depreciation of human capital. The skill level of each worker is unchanging. This is a simplification and we still obtain a sharp representation of the economic depreciation of human capital. In the next chapter (Technical change) we consider changes in human capital as training or education level changes. Current practice in national accounting considers labor services alone or divorced from a corresponding stock of human capital. Thus there is no depreciation of human capital in 'national income'. This is clear in our two input demographic model with K-capital and human capital, H. Births augment the stock of H and deaths diminish it.

In both of our models below, with labor represented as human capital, we end up with no wage income in the national accounts, only returns to human capital. In fact in each model our dollar-valued NNP can be viewed as market interest rate r_t multiplied by the market value of the capital goods in the economy. This means that we can label dollar-valued NNP as the stationary equivalent of current national wealth. From Weitzman (1976) we know that such representations suggest that NNP is a good measure of 'sustainable income'. So we achieve a Weitzman representation of NNP as sustainable income, but here dollar-valued NNP, not util-valued NNP. We have a solution to the problem of 'generalizing' Weitzman (1976) to a dollar-valued representation of the economy, rather than the familiar util-valued representation.

8.2   LEISURE IN THE NATIONAL ACCOUNTS

More leisure is, along with a longer average lifespan, one of the most conspicuous contributions to welfare of modern economic development. Leisure fits naturally into national product in a basic national accounts but is not in practice incorporated as part of product in the accounts. This is not a big problem if year-to-year changes in product are of interest, because leisure time has been holding steady of late. However, in measuring long-term growth in welfare, one should have included leisure in product in the two years being compared because, as we noted, leisure time has increased considerably since, say, 1900 in modern industrial societies.

In Chapter 6, we set out a model economy in which leisure time played a central role. The accounts are in Table 6.1 of Chapter 6 and leisure is accounted for in a transparent way. NNP includes the market value of leisure 'produced' over the accounting period and net national income includes the wage cost of 'producing' the leisure.[1]

We repeat: (a) leisure is not part of the current national accounts and (b) leisure fits very naturally in the natural accounts. Clearly leisure is left out in practice because it is tricky to estimate or observe. Non-laboring time can be devoted to training or may reflect unemployment 'activity'. A simple and still valuable measure of leisure would be holidays taken. This could be estimated with some confidence. European workers receive more annual leave than do their North American counterparts. Holiday or vacation time would still be convolved with unemployment time and the latter would have to be distinguished from the former.

And how should labor done in the home be dealt with? If a man marries his housekeeper, her dollar income disappears from the labor income in the economy. The man's expenditure bundle gets reallocated from consumption of domestic service in final demand to other forms of consumption and investment. Her former income disappears, as does the implicit value of her labor in household activity (child care, meal preparation, house maintenance and so on). The category of domestic service production, for this household, disappears. The housekeeper's expenditure on consumption and investment disappears from final demand (the households column) and her presence as labor income (in the households row) disappears. National product and income, in the national accounts, shrink by the same amount when the man marries his housekeeper. Actual 'product' is presumably unchanged by the marriage since, presumably, the ex-housekeeper does the same work around the home in her new role as wife.

There is then an obvious case for imputing for labor services done in the home in the national accounts. But this imputation has not been done, again because seemingly too much guesswork is involved or it would be too costly to do accurately.

8.3   KNOWLEDGE EMBODIED IN WORKERS

In this classic formulation of endogenous growth, some workers produce goods, $C + \dot{K}$, and some produce new knowledge, $\dot{A}(t)$. The knowledge gets embodied in each worker at zero cost, so that the effective labor supplied by $\hat{N}$ workers at time t is $A(t)\hat{N}$. Workers are then passive vessels for receiving new knowledge and, in our accounts, labor's value is *completely* captured by the value of the knowledge stock. The valuation of labor involves tracking the value of $A(t)$, not the number of workers. There is no wage bill anywhere in the accounts. It is as if the owners of $A(t)$ also *own* the workers and allocate them in order to maximize the return to owning $A(t)$. Workers get valued purely as providers of A-capital services, not as providers of labor services. Workers are instruments for owners of $A(t)$ to get their $A(t)$ into rental-earning situations.

Formally, we have new knowledge produced in

$$\dot{A}(t) = aA(N - N_1) \tag{8.1}$$

where N_1 are knowledge production workers, N is the economy's fixed endowment of workers, and a is a positive parameter. Goods are produced under constant returns to scale in

$$C(t) + \dot{K}(t) = F[K(t), A(t)N_1(t)] \tag{8.2}$$

where $C(t)$ are consumption goods and $\dot{K}(t)$ are investment goods. $K(t)$ is the current stock of K-capital yielding a service flow in production proportional to stock size, $K(t)$.

Planning or competition maximizes

$$\int_0^\infty U[C(t)]e^{-\rho t}dt$$

subject to (8.1), (8.2) and $A(0) = A_0$ and $K(0) = K_0$. ρ is the social discount rate. The current-value Hamiltonian for this optimization problem is

$$H = U(C) + \lambda(t)[F(K, AN_1) - C] + \mu(t)aA(N - N_1)$$

where λ and μ are util shadow prices (co-state variables) on K and A, respectively. The necessary conditions are

$$\frac{\partial H}{\partial C} = 0 \text{ or } U_C = \lambda \tag{8.3}$$

$$\frac{\partial H}{\partial N_1} = 0 \text{ or } \lambda F_Z = \mu a \tag{8.4}$$

where $Z = AN_1$

$$-\frac{\partial H}{\partial K} = \dot{\lambda} - \rho\lambda \text{ or } \rho - \frac{\dot{\lambda}}{\lambda} = F_K (= r_t) \tag{8.5}$$

$$-\frac{\partial H}{\partial A} = \dot{\mu} - \rho\mu \text{ or } F_Z N_1 + a(N - N_1)\mu/\lambda + (\frac{\dot{\mu}}{\mu} - \rho)\,\mu/\lambda = 0. \tag{8.6}$$

We multiply $(8.6)^2$ by A and represent $(\rho - \dot{\mu}/\mu)$ by r_t^A. (8.6) becomes

$$AN_1 F_Z + \frac{\dot{A}/\mu}{\lambda} = \frac{\mu A r_t^A}{\lambda} \tag{8.7}$$

which is the third row–column pair in Table 8.1. We make use of constant returns to scale in $F(\cdot)$ to obtain the row–column pair, goods, in Table 8.1.

The households column is the dollar-valued, linearized current-value Hamiltonian and can be viewed as NNP. $\dot{A}\mu/\lambda$ is the economic 'depreciation'

Table 8.1 National accounting matrix (knowledge embodied in labor)

Expenditures ↓ Receipts →	Goods	K-stock	A-stock	Households
Goods				$C + \dot{K}$
K-stock	KF_K			
A-stock	$AN_1 F_Z$			$\dot{A}\mu/\lambda$
Households		Kr_t	$\mu A r_t^A/\lambda$	

of A.[3] The households row comprises two dollar-valued stocks, each multiplied by an own interest rate. In balanced growth, essentially an asymptotic state,[4] r_t and r_t^A will be the same and then NNP would be interest on dollar value, $K + A\mu/\lambda$. Away from balanced growth, $r_t - r_t^A = \dot{\mu}/\mu - \dot{\lambda}/\lambda = \mu/\lambda d$ $(\mu/\lambda)/dt$, which reflects the changing asset prices ocurring because the ratio of K to A is changing. One could consider adding and subtracting $r_t\mu A/\lambda$ to the A-stock row–column pair to make NNI, $(K + \mu A/\lambda)\ r_t$ and NNP, $C + \dot{K} + d$ $(\mu A/\lambda)/dt$. Then NNP would be interest on wealth at all times. The cost of this approach is that asset price changes become part of NNP, a departure from current methodology.

8.4   DEMOGRAPHY AND DEPRECIATION

The notion of labor services entering the production function independently of the people in the economy is a poor formulation. It makes more sense to view labor services provided as a linear function of the population *per se* as we do with K-capital. That is, we have $C + \dot{K} = F(K, H) - \delta K$ where H is the stock (number of workers or people) and the stock yields a flow of labor services per unit of time. K and H are viewed symmetrically. Then one postulates a demographic process such as

$$\dot{H} = \theta(C/H) - \gamma H \tag{8.8}$$

where γ is the exogenous withdrawal (death) rate and $\theta(\cdot)$ is the births of new laboring people, as a function of per capita consumption. We assume $\theta(0) = 0$, and that $\theta(\cdot)$ is increasing and concave in per capita consumption. And

$$\dot{K} = F(K, H) - C - \delta K \tag{8.9}$$

where δ is the constant rate of decay of K-capital, C is aggregate consumption and production function $F(\cdot)$ exhibits constant returns to scale.

We assume that 'the market' or a planner acts to maximize

$$\int_0^\infty U(C)e^{-\rho t}dt$$

subject to (8.8), (8.9) and $K(0) = K_0$ and $H = H_0$. ρ is the constant rate of discount of utility. It makes sense to think of 'adjustment' being from small initial values of K and H to the larger steady-state values. The current-value Hamiltonian for our maximization problem is

$$H^C = U(C) + \lambda(t)[F(K, H) - C - \delta K] + \mu(t)\left[\theta\left(\frac{C}{H}\right) - \gamma H\right].$$

Necessary conditions are

$$\frac{\partial H^C}{\partial C} = 0, \text{ or } U_C = \lambda - \mu\theta'(\cdot)/H \tag{8.10}$$

$$-\frac{\partial H^C}{\partial K} = \dot{\lambda} - \rho\lambda, \text{ or } \rho - \frac{\dot{\lambda}}{\lambda} = F_K - \delta \tag{8.11}$$

and we express $\rho - \dot{\lambda}/\lambda$ as r_t,

$$-\frac{\partial H^C}{\partial H} = \dot{\mu} - \rho\mu, \text{ or } -\lambda F_H - \mu\theta'(\cdot)\frac{C}{H^2} + \mu\gamma = \dot{\mu} - \pi\mu \tag{8.12}$$

and

$$\lim_{t \to \infty} \lambda(t)K(t)e^{-\rho t} = 0,$$

$$\lim_{t \to \infty} \mu(t)H(t)e^{-\rho t} = 0.$$

We multiply (8.11) by K/λ to create the second row–column pair in Table 8.2. We set $\rho - \dot{\mu}/\mu = r_t^H$, an own interest rate. We multiply (8.12) by H/λ to create the third row–column pair in Table 8.2. The first row–column pair is the current revenue equals input costs for goods producers.

We clarify the households column by adding and subtracting $\mu\theta(\cdot)/\lambda$. Then the households column becomes

$$C + \dot{K} + \dot{H}\mu/\lambda - (\theta - \theta'C/H)\mu/\lambda$$

Table 8.2   National accounting matrix (endogenous population growth)

Expenditures ↓ Receipts →	Goods	K-capital	H-capital	Households
Goods				$C + \dot{K} + \delta K$
K-capital	KF_K			$-\delta K$
H-capital	HF_H			$-\mu\gamma H/\lambda + \mu C\theta'/(H\lambda)$
Households		Kr_t	$Hr_t^H\mu/\lambda$	

The last term is an income adjustment arising because $\theta(\cdot)$ is not linear in C/H. This term belongs in national income. When moved, we are left with

$$C + \dot{K} + \dot{H}\mu/\lambda$$

as NNP (the dollar-valued, linearized current-value Hamiltonian). And NNI becomes (from the households row)

$$Kr_t + Hr_t^H\mu/\lambda + (\theta - \theta'C/H)\mu/\lambda,$$

a familiar entity. The stock of workers, H, enters income as interest on capital value, $H\mu/\lambda$, where the interest rate is its 'own rate'. Human capital has a 'depreciation' term in NNP, corresponding to the value of the net change in the stock.[5]

The above model is a type of von Neumann (1945) model because it achieves, with an appropriate $U(C)$ function, a balanced stationary state in terms of capital goods K and H. Von Neumann formulated a model of an economy in terms of capital goods alone, in which equilibrium was a proportional growth across periods of the capital stocks. He abstracted from the details of human capital 'spawning' more human capital and of flow product being divided into new K-capital and current consumption. Our model could be turned into a balanced growth model if δ, the decay factor on K-capital, were set at zero.

8.5   CONCLUDING REMARKS

First, we considered the matter of leisure and the services of 'home-makers' in the national accounts. Currently these are major items, purposefully neglected. The grounds for leaving these items out turn on practicality, not logical coherence. If good-quality data could be amassed at a reasonable cost, these items should be placed into the national accounts. It was in Chapter 6 that we considered the matter of leisure in detail.

We broke new ground when we considered the accumulation of embodied skill or knowledge in workers because we ended up with a clear statement of NNP being interest on the dollar value of wealth. We solved the problem of arriving at the dollar measure of NNP being sustainable 'income' in place of the util measure of NNP as in Weitzman (1976). It turned out that knowledge capital made labor flow income redundant and net national income had no wage term in it, only interest income on the knowledge stock.

Similar results emerged when we considered demography in our final model. Dollar-valued NNP was again interest on the value of dollar wealth in the economy. We constructed our model to have labor services in product flow directly from the stock of workers. That is, our model was constructed from inputs that were purely capital, not flows *ab initio*. We observed, then, that by breaking away from the approach which treats labor services in production directly as flows, separate from stocks of workers, we could achieve the classic result of dollar-valued NNP being interest on the dollar value of wealth.

NOTES

1. Dasgupta et al. (1995) correctly point out that 'labor income should not be included in the national product measure' (p. 121) and proceed to treat this matter formally, along with human capital (pp. 145–6) but fail to remark that leisure time should be in the 'product measure'.
2. Equation (8.6) reduces to $\rho - aN = \mu/\mu$ when (8.4) is used. In *growth*, U_C should decline and hence $\mu(t)$ should decline. Hence $aN - \rho$ must be postive.
3. To obtain estimates of the marginal value of better education, one needs to have agents dividing their time between work, learning and leisure. See, for example, Razin (1972a, 1972b) and Aronsson et al. (1997, Chapter 5). The latter direct attention to the depreciation of human capital. Our economic depreciation term would be relevant to their analysis of 'the utility value of additional human capital' (pp. 80–81).
4. One needs $U(C) = C^{1-\sigma}/(1 - \sigma)$ for $\sigma > 0$ for such balanced growth to be achievable.
5. Usher (1980, pp. 109–10) considers depreciation of human capital in a growth-accounting exercise. He considers education as being capital-augmenting and considers death, rather indirectly, as capital-depleting. Family size is a crucial dimension of depreciation in Usher's formulation.

REFERENCES

Aronsson, T., P.-O. Johansson and K.-G. Löfgren (1997), *Welfare Measurement, Sustainability and Green National Accounting*, Cheltenham: Edward Elgar.
Dasgupta, P., B. Kristrom and K.-G. Maler (1995), 'Current issues in resource accounting', in P.-O. Johansson, B. Kristrom and K.-G. Maler (eds), *Current Issues in Environmental Economics*, Manchester: Manchester University Press, pp. 117–52.
Razin, A. (1972a), 'Optimum investment in human capital', *Review of Economic Studies*, **39**, 455–60.
Razin, A. (1972b), 'Investment in human capital and economic growth', *Metroeconomica*, **24**, 101–16.
Usher, Dan (1980), *The Measurement of Economic Growth*, Oxford: Blackwell.
von Neumann, John (1945), 'A model of general equilibrium', *Review of Economic Studies*, **13**, 1–9, translated from a 1938 German publication by G. Morgenstern.
Weitzman, M.L. (1976), 'On the welfare significance of national product in a dynamic economy', *Quarterly Journal of Economics*, **90**, 156–62.

9. Technical change

9.1 INTRODUCTION

The development of modern national accounting methodology coincided with the 'entrenchment' of a Keynesian macroeconomic model. If management of aggregate demand by government agents, acting in the interests of members of the nation, was the desideratum, then good quality data were seen to be necessary. Hence the coincidence of the arrival of the view of managing aggregate demand and the modern national accounts. Somewhat separately, observers had long been interested in representing their view of an economy with data. The physiocrats are a good example. There is presumably the view that if my empirical representation is clear, I shall win adherents to my view of how the economy works. Of course if one knows 'how the economy works', one should be able to predict where it is going or what is the mechanism of growth and development. The three ingredients of growth and development have long been acknowledged to be capital accumulation, the improvement in techniques, and institutional change. The way these ingredients interact to yield rapid and sustained economic growth and development has never been agreed upon by all observers. Hence the need for a detailed portrait of an economy – a data-based portrait. The correct data-based portrait would seemingly make clear details of the mechanisms of economic growth and development.

The fact is that the modern national accounts themselves provide few hints as to underlying mechanisms of growth and development. The search for sources of growth involves linking together data from a sequence of national accounts. An extremely careful study of a national accounts for a particular year reveals very little about growth and technical progress. This becomes clear in our analysis in Tables 9.1 and 9.2. Data in modern national accounts are observations in need of analysis, if the nature of capital accumulation and technical progress is what is being investigated. In fact we end up saying that if technical progress is of type x, the national accounts will assume a particular character reflecting the prior assumption that technical progress is of type x. If the national accounts data could be collected in some 'neutral' fashion, statistical inference should be able to discern the nature of the underlying process of technical change. But data collection can never be neutral. What is selected for collection and how the data are assembled and aggregated reflect a prior model of the underlying economy. We avoid the inference problem by focusing on a national accounts, given the process of technical change specified *a priori*.

An apparent virtue of Solow's (1957) classic measurement of technical progress in manufacturing in the United States was its parsimony in assumptions about the microeconomics of technical change.[1] He seemed to be getting estimates which were meaningful, independently of the nitty-gritty of the processes at the level of plants and firms. It was illusory, as many observers realized, to think that the data were speaking for themselves. And, not surprisingly, his work provoked a torrent of research which could be described, roughly speaking, as linking estimates of technical progress in aggregate data to processes of technical change at the plant and firm level. The researcher is interested in the mechanism, at the micro-level, generating the technical progress and in how the technical progress is 'capitalized' in (a) lower prices of outputs, (b) higher profits for 'higher-tech' firms and (c) higher wages for workers in sectors experiencing rapid technical progress. The volume of research in this area remains large and we get a glimpse of a bit of it when we report on the Romer (1990) analysis below.

Romer's model has skilled workers 'capitalizing' new knowledge in wage increments and this process is external to the complete funding of new knowledge production by durable input producers. Hence, as with many models, workers benefit greatly from R&D and it remains difficult to design a mechanism to get funds flowing from these beneficiaries back to the producers of new knowledge. Hence a role for the publicization of the production of new knowledge or, at a minimum, a need for a tax on beneficiaries, with the revenue being directed to the producers of new knowledge. And in modern industrial economies, much new knowledge production is heavily subsidized by the government but the corresponding revenue stream is not linked directly to individuals who benefit most from the new knowledge. The subsidies are funded from general government revenue.

Romer (1990) has households lend to his durable input producers in order that the latter can acquire the new designs from the R&D sector. This means that, indirectly, household savings are fully supporting the current R&D activity. It is unusual for new knowledge producers to be able to get funding, certainly directly, from arm's-length borrowers. R&D activity is intrinsically a risky investment and there is the added moral hazard problem in that well-funded, highly skilled R&D workers may not exert 'optimal' effort. An alternative source for funding current R&D activity is license fees, based on past successful inventions. In this scenario, the R&D sector itself becomes the lender to 'purchasers' of new knowledge, and certain incentive problems are eliminated.

The endogenous growth model with only labor-augmenting technical change was reported on in Chapter 8. The funding of R&D was solved in this case by the owners of knowledge capital claiming all of wage income as their rightful return to capital! Wages are bound up in rentals deriving from the current knowledge stock. Formally there is no residual wage income for the workers. To make this model reflect the real world, in some sense, workers would have to be the owners of the knowledge stock. A worker and his/her human capital would be tied in a unit. Even then workers would have to work out a mechanism for clearing off part of their current wage income (return to knowledge capital) in order to support the current production of new knowledge.

We consider two types of exogenous technical change and then turn to Romer's (1990) framework of endogenous technical change. We set out the accounts for this model and turn to a simpler version, without labor productivity growth and monopolistic competition.

9.2 LABOR-AUGMENTING EXOGENOUS TECHNICAL PROGRESS

We suppose that stock $\dot{A}(t)$ emerges spontaneously, requiring no inputs. $\dot{A}(t) = \gamma A(t)$ for $\gamma > 0$. We can identify stock $A(t)$ with efficiency improvement in labor, N, in the production relation

$$\dot{K}(t) = F[K(t), A(t)N] - C \qquad (9.1)$$

N is the constant labor force, $K(t)$ is machine capital, $C(t)$ is aggregate consumption and production function $F(\cdot,\cdot)$ exhibits constant returns to scale and smooth substitution between inputs. We have the planning problem, maximize

$$\int_0^\infty U[C(t)] \exp(-\rho t)dt$$

subject to (9.1), $K(0) = K_0$, and $A(0) = A_0$ and $\dot{A} = \gamma \dot{A}$. $U(C)$ is a concave utility function with $U(0) = 0$ and satisfying Inada regularity conditions for C near zero. The current-value Hamiltonian for our planning problem is

$$H(t) = U(C) + \lambda(t)\{F[K(t), A(t)N] - C\} + \mu(t)\gamma A(t)$$

where $\lambda(t)$ and $\mu(t)$ are co-state variables corresponding to state variables $K(t)$ and $A(t)$. Necessary conditions are

$$\frac{\partial H}{\partial C} = 0 \text{ or } U_C(t) = \lambda(t), \qquad (9.2)$$

$$-\frac{\partial H}{\partial K} = \dot{\lambda} - \rho\lambda \text{ or } \rho - \frac{\dot{\lambda}}{\lambda} = F_K(t), \tag{9.3}$$

$$-\frac{\partial H}{\partial A} = \dot{\mu} = \rho\mu \text{ or } \rho - \frac{\dot{\mu}}{\mu} = \lambda NF_Z(t)/\mu + \gamma \tag{9.4}$$

and

$$\lim_{t\to\infty} \lambda(t)\, K(t) \exp(-\rho t) = 0,$$

$$\lim_{t\to\infty} \mu(t)\, A(t) \exp(-\rho t) = 0.$$

The interest rate is $r_t = \rho - \dot{U}_C/U_C$. Euler's Theorem allows us to write

$$C(t) + \dot{K}(t) = K(t)F_K(t) + A(t)NF_Z(t)$$

for $Z \equiv AN$. This equality becomes the first row–column pair in our national accounting matrix in Table 9.1. The second row–column pair is $KF_K = K_r$ and the third row–column pair is equation (9.4), rearranged.

Row sums equal column sums by construction in Table 9.1. So-called 'receipts' are associated with the row entries and so-called 'expenditures' with column entries. Since we have inputted the first three row sums and column sums correctly, the households column must equal the households row. We identify the latter with national income or payments to primary factors and the former with national product or the value of expenditures.

The column entries are the dollar-valued linearized current-value Hamiltonian and have an accepted interpretation as dollar-valued NNP. $\dot{A}\mu/\lambda$ is the value of current 'investment' in stock $A(t)$.

Table 9.1   National accounting matrix (labor-augmenting, exogenous technical progress)

Expenditures ↓ Receipts →	'Goods' production	K-capital	Labor	Households
'Goods' production				$C + \dot{K}$
K-capital	KF_K			
Labor	ANF_Z			$\dot{A}\mu/\lambda$
Households		$r_t K$	$(\rho - \dot{\mu}/\mu)A\mu/\lambda$	

Value-added or net national income (NNI), the households row, represents a problem because ρ and $\dot{\mu}$ are unobservable. $(\rho - \dot{\mu}/\mu)\ (\equiv r_t^A)$ is the own rate of interest on the A asset. An accountant would end up inputting for $(\rho - \dot{\mu}/\mu)$ $A\mu/\lambda$. This is not the desired procedure. (In fact, $\dot{A}$ exogenous technical progress, would also have to be estimated since it would not be observed. $\dot{A}$ would be a residual component of national product.) We turn to replacing $(\rho - \dot{\mu}/\mu)\ A\mu/\lambda$ with observables. For dollar stock value $V_t = A(t)\mu(t)/\lambda(t)$ we have

$$\frac{dV_t}{dt} = \left(\frac{\dot{\mu}}{\mu} - \frac{\dot{\lambda}}{\lambda} + \frac{\dot{A}}{A}\right)\frac{\mu A}{\lambda}$$

$$= \left(\frac{\dot{\mu}}{\mu} - \rho\right)\frac{\mu A}{\lambda} + r_t V_t - \frac{\dot{A}\mu}{A}. \tag{9.5}$$

Equation (9.5) provides us with an expression for $(\dot{\mu}/\mu - \rho)\ \mu A/\lambda$ in NNI. Equation (9.5) is an instance of the Irving Fisher relation $dV_t/dt = R_t V_t - yt$ where y_t is the current flow income from the asset with market value, V_t. One checks this by noting in Table 9.1 that $(\dot{\mu}/\mu - \rho)\ \mu A/\lambda - \dot{A}\mu/\lambda$ equals ANF_Z, this latter being current income from asset $A(t)$. We replace $V_t r_t^A$ in the households row with $V_t r_t$ and $\dot{A}\mu/\lambda$ in the households column becomes $\dot{A}\mu/\lambda + (r_t - r_t^A)V_t$. We end up with the new expression

$$K(t)r_t + V_t r_t$$

for NNI, and

$$NNP^R = C(t) + \dot{K}(t) + dV_t/dt$$

$$= NNP^H + A(t)d(\mu/\lambda)/dt$$

for net national product. Capital gains term, $A(t)d(\mu/\lambda)/dt\ [\equiv (r_t - r_t^A)V_t]$ is the orphan here. If one sticks with NNPH for net national product, the capital gains term becomes a negative entry in net national income and if one espouses NNP^R for net national product, the capital gains term becomes a positive entry in net national product. NNP^H is the linear approximation to the current-value Hamiltonian. The capital gains term is zero when the ratio, K/A, is unchanging and thus a non-zero capital gains term is reflecting a changing stock ratio along the path which the economy is moving. In balanced growth,[2] K/A is constant and the capital gains term is zero and $NNP^R = NNP^H$, with NNI the same for the two versions of NNP.

Labor needs a mechanism to capture the productivity increments in the wage. It is by no means automatic that a productivity improvement in labor will show up in wage increments, although our national accounts portrait of the economy implies that this is so. The measurement of technical progress starts with the larger increase in 'output' compared with the physical increase in an input or index number representing a group of inputs, between two dates. Here one is confronted with problems in defining 'output', usually a basket of commodities, and with the increase in the 'input', which should be considered with other inputs held constant, a huge task of normalization. The applause goes to those who carry out the measurement in a believable way. A very crude measure of productivity increase is yielded when one divides the dollar increase in output, inflation adjusted, by the increase in person-hours paid for in the economy. This measure of 'productivity increase' has been appealed to over many decades. The obvious problem is that one cannot tell how much of the measured 'productivity increase' is a result of (a) an improvement in labor efficiency, (b) an increase in K-capital, unimproved, and/or (c) an increase in the efficiency of K-capital. The sophisticated alternative is a measure of 'total factor productivity', the ratio of the increase in 'output' to the composite comprising weighted increases in inputs. The increases themselves are measured in physical, not dollar, values.

One source of exogenous technical change might be 'learning by doing'. A worker can become better at his/her job by spending time working at it. In this case output-productive activity is mixed with learning or the improvement in the productive quality of the input. Arrow (1962) formalized this view in a growth model and extensions were developed by Levhari (1966). Productivity-enhancing experience (efficiency) was made a function of cumulative past investment in machines. For the Cobb–Douglas case, one has current output with vintage v of capital in

$$Q_{v,t} = \xi(G_v{}^n N_{v,t})^\alpha I_v{}^{1-\alpha}$$

where I_v is current investment and G_v is cumulative past investment. $N_{v,t}$ are workers. n and α are positive parameters. Given the marginal productivity of labor the same over all vintages, one can aggregate over vintages to get

$$Q_t = \left(\frac{1-\alpha}{\alpha_n + 1 - \alpha}\right)^{1-\alpha} \xi G_t{}^{\alpha n + 1 - \alpha} N_t{}^\alpha$$

where N_t is the current supply of labor. Under the hypotheses of the labor supply growing at a constant rate and the savings rate constant, a balanced growth path can be obtained, with

$$Q_t = gG_t/[(1-n)s]$$

where g is the growth rate in Q_t and s is the savings rate.

9.3 EXOGENOUS TECHNICAL PROGRESS

We first consider the case of technical index s shifting the production function $F(K, N, s)$ where

$$C + \dot{K} = F(K, N, s)$$

and $ds/dt = 1$ and $F(\cdot)$ exhibit constant returns to scale, so that $C + \dot{K} = KF_K + NF_N + sF_s$. In this formulation sF_s is a residual income flow accruing to households as 'profit'. (This is very similar to the 'producer surplus' which households receive when there are not constant returns to scale in production.) We shall introduce a util-valued shadow price on stock s since s could be viewed as knowledge increasing exogenously as time passes.

We assume that the market or a planner maximizes

$$\int_0^\infty U[C(t)]e^{-\rho t}dt$$

subject to $\dot{K} = F(K, N, s) - C$ and $K(0) = K_0$, where ρ is the discount rate and $U(\cdot)$ is a concave utility function with $U(0) = 0$ and $U_C(0) = \infty$. N, the labor force, is treated as constant. The current-value Hamiltonian for this problem is

$$H(t) = U(C) + \lambda(t)[F(K, N, s) - C] + \mu(t)$$

where λ is the co-state variable corresponding to state $K(t)$ and μ is the co-state variable corresponding to state $s(t)$. The necessary conditions are

$$\frac{\partial H}{\partial C} = 0 \text{ or } U_C = \lambda$$

$$-\frac{\partial H}{\partial K} = \dot{\lambda} - \rho\lambda \text{ or } \rho - \frac{\dot{\lambda}}{\lambda} = F_K$$

$$-\frac{\partial H}{\partial s} = \dot{\mu} - \rho\mu \text{ or } \rho - \frac{\dot{\mu}}{\mu} = \lambda F_s/\mu$$

and

$$\lim_{t \to \infty} e^{-\rho t}\lambda(t)K(t) = 0,$$

$$\lim_{t \to \infty} e^{-\rho t}\mu(t)s(t) = 0.$$

This turns out to be a subtle model because although $s(t)$ moves autonomously, the level of $s(t)$ affects λ and thus the rate of interest $r_t (= \rho -$

$\dot{U}_C/U_C$) and the rate of accumulation of $K(t)$ and thus the current level of $C(t)$. In other words, though s moves exogenously, its value feeds back on the evolution of all variables in the economy.

We define $\rho - \dot{\mu}/\mu$ as r_t^S. Thus $sF_s = sr_t^S\mu/\lambda$. This becomes the fourth row–column pair in Table 9.2. The accounts are laid out in Table 9.2.

The novelty is that there is residual income attributable to technical progress in the households row. It is standard for such a model to consider

$$\frac{\dot{Q}}{Q} = \left(\frac{NF_N}{Q}\right)\frac{\dot{N}}{N} + \left(\frac{KF_K}{Q}\right)\frac{\dot{K}}{K} + \text{residual}$$

where $Q = F(K, N, s)$ and here residual is $sF_s/Q \cdot \dot{s}/s = F_s/Q$. The residual is essentially the share of technical progress in current product. Solow (1957) estimated F_s/Q to be about 2 percent for the manufacturing sector in the United States over about three decades. Critics have argued that the residual in fact has a value of approximately zero when careful attention is paid to the scope and magnitude of observable inputs. This latter view implies that technical progress is endogenous or generated within the economy, rather than being exogenous. Observe that if F_s/Q is positive and approximately constant, then, under constant returns to scale, the share sF_s/Q must always increase and come to 'claim' most of the income accruing to inputs. Since this has not been observed, one must abandon constant returns to scale in $F(\cdot)$ if one wishes to claim that F_s/Q is positive and approximately constant. A natural candidate production function is $Q = Ae^{gt}\psi(K, N)$, where g is the constant rate of exogenous technical change and A is a positive parameter. This leads to the equation

Table 9.2   National accounting matrix (exogenous technical progress)

Expenditures ↓ Receipts →	'Goods'	Labor	K-capital	S-capital	Households
'Goods'					$C + \dot{K}$
Labor	NF_N				
K-capital	KF_K				
S-capital	sF_s				
Households		NF_N	Kr_t	$\mu sr_t^S/\lambda$	

$$\frac{\dot{Q}}{Q} = \frac{N\psi_N}{\psi}\frac{\dot{N}}{N} + \frac{K\psi_K}{\psi}\frac{\dot{K}}{K} + g$$

Hence ψ_N and ψ_K are proportional to the wage and 'productivity' of K-capital, respectively, under constant returns to scale in $\psi(\cdot)$.

Kemp and Long (1982) and Weitzman (1997) observed that since exogenous technical change is a non-autonomous element in the economy's evolution, one has the relation

$$H(t) + \int_t^\infty e^{-\rho(z-t)}\lambda(z)F_s(z)dz = \rho V(t)$$

where $H(t)$ is the current-value Hamiltonian and $V(t)$ is the optimal value of the program beyond t. (See Aronsson et al., 1997, pp. 49–54.) Since the integral is positive, we have the result that the current-value Hamiltonian is an underestimate of $\rho V(t)$, society's 'sustainable income'. Weitzman (1997) estimates $\int_t^\infty(\cdot)dz/H(t)$ to be about 0.5. Hence the current-value Hamiltonian is a large underestimate of 'sustainable income'. To arrive at this result, Weitzman relies on a 2 percent estimate of exogenous technical progress, a 'fragile' assumption.

9.4   ENDOGENOUS LABOR PRODUCTIVITY GROWTH

This case was reported on in detail in the previous chapter. That report could be inserted here in order to round out our analysis of endogenous technical change in this chapter.

9.5   ENDOGENOUS GROWTH WITH DISTINCTIVE NEW MACHINES

The Romer (1990) model has new knowledge embodied in skilled workers, in the same way that we observed it above. But new knowledge also gets crystallized in a collection of new designs and at each date one new design is embodied in each new capital good. Current vintages of capital are identical but every vintage is distinct and *one vintage of capital good is an imperfect substitute for another in goods production.* Imperfect substitutability implies some market power and rental price gets marked up above the cost of durable capital K embodied in the produced input. The mark-up ends up financing the once-over cost of a new design embodied in each produced input.

We present a generic Romer model and consider two solutions. In the first, households lend to input producers in order that they can acquire the new designs embodied in their new inputs. In the second solution, R&D workers lend to the input producers for the acquisition of the new designs. The different institutional arrangements for funding R&D yield different balanced growth paths and growth rates as well as different national accounts.

The following three equations tell one much about the Romer model.

$$Y(t) = H_Y^\alpha A(t) x^{1-\alpha},$$

where $Y(t)$ is current produced output of final goods. These goods can be consumed, transformed into K-capital, and/or let out as loans, for use next 'period'. H_Y are skilled workers involved in the production of $Y(t)$. The economy has a fixed number H of such workers. The balance, H_A, work in the R&D sector.[3] Wages, $w(t)$, are equalized by 'migration' of workers between sector. $A(t)$ is the number of durable input firms that have received a new design, embodied in some K-capital, up to date t. At each date $\dot{A}(t)$ new designs are produced in the R&D sector and $\dot{A}(t)$ new durable input firms come into existence. x is the flow of services from a vintage of durable input firms, each vintage being distinct. The services of a firm of one vintage is an imperfect substitute for the services of a firm of another vintage. x gets defined in

$$x = K(t)/[\eta A(t)],$$

where $K(t)$ is the cumulative, perfectly durable K-capital at date t and η is a positive parameter. The production function for new designs is the right-hand side of

$$\dot{A}(t) = \delta A(t) H_A$$

where δ is a positive parameter. Note that $A(t)$ represents (a) the number of durable input firms which have bought a new design, up to date t, (b) the number of designs (inventions) that have been created and embodied in K-capital up to date t, and (c) the stock of knowledge at date t. The stock of knowledge is an efficiency index in labor services. This means that wages and labor productivity grow at rate $\dot{A}(t)/A(t)$.

A key mechanism in Romer (1990) is that each design-taker, a durable input firm, pays for its new design, costing P_A with discounted profits, π/r. r is the interest rate. It is endogenous. Profits arise because each firm can mark up its rental charge to goods producers as each firm has some market power since each vintage of durable input is an imperfect substitute for another vintage in goods production. The ith durable input commands rental

$$p(i) = (1 - \alpha) H_Y^\alpha x(i)^{-\alpha}$$

and

$$\pi = \max_{x(i)} p[x(i)]x(i) - r\eta x(i)$$

yielding

$$p(i) = r\eta/(1 - \alpha)$$

and $\pi = \alpha p(i)x(i)$. $(1 - \alpha)p(i)x(i)$ flows as rental from the durable input firms of type i to owners of 'machine' capital for the K-capital embodied in the $x(i)$ durable input suppliers. All the $x(i)$s are treated as of the same size across types or vintages. Hence we have a generic x and p for our model.

Given wages equal in the two sectors, we obtain

$$H_Y = r/(1 - \alpha)\delta.$$

Since $\dot{A}(t)/A(t) = \delta H_A \equiv g$, and $H = H_A + H_Y$, we obtain $g = \delta H - r/(1 - \alpha)$ or

$$r = (1 - \alpha)(\delta H - g).$$

If g were equal to r, then $\dot{K} = rK$ or all of K-stock rentals would be being plowed back into new K. Thus g equal to r provides a plausible ceiling on the growth rate. There is a utility function $u[C(t)]$ of the form $C^{1-\sigma}/(1 - \sigma)$ and a discount rate ρ. The market rate r, is defined by $\rho - \dot{U}_C/U_C$. That is

$$\rho + \frac{\sigma \dot{C}}{C} = r.$$

Macroeconomists often set σ at 3.5

We now take up Romer's solution of the model, with households funding the R&D sector via loans to new durable input firms, and the national accounts for his formulation. Households save, $S(t)$, and part, $\dot{A}(t)P_A$, is lent to the $\dot{A}(t)$ new durable input firms for new designs and the rest, $\dot{K}(t)$, is directly invested in new durable input firms. Current saving is, then, completely taken up financing the new durable input firms.

This model solves by setting $\dot{C}(t)/C(t)$, which via the utility function is equal to $r - \rho/\sigma$, equal to g. Then the rate of balanced growth for the system is

$$g = \frac{\delta h - \Lambda \rho}{\sigma \Lambda + 1}$$

for $\Lambda \equiv 1/(1 - \alpha)$. Note that $\sigma > 1$ is sufficient for this growth rate to be less than the ceiling rate above. It is also sufficient for the growth rate in utility, $(1 - \sigma)g$, to be less than ρ, the discount rate.

Goods output at date t equals the value of inputs in

$$Y(t) = w(t)H_Y + A(t)px$$

$$= w(t)H_Y + rK(t) + rP_A A(t)$$

because product exhaustion occurs at the endogenous prices. This can be checked by the reader. Total current product is $Y(t) + P_A \dot{A}$ equal to $w(t)H + rK(t) + rP_A A(t)$. Product is expended on $C(t) + \dot{K}(t) + L(t)$, where $L(t)$ are current loans equal to $P_A \dot{A}$. Net national product is this expenditure less the economic depreciation of the $K(t)$ and the $A(t)$. The national accounts for this model are set out in Table 9.3, where net national product is the households column. Its sum equals the households row sum. The row is net national income. The accounts here are quite uncomplicated.

One would like to have input levels multiplied by the appropriate value of marginal products in the first column in Table 9.3. Unfortunately such a representation is difficult to arrive at. Hence we make do with direct flow payments to inputs in column 1. The same is true for column 2. In a sense, households choose a level of saving in this model and then that level gets split between $\dot{K}(t)$ and $P_A \dot{A}(t)$ in order that $x (= \dot{A})$ new durable input firms are appropriately assembled. Workers produce new designs, $\dot{A}$, and 'goods' producers produce the $\dot{K}$ needed to embody the new designs. Since only balanced growth is being considered, the ratio of A to K is constant and there are no relative asset price changes (capital gains) to keep track of.

9.6 ROMER (1990) WITHOUT ENDOGENOUS LABOR PRODUCTIVITY GROWTH

The first-best version of Romer's model (see his Appendix) has new knowledge produced in $\dot{A}(t) = aAN^R$ and goods produced in

$$\dot{K}(t) + C(t) = \eta^{\alpha-1}A(t)^{\alpha}(N - N^R)^{\alpha}K(t)^{1-\alpha}.$$

Formally this model is the Cobb–Douglas version of the model of endogenous growth with labor-augmenting technical change set out in Chapter 8. Hence the first-best model is the same as the model analyzed there, except for the specialization of the production function to the Cobb–Douglas form. There is no mark-up by durable input providers to fund the R&D sector. A portion of the returns to knowledge capital (wage income) funds the R&D sector.

Table 9.3   National accounting matrix (Romer, 1990)

Expenditures ↓ Receipts →	Consumption goods	$\dot{K}$ goods	New designs	Labor	K	A	Households
Consumption goods							$C + \dot{K}$
$\dot{K}$ goods							
New designs							$\dot{A}P_A$
Labor	wH_Y		wH_A				
K	rK						
A	rAP_A						
Households				wH	rK	rAP_A	

9.7   ROMER (1990) VARIANTS

A central idea in Romer (1990) is the presence of high-tech durable inputs in the production of consumption and investment goods, with new investment goods going into durable input production. It is not difficult to construct a first-best economy with these high-tech inputs in 'goods' production. This model can be considered a platform on to which other elements can be added.

We have durable inputs produced in

$$D = f(K, N_1). \tag{9.6}$$

We have the stocks of new capital, stock K, in the high-tech intermediate goods sector, and of old capital, stock M, in 'goods' production. Old capital gets augmented by the trickle down δK and each period from the stock of new capital.[4]

$$\dot{M} = \delta K - \alpha M \tag{9.7}$$

where α is the current rate of 'decay' of old capital. New capital has its stock grow in

$$\dot{K} = R - \delta K \tag{9.8}$$

where R is current production of new capital in

$$R = F[M, f(K, N_1), N - N_1] - C. \tag{9.9}$$

The market acts to maximize $\int_0^\infty U(C)e^{-\rho t}dt$ subject to (9.7), (9.8), (9.9), and $M(0) = M_0$ and $K(0) = K_0$. Our Lagrangian is

$$L(t) = H(t) + \lambda(t)\{F[M, f(K, N_1), N - N_1] - C - R\} \tag{9.10}$$

where

$$H(t) = U(C) + \eta(R - \delta K) + \mu(\delta K - \alpha M).$$

The necessary conditions include

$$U_C = \lambda \tag{9.11}$$

$$\eta = \lambda$$

$$F_f f_{N_1} = F_Z \tag{9.12}$$

$$\rho - \frac{\dot{\eta}}{\eta} = F_f f_K \frac{\lambda}{\eta} + \delta \frac{\mu}{\eta} - \delta \tag{9.13}$$

$$\rho - \frac{\dot{\mu}}{\mu} = F_M \frac{\lambda}{\mu} - \alpha \tag{9.14}$$

where $Z = N - N_1$. The novel relation here is the equality in prices of new capital η and 'goods', λ. In view of this (9.13) and (9.14) can be written as

$$Kr_t = F_f f_K K + K\mu\delta/\lambda - K\delta \tag{9.15}$$

$$Mr_t^M \, \mu/\lambda = MF_M - \alpha M\mu/\lambda. \tag{9.16}$$

Equation (9.16) becomes the second row–column pair in Table 9.4 and (9.15) becomes the fifth row–column pair in Table 9.4. (9.12) becomes the fourth row–column pair.

Consider the households column. f gets consolidated and $R - \delta K = \dot{K}$ and $\delta K - \alpha M = \dot{M}$. Hence the households column reduces to

$$NNP = C + \dot{K} + \dot{M}\mu/\lambda.$$

This is the dollar-valued linearized current-value Lagrangian. And NNI is

$$Mr_t^M \, \mu/\lambda + NF_Z + r_t K,$$

a familiar collection of interest flows on capital and labor income or value. Since r_t^M is an own rate, an unobservable, we can express $Mr_t^M \, \mu/\lambda$ as

$$r_t M \, \mu/\lambda - (r_t - r_t^M)M\mu/\lambda$$

in NNI. The second term is capturing the percentage change in the price of M-capital relative to K-capital.

This variant of Romer (1990) is a first-best. There is not a monopolistically competitive high-tech sector. We have left the new knowledge sector out. It is straightforward to have knowledge capital A produced and attached to labor. Then we could achieve balanced growth with decay rate α set at zero and have a model very similar to Romer (1990).

Table 9.4 *National accounting matrix (high-tech intermediate goods)*

Expenditures ↓ / Receipts →	'Goods' production	M-capital	Intermediate goods	Labor	K-capital	Households
'Goods' production						$C + R$
M-capital	MF_M					$-\alpha M\mu/\lambda$
Intermediate goods	fF_f					$-fF_f$
Labor	$(N - N_1)F_Z$					$N_1 f_{N_1} F_f$
K-capital						$Kf_K F_f - K\delta + K\delta\mu/\lambda$
Households		$Mr_t^M \mu/\lambda$		NF_Z	$r_t K$	

9.8   CONCLUDING REMARKS

We considered two types of exogenous technical change and two model
economies with prominent endogenous technical change. The national
accounts were set out for three cases. Technical change, endogenous and
embodied in labor, was reported on in detail in Chapter 8. Technical change
shows up in the accounts in a somewhat indirect fashion. One would learn
relatively little about how an economy was being influenced by technical
change by scrutinizing its accounts at any particular date. One needs a series
of accounts as inputs for an analysis of technical change and then one needs a
model of how the data are generated before one can estimate the impact of
technical change on the performance of the economy. Solow's (1957) work
took data essentially from the national accounts and inserted them into a
model of the process of technical change and extracted estimates for his
model, estimates of 'total factor productivity' for the US manufacturing
sector. National accounts data provide a modest means toward measuring
technical change but they tend to represent the tip of an iceberg: the model
generating the data is under water and the details of its shape are very hard to
infer. We took up exogenous labor-saving technical change and Hicks-neutral
exogenous technical change. Delicate questions of input pricing emerge as
central concerns. Issues of income distribution are closely tied up with those
of technical change. Relative incomes reflect which owners of inputs can cap-
italize on the free flow of productivity improvement.

Our final accounting analysis dealt with Romer's (1990) model of new
designs, produced in the R&D sector, and embodied in new durable inputs for
final goods production. Investment in new designs, in the expansion of the
knowledge stock, was financed by the savings of households. Romer
exploited a monopolistic competition argument in order to get producers of
new durable inputs earning a surplus. The surplus flowed as interest income
to owners of the knowledge stock. We reformulated Romer's model as a first-
best economy with two vintages of machine capital, no endogenous growth in
labor's productivity, and no monopolistic competition. The analysis was quite
straightforward, as were the accounts for the economy.

NOTES

1. Griliches (1996) reports on the history of research along Solowian lines in the decades preced-
   ing 1957. Solow provided a methodology for measuring economic growth at the level of the
   nation, and the intensification of the Cold War created a strong demand for estimates of the
   growth rates for different countries.
2. For $U(C) \equiv C^{1-\sigma}/1 - \sigma$ with $\alpha > 0$ and finite, $\dot{\lambda}/\lambda = -\sigma\dot{C}/C$ and an optimal balanced growth
   path exists.

3. We have left unskilled workers out of our version of Romer (1990) because their presence is completely passive there.
4. Jorgenson (1974) has a good treatment of many vintages of one type of capital good.

REFERENCES

Aronsson, T., P.-O. Johansson and K.-G. Löfgren (1997), *Welfare Measurement, Sustainability and Green National Accounting*, Cheltenham, UK: Edward Elgar.
Arrow, K.J. (1962), 'The economic implications of learning by doing', *Review of Economic Studies*, **29** (3), 155–73.
Griliches, Zvi (1996), 'The discovery of the residual: a historical note', *Journal of Economic Literature*, **34** (3), September, 1324–30.
Jorgenson, D.W. (1974), 'The economic theory of replacement and depreciation', in Willy Sellekaerts (ed.), *Econometrics and Economic Theory: Essays in Honour of Jan Tinbergen*, White Plains, NY: International Arts and Sciences Press Inc., 189–222.
Kemp, M.C. and N.V. Long (1982), 'On the evaluation of social income in a dynamic economy: variations on a Samuelsonian theme', in G.R. Feiwel (ed.), *Samuelson and Neoclassical Economics*, Boston: Kluwer-Nijhoff, pp. 185–9.
Levhari, D. (1966), 'Extensions of Arrow's learning by doing', *Review of Economic Studies*, **33** (2), 117–32.
Romer, Paul (1990), 'Endogenous technical change', *Journal of Political Economy*, **98**, 71–102.
Solow, R.H. (1957), 'Technological progress and productivity change', *Review of Economics and Statistics*, **39**, 312–20.
Weitzman, M.L. (1997), 'Sustainability and technical progress', *Scandinavian Journal of Economics*, **99** (3), September, 355–70.

10. Recapitulation and questions about implementation

10.1 INTRODUCTION

Original to this monograph is (a) the incorporation of capital goods in the national accounts via our National Accounting Matrices (NAMs) and (b) our treatment of financial services in Chapter 2 for the national accounts. These innovations in the large lead to many smaller and important innovations for the practice of national accounting. First, capital goods price changes appear inevitably on the income side of the national accounts. This means that a complete national accounting will require the collection or estimation of such price changes and the incorporation of the changes in the income side of the accounts. This is a demanding task and appears to have been avoided to the present by the restriction of attention to dealing with one type of capital good, namely generic machines and structures. Once natural capital or human capital is introduced into the national accounts, relative price changes of capital goods emerge and must be incorporated in the income side of the accounts. Second, we have noted that certain inherent non-linearities (inhomogeneities) arise when, say, renewable resources are incorporated in the national accounts. These non-linearities create residual income entries in the income side of the accounts. Hence there are new estimations required on the income side when certain non-traditional capital goods are entered in the national accounts. These residuals are analogous to those emerging when there are non-constant returns to scale in production.

We arrived at these conclusions because we derived the expenditure or product side of the accounts simultaneously with the income or value-added side of the accounts. Our NAM was the device or vehicle for carrying out this simultaneous derivation. Our NAM, a special case of Richard Stone's (1973) well-known SAM (social accounting matrix), is a somewhat sophisticated double-entry book-keeping system. Certainly we feel that getting national accounting procedures right can be quite difficult when questions are taken up and are not dealt with in a joint analysis of the expenditure and income implications.

The introduction of natural capital in the national accounts has been linked directly in recent years to the introduction of new depreciation entries in NNP. We endorse this development whole-heartedly. These depreciation entries emerge naturally in the linearized, dollar-valued, current-value Hamiltonian, which we have relied on, for the most part, to be our NNP. In this regard we are working in the mainstream. However, the actual derivation of the appropriate depreciation terms can be tricky and our analysis carries out these derivations repeatedly. We have then a catalogue of sorts of economic depreciation formulas for national accounting.

In this chapter we reflect on the matter of carrying out the reforms or extensions we have developed above in a formal way. If one views the national accounts as a cake, it is appropriate to view their production as (a) getting the ingredients right, in quantity and quality, and (b) getting the recipe (mixing and baking procedures) right. This has been a volume about (b). The marketplace is supposed to generate the right quality of data. Roughly speaking, if the markets are working and collectors amass the market data carefully, many observers feel that the cake is bound to come out right. But there are observers who feel that the procedures for mixing and baking are seriously flawed. For example, one can easily argue that imputing for the labor of home-makers or for the value of leisure time would improve the national accounts considerably. But each of these imputations would involve surveys and delicate estimations which would be very costly to obtain 'reliably'. Market-generated data are not lying about waiting to be collected and processed. The critic would argue here that the quality of the existing ingredients is fine but the cake is inadequate because not enough ingredients were amassed. The cake recipe could be said to be wrong because it called for too few ingredients. But in this case the extra ingredients must be worked up by indirect means, by surveying and estimating, because the market is not providing the full set of ingredients required. This provokes critics from the other camp who argue that ingredients not directly shown up in the marketplace are inadequate and the final cake will be seriously flawed if indirect market data are used. These critics argue that it is when users see that the ingredients have been obtained by indirect means that they lose confidence in the whole exercise of national accounting. The basic philosophy is that if the data are taken from observable and direct market transactions, they must be 'valid' and the resulting aggregates will be meaningful. Hence the resistance to include the labor services of home-makers because their wages and hours worked are not directly registered in the marketplace.

An easy criticism of this view is that the purity of the data going into the aggregates is no guarantee that the aggregates are communicating what users wish to be informed about. Our monograph is about arriving at the aggregates and our argument is that it is a delicate task to get aggregates that are easily interpretable as 'the best measure of recent economic activity in the nation'. A national accountant would argue that his/her activity involves working with a system that is something of a compromise with the ideal because the ideal involves details which are too costly to implement. There is the do-able and the ideal, and one can function acceptably in the intermediate zone. There remains the question of the quality of the data, whether those generated in the marketplace are intrinsically the perfect ingredients in their own right, even though the cake may be made with too few data. This is a third and not unimportant issue. For example, if the model of the economy which underlies the national accounts is a first-best, competitive model and the actual state of affairs is imperfect competition in many sectors, the data collected will be wrong for the accounts, as structured. And the aggregates will be the wrong relative sizes. One sector may be excessively small because prices are well above marginal costs, not because 'there is a lack of productive activity' there. The home-maker's services imputation problem is different. A sector gets left out of the aggregates because the market does not generate a complete set of data for the accounts and this in turn leads to a 'rough and ready' recipe, one based on the limited data churned out by the marketplace. This monograph has set out various ideal recipes and left open the question of whether market data are available to make the cake. This is not entirely accurate because much of economics is built up with basic market prices and quantities as the primitives to inject into the models, and we are working within standard economics. Here we ask whether changes in the traditional accounts are necessary. Is the repair worth the cost? Are the recommended changes 'second order of smalls' or will they have first-order impacts? And finally, are the data required for our ideal accounts currently available?

10.2   INCORPORATING CAPITAL GAINS IN NET NATIONAL PRODUCT

Asset prices can change systematically, in ways we have been labelling 'anticipated', given no inflation, or in response to unanticipated shocks. Hicks argued for unanticipated capital gains, or windfalls more generally, to be included as income only in the form of interest on the windfall and not as the capital value of the windfall itself. The idea is that an unanticipated capital gain represents an unanticipated increase in current wealth. For an individual, this increase in wealth translates into extra sustainable consumption and a good measure of this extra sustainable consumption is the windfall multiplied by the interest rate. Alternatively a future stream of extra consumption is represented currently by its discounted value, namely the 'windfall' current wealth. It is reasonable to argue that the *sum* of all *unanticipated* capital gains and losses in the current period should be zero. This suggests that the *sum* of all current capital gains and losses will be the *anticipated type*. This provides the national accountant with a procedure for incorporating capital gains into net national product. Of course, to the extent that the unanticipated capital gains sum systematically to a non-zero entity, our procedure will yield unsatisfactory results in practice. This is well worth investigating. There does seem to be the possibility of including capital gains and losses in the national accounts in a satisfactory way, without large direct costs or indirect costs in the form of imputation procedures.

10.3   INTEGRATING THE FINANCIAL-CAPITAL CONSTRAINTS

In Chapter 2 we set out a revised set of flow accounts for a nation based on the idea of integrating flow representations of the financial-capital accounts of firms and households into the traditional real flows accounts. The idea here is that banks, broadly conceived, consume primary factors, labor and capital, in providing lending (intermediation) services and check-writing (transactions) services. These services are intermediate since no household consumes these services for themselves. They are a means to an end, namely directly consumed goods and services. And the market price of a widget includes the expenditure by the producer of the widget for lending services and for deposit services provided by banks. The accountant's task becomes one of rationalization or of moving the value of inputs used up by banks in providing the services to the widget producer 'back' into the accounts of the widget producer. This rationalization eliminates double counting. It replaces an intermediate input entry with its primary input value.

By integrating the financial-capital accounts of firms and households with the traditional flow accounts, we ended up with 'formulas' for doing the rationalization sketched above. In principle, we could take the accounts of any firm and replace the value of its purchases of banking services with the corresponding primary inputs used in producing those services, in the banking sector. But this would be a make-work project since the values of the banking services are in the prices of widgets. One simply has to net the value of those services out of the banking sector in order to avoid double counting when one does the final aggregation to obtain net national product. (Scale economies could create messy wedges here.) However, with respect to households, matters are different. Their dollar expenditures include a payment for the services of banks in providing loans (mortgages and consumer loans) but not for the services of check-writing because banks charge for much of such services indirectly, by paying 'artificially' low deposit rates to the depositors.

Households receive check-writing services and pay for them by forgoing the market rate of interest on their funds held in check-writable accounts. Hence the need to impute a dollar flow into the household accounts equal to the cost to the banks for providing the deposit services. These costs are the net value of bank output, after all the services to firms have been netted out. We described this above. Alternatively, the deposits of households, multiplied by the spread between the market rate of interest and the deposit rate, will reflect the costs of these services. The imputation can be done with this 'formula'. Once this is done, the value-added of banks will have been completely rolled into the accounts of users of bank services. The only nominal final part of bank output will be in the household expenditures. The rest of the value of bank output will be buried in the prices of goods and services. And this household expenditure for financial services is done to obtain consumables and should be incorporated as, say, a transactions cost for obtaining those final goods, the consumables.

The cash-strapped national accountant would say: now that we know what to do, let's do it and leap over the data-extensive step of sorting out the financial-capital accounts of all firms and households. In fact this is what current practice is, in principle. The accountant does the 'rationalization' of the value of bank product as described above and never collects data for the financial-capital accounts. This is acceptable if the implementation is done with due care. However, we observed one other new bit when we integrated the financial-capital constraints with the traditional flow accounts: namely mark-ups in national income for equity-holding by households. These entries were the value of equities in the economy, multiplied by the premium over the market rate of interest that equities commanded. These values have presumably been mis-labelled as a return associated with scale economies or with 'profits' in some sense. Again, the cash-strapped national accountant would say: now that we see where and what the new entries are, we can incorporate them into the national accounts without having to collect all the data from firms and households on their financial-capital constraints. Quite so.

The practicalities of implementing our recommendations on financial-capital constraints seem straightforward and free of large expenditure on new data collection and processing. There remains a new issue. A user of the national accounts would have to understand why the entries were where they were and why they were of the magnitude they were. There would be the need for a user's guide with all the details of dealing with the financial-capital constraints spelled out. Roughly speaking, the longer and more complicated the user's guide, the more non-intuitive are the basic accounts. This represents yet another trade-off, namely doing things in the correct way and not obliging non-experts to grapple with the details of why things are done the way they are. Presumably a major *desideratum* in national accounting is 'accessibility' or 'user-friendliness' or the avoidance of 'counter-intuitiveness'. One wants to avoid creating a class of professional interpreters of the national accounts.

Our Chapter 2 and its treatment of financial-capital constraints dealt with an abstract economy in a steady state. We side-stepped dealing with capital gains, anticipated or not, on assets. This approach bought us much simplification, but at a cost of realism. Toward the end of Chapter 2 we returned to a real framework for a growing economy. We took up intermediation costs and arbitrage costs in that economy and observed how these costs were capitalized in capital goods prices and how these costs entered into terms for economic depreciation. The costs of intermediation (moving current savings to investment projects) remained explicit. There remains the cautionary tale here for the accountant: be on guard against double counting because the chances are that much of the costs of arbitrage and intermediation is embodied by the market in capital goods prices and should not make a separate appearance in the national accounts.

10.4 NATURAL RESOURCE CAPITAL

Making the national accounts greener has been much talked about over the past ten years. One way to confront natural capital and national accounting is to reflect on the accounts for a nation specialized in oil exporting. Current 'high income', much from oil rents, will run out some day, and this suggests that current oil income is an overestimate of sustainable income. With his usual clarity, Hicks suggested treating discounted future oil income as a current fund of *capital* and treating current sustainable income as what the interest flow would be if that capital were sitting in a bank.[1] This is converting the value of oil reserves remaining into a 'sustainable equivalent' income stream. We had much to say about this in Chapter 4. The decline in fish stocks, timber stands, biodiversity and so on is another diminution in natural capital that should be factored into the current level of sustainable income. And finally the pollution of airsheds and watersheds represents a loss of services from 'environmental capital' and this too should be factored into the current level of sustainable income. Part of the movement to green the national accounts involves adjusting market prices with Pigouvian wedges, wedges reflecting negative externalities associated with pollution. This idea is reasonable in theory but is seemingly unreasonable in practice. Careful estimation of the wedges would be hugely costly and any departure from the utmost in rigor would cause the national accounts to be dismissed as 'just made up'.

The primary task in greening the national accounts is introducing depreciation or disinvestment entries for natural capital. Markets generate much of the requisite data. One needs quantity of stock lost over the period multiplied by the unit net price (market price net of marginal costs of 'extraction', broadly defined). With oil, for example, the stock lost is current net usage and the unit value is market price less marginal extraction cost. This is the general 'formula' in the utility NNP. Refinements to this formula are necessary for dealing with capital gains on current usage, as well as for dealing with current discoveries of new stock (see Chapter 4). There has been considerable hands-on activity in greening certain national accounts already.[2] William Nordhaus (1999) recently chaired a committee which prepared a report for the National Science Foundation (Washington, DC) on principles of greening the national accounts for the United States and his recommendations could be viewed as a point of departure as to how it should be done. However, there is no reason to believe that capital gains and arbitrage activity would be dealt with in that report in the way we recommend dealing with them here, and we do not suggest that the Nordhaus report is a substitute for our 'report' here. The Nordhaus report could serve as an introduction to our Chapters 4 and 5. Our work here is new in its treatment of capital gains on stocks. Our approach yields an entry in national income for natural stocks which corresponds with Hicks's concept of 'permanent' or 'stationary equivalent' income for depletable stocks (Chapter 4). And our entry for economic depreciation of natural stocks is an extension of current practice for new types of capital.

We did not report on the issue of the boundary of green capital for inclusion in the national accounts. For example, biodiversity can be viewed as a species of natural capital and its depletion can be viewed as reducing future potential output somewhat. Should the national accounts be reporting on the current depreciation in this natural stock? Or suppose that average annual sunshine is reduced to a region because of global climate change. Should this depletion show up in NNP? The general rule is that if services from the capital are moving through the marketplace, one should include the corresponding stock change in the national accounts. This opens the door very wide for inclusion of various types of natural capital, but that may be the proper way to deal with the issues of large-scale environmental change.

NOTES

1. He proposed defining depreciation as the difference between current actual flow income from oil sales and what the sustainable income would be. Recall the report on this in Chapter 4.
2. See, for example, the empirical work in Lutz (1993), particularly Chapters 6 and 7.

REFERENCES

Lutz, Ernst (ed.) (1993), *Toward Improved Accounting for the Environment*, Washington, DC: World Bank.

Nordhaus, William (1999), *Nature's Numbers: Expanding the National Economic Accounts to Include the Environment*, Washington, DC: National Science Foundation.

Stone, Richard (1973), 'A system of social matrices', *Review of Income and Wealth*, **19** (2), 143–66.

Index

asset balance 15, 17–47, 207–9
asset pricing *see* capital goods; price
    changes, capital goods

balance of payments 158, 163
balanced growth 11, 34, 56, 63, 138,
    181–2, 184, 190, 195, 197, 200
banking *see* financial services
bequests 137–8
Benthamite utility functional 76–8

capital account (firm) 15, 17–47, 207–9
capital gains *see* price changes, capital
    goods
capital goods 45, 59–68, 83, 145
central bank 42
Chichilnisky Criterion 76–8
constant consumption *see* sustainability
conventional national accounting *see*
    traditional national accounts

data 179, 186–8, 191, 193, 205–6, 208–9
deforestation 138–44
demography 178, 182–4
depreciation 8, 12, 15, 61, 67–73, 86–90,
    115–17, 133–7, 141–51, 163–5,
    172, 181, 184, 197, 205, 209–10
    see also macrodepreciation
discount rate 14, 51, 58–61, 68–9, 76–80
discovery 110–15
double dividend 145
durable exhaustible resources 102–10
Dutch Disease 169–76

equity 15, 17–47, 208
exchange rates 158, 163
exhaustible resources 10–11, 64–76,
    83–121, 124, 158–76, 208–9
exploration activity 110–15

financial services 17–47, 207–9
fishing 128–33, 145–55
forests 124–8, 138–44

GNI 4–5
GNP 4–5
government 6
government debt 42
green national accounting 1, 13, 115,
    145–55, 208–9
Gross National Product (GNP) 4–5
Gross National Income (GNI) 4–5

HNNP *see* NANNP
Hicksian Income 8, 49, 208–9
Hicksian Net National Product *see*
    NANNP
homemakers 178–80, 205–6
Hotelling Rent 91
Hotelling Rule 67
human capital 7, 178–85, 204

imperfect competition 14, 194–202
interest rate 7, 12, 14, 33, 60–67, 89–91,
    193, 200, 208
interest rate, own 12, 63–7, 128, 137,
    140–41, 184, 200
interest rate spreads 15, 17, 29–33,
    38–40, 208
intermediate goods 9–10, 17, 209
    see also financial services;
    technology; transactions;
    transportation
inventory 110–17
Investing Resource Rents 71, 74, 88–91,
    98–100, 172–4
investment 55, 67–8, 143–4, 174–5

knowledge capital 11, 61–3, 178,
    180–82, 186–202

labor 7, 178–85
land use 137–44
leisure 146–54, 178–85, 205
lending 17–47

macrodepreciation 89, 91, 94

NAM 4
NANNP 91, 98, 100–101, 144
National Accounting Matrix 4
National Accounting Net National
    Product *see* NANNP
natural resource stock 13, 40, 60, 75–6,
    83–4, 102–5, 110–21, 133–7, 146,
    204–5, 209–10
Net National Income 8
Net National Product 8, 145
NNI 8
NNP 8, 145
Non-Hicksian Net National Product *see*
    UNNP

overlapping generations 75–6, 137–8

pollution 133–7
population growth 178, 181–4
price changes, exogenous 88–9, 119–21,
    158, 162–3, 169–75
price changes, capital goods 1, 11–15,
    49–50, 61–73, 83–115, 132, 137,
    138–44, 158, 165, 174–5, 190,
    197, 204, 206–10
profit 1, 5–6, 14–17, 115, 121, 187, 195,
    208

R-Percent Rule 74–5
R&D (research and development)
    187–8, 195–8
recycling 105–10
renewable resources 10–11, 124–44,
    204, 209
rent 91, 143, 146
rental 7, 22, 87, 105–8, 188, 194–5
returns to scale, non-constant 5–6, 10,
    14, 87, 128–33, 204, 207–8
risk 5, 15, 21–22, 38

SAM 4, 204
S-shaped growth 124
savings 39–46, 53, 72–3, 99, 196
Social Accounting Matrix 4, 204
stationary equivalent 63
stochasticity 78–80, 119–21
stock, natural resource *see* natural
    resource stock
substitution 79, 194
sustainability 8, 50, 53–80, 88–91,
    98–100, 145, 155, 158, 162–3,
    184–5, 194, 206, 209

tax, income 76
tax, inheritance 76
tax, Pigouvian 133–7, 145–55, 209
tax, Samuelson 115–17
technical change, endogenous 11–12,
    180–82, 186–8, 194–201
technical change, exogenous 13, 75,
    186–94
technology 194–200
terms of trade 74, 75, 88–9, 158, 163,
    169–76
Tobin's q 3
trade 74–5, 154, 158–76
tragedy of the commons 154
traditional national accounts 1–3, 12,
    145–6, 178–80, 186–7, 202, 204–6
transactions costs 27, 43–5
transportation costs 10, 27, 46
tree harvesting 124–8, 138–44

uncertainty 78–80, 119–21
UNNP 57–60, 91, 94, 102, 144, 162,
    179, 184, 210
Util-Valued Net National Product *see*
    UNNP

value-matching 118–21

wage 7, 154–95
wealth 42–5, 52–8, 79

ZPIA (zero-profit intertemporal
    arbitrage) 1, 7